Employee Participation
and
Labor Law
in the
American Workplace

Employee Participation and Labor Law in the American Workplace

Raymond L. Hogler
AND
Guillermo J. Grenier

Q

QUORUM BOOKS
New York
Westport, Connecticut
London

Library of Congress Cataloging-in-Publication Data

Hogler, Raymond L.
   Employee participation and labor law in the American workplace /
Raymond L. Hogler and Guillermo J. Grenier.
      p.   cm.
   Includes bibliographical references and index.
   ISBN 0–89930–752–3 (alk. paper)
   1. Industrial management—Employee participation—Law and
legislation—United States.   2. Labor laws and legislation—United
States.   3. Industrial management—United States—Employee
participation.   4. Company unions—United States.   5. Trade-unions—
United States.   6. Industrial relations—United States.
I. Grenier, Guillermo J.   II. Title.
KF3369.H64   1992
344.73'01—dc20
[347.3041]   91–36333

British Library Cataloguing in Publication Data is available.

Library of Congress Catalog Card Number: 91–36333
ISBN: 0–89930–752–3

First published in 1992

Quorum Books, One Madison Avenue, New York NY 10010
An imprint of Greenwood Publishing Group, Inc.

Printed in the United States of America

∞

The Paper used in this book complies with the
Permanent Paper Standard issued by the National
Information Standards Organization (Z39.48–1984).

10 9 8 7 6 5 4 3 2 1

For Louis Hogler

a charter member of Local No. 6417, United Mine Workers of America, organized under the Blue Eagle in August 1933, Somerset, Colorado

and to Nelida and Guillermo Grenier

Contents

Preface ix

1. Introduction 1

2. From Employee Representation to Trade Unionism 13

3. The Legal Context of Worker Participation 65

4. Participation in the Modern Workplace 99

5. Changing Labor Law 125

6. Conclusion: Lessons from the Steel Industry 169

Bibliographical Note 173

Index 177

Preface

Employee participation is increasingly promoted as the future of workplace organization in the United States. In their quest for superior methods of motivating workers and improving productivity in a global economy, employers afford growing acceptance to involvement programs. But if ideas of industrial democracy have a future in America, it is equally true that they have a past—an enduring and important one. During the period between the two world wars, for example, combinations of workers organized by management challenged independent trade unions in the coverage of employees. Senator Robert Wagner, the chief author of the National Labor Relations Act (NLRA), vehemently opposed the company-dominated employee organizations as inimical to a system of genuine collective bargaining, and in 1935 Congress declared them illegal.

Interest in participation languished through the 1950s and early 1960s. But particularly over the past two decades, managerial technique has emphasized participation as an important component of human resource management. The relevant provisions of our labor law, however, remain antagonistic toward participation plans sponsored and directed by employers. For that reason, many critics urge that our law should be modified to permit such plans. Organized labor, at the same time, becomes progressively weaker and unable to mount a viable response to managerial dominance over workers. Removing all impediments to the internal organization of workers within the firm would assuredly contribute to labor's deterioration. That point is inescapably clear from the history of participation.

This study proposes a solution to the dilemma. It begins with an elaboration of the problem itself: the fundamentally malleable nature of employee participation schemes and their potentiality for thwarting the collective interests and aspirations of workers. Because "participation" is a concept protean in scope, a historical context is essential to its understanding, and a chapter of the book is devoted to a development of that history. After 1935, the central issue of participation is legal, rather than historical; accordingly, we trace the evolution of the law surrounding section 8(a)(2) of the NLRA from the Wagner Act to the present. Contemporary usages of participation are examined in a case study that documents the failure of labor law in guaranteeing workers their basic right to freedom of choice in representation matters. To provide an adequate framework for our proposed legal reform, we trace the politics of labor law and industrial relations in the United States during the postwar era. We then present specific suggestions for legal change and policy arguments that support those suggestions. The rationale for statutory change is straightforward. If a goal of our political economy is enhanced democracy on the job, with its anticipated benefits, then Congress should act promptly to establish a legal climate ensuring that goal. The failure to do so will perpetuate an antiquated and ineffectual labor law.

Several institutions provided financial support for this project, including the Department of Labor Studies and Industrial Relations at Pennsylvania State University, the College of Business at Colorado State University, and the Center for Labor Education and Studies at Florida International University. Portions of the work were previously published in different form in *Hofstra Labor Law Journal*, the *Labor Studies Journal*, and in "Labor Law and Managerial Ideology: Employee Participation as a Social Control System," *Work and Occupations*, 18, no. 3, pp. 313–333, copyright © 1991 by Sage Publications. All of this material is used here with permission. A number of individuals read and commented on the manuscript in its different versions. We thank them for their assistance.

CHAPTER 1

Introduction

During the summer of 1936, the American steel industry experienced a temporary respite from the devastating early years of the Depression. Production in steel increased between mid-1935 and into 1937, with the index of factory employment on a 1923–25 base rising more than 51.6 percent. Those favorable economic conditions, and labor's alliance with the New Deal political coalition, were especially propitious for the Steel Workers Organizing Committee (SWOC), which, under the direction of John L. Lewis and the Committee for Industrial Organization (CIO), had commenced a union drive at the major steel enterprises.[1] Among the employers targeted by SWOC was the Bethlehem Steel Corporation, where an employee representation plan had been in existence since 1918. The plan, which SWOC leaders derisively referred to as a "company union," was of strategic importance in the campaign, and in July 1936 SWOC organizer Frank Fernbach devoted an entire radio address in the Bethlehem area to the subject of employee representation.

In his speech, Fernbach first assured the Bethlehem workers that SWOC intended no criticism of men active in the company union, who were merely attempting to better their working lives through any available avenue. The company unions, he continued, were called Employee Representation Plans (ERPs), but more realistically, they were the employer's "insurance against higher wages, shorter hours, and better working conditions." Fernbach reminded his audience that Bethlehem's ERP was inactive during the Depression, but when the National Industrial Recovery Act was passed in June 1933, the corporation had quickly resurrected the plan as a foil to independent trade unions. The consequence, according to Fernbach, was the steel workers "have been treated like flies. The companies have plastered their mills with fly paper company unions, and the steel workers cannot help but get stuck to the fly paper unions. If they try to keep off the fly paper—by refusing to vote—they are then on the spot." Ferbach went on to illustrate the shortcomings of the company unions with a number of specific examples drawn from the steel industry, and he urged his listeners to join with SWOC in "freeing ourselves from the fly paper company unions."

Despite the fact that company unions were the "babies of the Open Shop" and a means of combatting industrial unionism, Fernbach said, SWOC nevertheless was grateful to the Steel Institute and steel employers for creating them because the representation plans actually redounded to the benefit of union organizers in important ways. Most importantly, the elected company union representatives "learned a good deal about the needs of their fellow workers for a bona fide industrial union. They have become educated and trained in leadership. The company union starts steel workers to thinking. Now they have the best opportunity of their lives to become real union men." Implicitly, Fernbach acknowledged that even a form of collective dealing initiated by the employer provided a foundation for worker solidarity and group coherence.[2]

Fernbach's speech reflects the perspective of SWOC organizers toward representation plans elsewhere in the steel industry. At United States Steel, the elected employee representatives were the vanguard of the SWOC effort and were instrumental in the company's acquiescence to the recognitional demands of Lewis and the CIO. The employee representation plans played a central role in the unionization of the steel industry and eventually in the CIO's larger designs. For Lewis, as Irving Bernstein observed, "the organization of steel, the nation's basic industry and its citadel of antiunionism, was CIO's most urgent task, a necessary safeguard to the U[nited] M[ine] W[orker's] flank in the captive mines and the key to CIO success in other industries."[3] Clearly, then, company unions were essential to the objectives of the CIO. But company unions were not flimsy, ephemeral devices, either in steel or in other sectors of industry. Indeed, forms of worker participation appeared in the American workplace in the 1870s, and such plans had been a staple of managerial technique for nearly two decades prior to 1936. Employers routinely deployed representation systems as an antiunion strategy in the early 1930s; Bethlehem Steel Company's successful resistance to unionization for more than five years after the beginning of the SWOC drive amply attested to the continuing effectiveness of its ERP.[4]

The origins of employee participation, broadly defined as an internal, collective means of sharing power between owners and workers within a firm, can be traced to employers in the United States in the late nineteenth century. Although organizational techniques such as employee involvement and Quality Circle programs are sometimes viewed as particularly modern and are often attributed to the Japanese, the concept of participatory "industrial democracy" is more accurately associated with American management. In one well-known instance, for example, the Filene Department Store implemented a program in 1898 that, by 1903, had evolved into a comprehensive and elaborate scheme of participation known as the Filene Co-operative Association. Other significant plans prior to World War I included the "works council" at the Nernst Lamp Company in Pittsburgh; the "advisory committee plan" at the American Rolling Mill Company in Middletown, Ohio; the "industrial democracy" system at Packard Piano Company in Fort Wayne, Indiana; the "trade board" at Hart, Schaffner & Marx in Chicago; and the "shop forum" at the White Motor Company in Cleveland.[5]

But the most influential of the early employee representation plans was the one developed by John D. Rockefeller, Jr., at the Colorado Fuel & Iron Company (CF&I) in 1915. The Rockefeller Plan not only prompted national interest in workplace democracy throughout the United States, it also altered the nature of employee participation schemes in this country and shaped them to the end of antiunionism. Rockefeller created a resilient weapon to aid employers in fending off trade unionism, and his example persists in modern instances of corporate strategy. Reacting to the combined menace of the United Mine Workers of American (UMWA) and the impending intervention of the federal government in CF&I affairs, Rockefeller personally forged an organizational technique and an accompanying managerial ideology that, despite intense pressures, preserved the vital core of managerial prerogative within the firm.

In September 1913 the UMWA commenced a recognitional strike against CF&I and other Colorado coal operators. The strikers established tent colonies at various locations, including the strategic settlement at Ludlow. When the Colorado militia attacked the colony in April 1914, eleven children and two women were burned to death.[6] The virulent public reaction against the CF&I, and against Rockefeller personally, prompted Rockefeller to action. With the assistance of W. L. Mackenzie King, a Canadian expert on labor relations, Rockefeller developed an employee representation plan and personally inaugurated it at the CF&I mines in October 1915.

Rockefeller's motives, which were molded through his association with King, were complex and ambiguous. A majority of the CF&I workers ostensibly supported the plan; of a total 2,846 votes cast in a secret election, 2,404 (or 84 percent), were in favor of representation. The philosophy underlying the plan—at least the philosophy publicly espoused by Rockefeller—was that "the interests of the various parties in industry are identical and not opposed to one another, and that the industrial problem is largely the result of the loss of personal relations between owners and wage-earners." Elaborating on the purpose of the plan, President J. F. Welborn of CF&I added that "the intent of our representation plan has never been to use it as a subterfuge to combat unionism."[7]

But George West, a contemporary analyst of the strike and its ramifications, was more skeptical in his assessment of the situation. One of the fundamental causes of the labor dispute, according to West, was Rockefeller's indifference to the actual conditions in the mines owned by his company. Through the early months of the strike, Rockefeller urged Welborn to continue his policy of active resistance to and suppression of the union effort, regardless of the effects suffered by the miners and their families. Moreover, West concluded, the representation plan did not result in diminished managerial authority but rather was designed "to deceive the public and lull criticism, while permitting the Company to maintain its absolute power."[8] Testimony presented to the Industrial Commission made clear, in West's opinion, that Rockefeller had acted to dampen public support for President Woodrow Wilson's plan of conciliation, which would have involved a comprehensive scheme of labor relations with substantial incursion into managerial prerogatives. Despite such criticisms, the CF&I plan became a prominent feature in the industrial relations landscape and an enduring model for other employers.

During World War I, ERPs were established in a number of enterprises under the auspices of the War Labor Board. The Board's avowed purpose was to reduce strikes and labor conflict in specified industries, and its approach to labor relations was characterized by "a steady and almost severe insistence that collective dealing be established as a normal process in industry." To accomplish that objective, the Board issued more than 125 awards mandating installation of shop committees, and its influence persisted following the end of the war.[9] A number of employers voluntarily adopted plans after 1918, including such well-known concerns as American Telephone and Telegraph, Eastman Kodak, National Cash Register Company, and the Consolidation Coal Company.[10]

The continuity of Rockefeller's influence and the importance of certain individual figures in the perpetuation of representation techniques is typified by the Works Council at the International Harvester Company. Robert Ozanne, in his authoritative treatment of industrial relations at International Harvester, describes how in 1918 Rockefeller assisted the McCormicks by releasing Arthur Young, then in Rockefeller's employ, to direct the new industrial relations department at International Harvester. Young astutely prepared for the intense labor conflict that followed World War I by securing the services of his colleague at CF&I, Mackenzie King. "Together," Ozanne writes, "they drew up for International Harvester a slightly modified version of the Colorado Fuel plan. As the postwar strike activity began to crackle like fire around International Harvester, this plan was the backfire that Young set to protect the company from advancing unions."[11] Later, Young became a vice-president at U.S. Steel and was instrumental in establishing ERPs at that corporation in 1933 as the cornerstone of its antiunion strategy under the New Deal labor policies.

Throughout the 1920s, the ERP constituted an important dimension of employer welfarism. One leading historian suggests that the plans "seemed the capstone of welfare capitalism," and comments that "clearly [they] were intended to substitute for trade unions, both as a justification to the public and an answer to employee needs."[12] In addition, as the well-known industrial relations scholar Sumner Slichter concluded in 1929, welfare policies had the very important tendency to diminish workers' awareness of class. "Modern personnel methods are one of the most ambitious social experiments of the age," Slichter said, "because they aim, among other things, to counteract the effect of modern [technology] upon the mind of the worker and to prevent him from becoming class conscious and from organizing trade unions."[13] On a broader scale, employer welfarism helped to establish the legitimacy of corporate wealth and power and to defend wealthy and powerful corporations against attack in the political arena.[14]

Following the enactment of the National Industrial Recovery Act in 1933, and its encouragement of trade union organizations, participation plans were enthusiastically taken up by employers throughout the United States. Under the threat of a collective bargaining system sanctioned by the federal government, employers sought prophylactic measures against independent trade union representation. The steel companies generally implemented or renewed their employee representation plans, and, with the aid of the American Iron & Steel Institute, employers throughout the nation began to devise plans. By early 1935, employer-dominated organizations rivaled independent trade unions as a vehicle for collective dealings with workers.

In reaction to those developments, Senator Robert Wagner denounced company unions as the single greatest threat to free collective bargaining and urged their prohibition in the proposed federal statute then under consideration. Wagner believed that national trade unions would play a fundamental role in equalizing bargaining power between labor and capital and in redistributing wealth among classes. Those policy features of a federal labor law would meliorate conditions leading to economic depressions and the concomitant industrial strife. Company unions, because of their inherent limitations, were inadequate to fulfill Wagner's objectives. Section 8(2) of the National Labor Relations (Wagner) Act of 1935 consequently made it an unfair labor practice for an employer "to dominate or interfere with the formation or administration of any labor organization or contribute financial or other support to it."[15]

In its early decisions, the National Labor Relations Board, with the U.S. Supreme Court's approval, adhered closely to the literal text of the Act and interpreted the law and formulated remedies in a manner that effectively discouraged organizational structures based on concepts of collective dealing. The Board has remained remarkably consistent in its antipathy toward organizations of employees that are initiated by, or exist under the auspices of, the employer. Federal courts of appeals, which possess authority to review and enforce the orders of the Board, exhibit far greater solicitude toward managerial interests. Since the 1950s, the courts of appeals have shaped an ideology of participation based on "employee freedom of choice" and labor-management "cooperation."[16] Those doctrines have growing appeal in the modern economic environment.

Beginning in the 1970s, American employers showed renewed interest in participation systems. Declining productivity, worker dissatisfaction, and relentless, global competition all have contributed to a search for improved forms of work organization; using the modern terminology of "employee involvement" and "Quality Circles," managers have introduced various methods of worker participation in the enterprise to address those issues. But, problematically, the managerial methods have a close structural resemblance to the systems condemned by the Supreme Court under the Wagner Act. As a result, the legality of employee involvement programs in the nonunion setting has become one of the most disputed of labor law issues, and scholars advance divergent opinions as to whether section 8(a)(2) invalidates all forms of collective organization or whether it should do so as a matter of policy.[17] In light of the conflicting decisions of the Board and the courts, and the ambiguous and contradictory legislative history of the Wagner Act and the Taft-Hartley amendments of 1947, the legal question seems intractable without further legislative direction. One of the leading scholars of the National Labor Relations Act summarizes the state of affairs: "Legislative confusion and contradiction concerning the Act's purpose, due to inconsistencies among several of its important provisions, have given those charged with implementing the Act great freedom to apply their own values and beliefs in construing its proper purposes."[18]

A similar discourse has emerged among proponents of employee involvement schemes in the workplace and their critics, in both union and nonunion contexts. Some labor relations experts assert that labor-management cooperation is essential to America's competitive economic position. In his study of American economic policy, former Secretary of Labor Ray Marshall argued that "improved U.S. economic performance and competitiveness require greater worker participation."[19] Similarly, an influential and popular book on management theory compared Japanese management styles with American organizations and concluded that the most important characteristics of the Japanese system is "their participative approach to decision making."[20] Increased employee involvement in the workplace is viewed as a means of meliorating the adversarial positions of management and organized labor in American industry.[21] Of direct application to the shop floor, even the "notoriously hierarchical" General Motors (GM) is now "waking up with the repentant fervor of Ebenezer Scrooge on Christmas morning. The world's largest industrial company proclaims that it has discovered the real path to corporate health: listening to, and trusting, its people."[22] GM's new approach is critical to its Saturn project. According to a recent report, "the core of Saturn's system is one of the most radical labor-management agreements ever developed in this country, one that involves the United Auto Workers in every aspect of the business. . . . Beyond sharing power at top levels, the labor agreement established some 165 work teams, which have been given more power than assembly-line workers anywhere else in GM or at any Japanese plant."[23]

Other writers, however, point out that employee involvement programs and quality circles embody sophisticated techniques of social control over workers. Those commentators view participatory schemes as a subtle, insidious instrument of managerial power used in some instances to deflect potential unionizing efforts among workers and undermine collective action.[24] In a union setting, participation may erode the effectiveness of collective bargaining relationships and contractual protections against onerous working conditions.[25] Workers themselves exhibit a fragmentation of opinion, and dissident members of the United Auto Workers (UAW) Union threatened to form a separate organization to oppose the union's program of "cooperation" with automobile manufacturers.[26]

American labor law is at best confusing and ambivalent with respect to managerial prerogatives in imposing forms of organization upon workers. Labor law delimits the articulation of managerial and worker power at every level of the enterprise, yet contemporary jurisprudence often disregards compelling accounts of how managerial power in the guise of industrial democracy molds the attitudes and values of workers. Federal courts of appeal propound a vision of employee "free choice" that is often contradicted by the actualities of working life set forth in historical and contemporary studies. Absent any grounding in the real circumstances of employment, the judicial dogma is at once disingenuous and dangerous.

Explicit in the managerial arguments supporting employee involvement programs is the contention that employee expressions of choice should be effectuated, even when employees favor company-sponsored organizations over trade union representation. But more is at stake than the abstract notion of "choice." The historical record is replete with instances in which employers have defined the choices of workers with respect to their collective activities, and modern scholarship substantiates the managerial capacities for such strategies. One leading analyst of organizational behavior, for instance, remarks of the popular "Theory Z" style of management that "the attractiveness of the Theory Z organization is not due to any inherent improvement it offers in organizational effectiveness. Top management will be attracted to the Theory Z concept because it increases their control while giving the impression of lessening it."[27] By embedding managerial power within a context of work group "autonomy," employers can advance their own goal of deflecting potential threats of collective worker action and maintaining a less visible, but certainly no less effective, structure of bureaucratic power.

This book explores the relationship between labor law, forms of industrial organization, and power in the workplace. Our approach focuses initially on the origins of employee representation in American industry, with particular attention to the Rockefeller Plan at Colorado Fuel & Iron. Tracing the permutations of employee representation from Ludlow through the War Labor Board to the steel industry, we examine the formation of the plan at the Midvale Steel Company in 1918 under the sponsorship of William Dickson. Dickson illustrates more clearly than any other manager of the pre-Wagner period the shifting, contradictory motivations that drove programs of employee representation. The steel industry, following the example of the Midvale and Bethlehem companies, subsequently provided national leadership in the development of company unions after enactment of the National Industrial Recovery Act of 1933.

Between 1935 and 1937, under the stimulus of unique political and economic conditions, American workers overwhelmingly chose to engage in formal collective bargaining arrangements. As one aspect of that movement, rank and file steelworkers at U.S. Steel subverted the company's ERPs and influenced Myron Taylor, chairman of the corporation, to recognize and deal with an independent trade union. Our account of that activity is based on the personal recollections of the workers who controlled the SWOC drive within the key Carnegie-Illinois subsidiaries.

Examining the nature of participation in the modern workplace, we develop two related lines of analysis. The first is the evolution of the law interpreting sections 8(a)(2) and 2(5) of the National Labor Relations Act, which we trace from the 1930s using Board and appellate case law and academic commentary. The second perspective deals with the impact of managerially sponsored organizations of workers on trade unionism. In that regard, we consider theoretical aspects of participation programs as well as the assessments of contemporary union organizers who have encountered them in the context of an ongoing campaign. To ground the general observations regarding power, control, and participation plans, we provide a case study of a major firm that successfully relied on internal work groups as an antiunion device. The combination of legal and sociological analysis illuminates theory and practice, organizational structure, and individual behavior.

We then present an argument for reform of the National Labor Relations Act. Our point of departure is organized labor's escalating decline over the past two decades. According to many authorities, the leading cause of that decline is managerial opposition to unions,[28] and the federal labor law, as uncontrovertible evidence shows, is largely impotent to constrain employer misconduct directed against union organizing drives. The most useful approach to the matter of worker participation and the law is through a statutory framework that takes into account employer resistance to union organization and provides effective legal countermeasures. But, realistically, any proposal to alter the balance of power in the employment relationship must confront political limits. Capitalists in the United States can mobilize, and have demonstrably mobilized in the past, to defeat any legislative initiatives that are unacceptable to them. Their ability to do so was evident in 1947 and 1977, and the political strength of capital was further consolidated during the 1980s. Accordingly, compromise is the key to any legal reform.

Based on the premise that change is both necessary and attainable, we suggest the repeal of section 8(a)(2) of the National Labor Relations Act. This repeal should be accompanied by the amendment of section 9 to impose upon employers a duty of recognition and bargaining whenever a labor organization proves majority support through authorization cards, regardless of whether an election is held. Although quite modest in scope, those two changes would adequately protect the legitimate interests of employers in implementing new forms of work organization, and the legitimate interests of employees to engage in collective activities. If "cooperation" and "competitiveness" are the dual hallmarks of a successful global economy, then policies must be developed to promote those objectives in a fair and equitable manner. The present situation, in which management risks unlawful conduct when establishing workplace participation programs and unions have diminished hopes of winning a Board election in the face of an extended company campaign, has little to recommend it from the point of view of either labor or management. But modification of our labor law can succeed only to the extent that it is predicated on the mutual protection of labor and capital.

Toward the objective of reform, the historical development of employee representation plans is essential to an understanding of the contemporary industrial situation and to the formulation of viable policies accommodating the needs of workers and employers. From Rockefeller's public relations triumph through the antiunion strategies of major employers in the steel industry to the programs of modern corporations such as the Ethicon subsidiary of Johnson & Johnson, worker participation has often served as a valuable conduit of managerial power in the workplace. Precisely because of workers' desires for autonomy and self-fulfillment, the ideological appeal of "industrial democracy" retains the vitality it possessed in the first decades of this century. Consequently, modern organizational design often reflects the tension between individual "freedom of choice" and workers' collective action as a means of securing economic strength for workers in furtherance of our express legislative policies.

According to some critics, the fundamental purpose of the NLRA—that is, "encouraging the practice and procedure of collective bargaining"[29]— has been rendered obsolete by the dictates of efficiency in a modern global economy. Even if that contention has some validity, trade unionism nonetheless deserves continued statutory support. Rather than playing only an economistic role of achieving monopoly wage gains, unions can also fulfill an important social function in the modern workplace by translating concepts of democracy into more durable form. The federal government has announced its commitment to labor management "cooperation" in the interest of restoring America's competitive position.[30] Such a commitment might appropriately be embodied in legislation that renews the undertaking of the Wagner Act to American workers. The self-actualization of workers through a democratized workplace was, arguably, a central theme of the NLRA. Cooperation by workers demands in return assurances against the employer's exploitation, in the 1990s as well as in the 1930s. Where collective action is organized and directed by the employer, "freedom of choice" becomes the merest vacuous platitude that obscures the legal rights of workers, dampens their aspirations toward meaningful autonomy, and dulls the attraction of independent unionism. The democratic process rests on the availability of meaningful options, and without legal reform, workers' options are dubious at best. Section 8(a)(2) is a linchpin of modern labor-management relations. It also offers a viable path to the transformation of our industrial relations system.

NOTES

1. Irving Bernstein, *Turbulent Years: A History of the American Worker, 1933–1941* (Boston: Houghton Mifflin, 1970), 448. In November 1938, the Committee become the Congress of Industrial Organizations (697).

2. "COMPANY UNIONS—Open Shop Babies—The Fly Paper of the Institoot -[sic]," typescript in Harold J. Ruttenberg Papers, Box 4, Folder 6, Labor Archives, Pennsylvania State University. The manuscript is undated, but Fernbach refers to .events that took place in July 1936 as occurring "a couple of weeks ago."

3. Bernstein, *Turbulent Years*, 435.

4. In September 1937, SWOC filed numerous unfair labor practice charges with the National Labor Relations Board against Bethlehem and, among other determinations, the Board concluded that Bethlehem's ERP violated Section 8(2). *Bethlehem Steel Co.*, 14 N.L.R.B. 539 (1939). Bethlehem contested the Board's decision in federal appellate court, and SWOC began another organizing campaign in October 1940. An NLRB election was held at the Sparrows Point plant in September 1941; workers overwhelmingly voted for union representation. Mark Reutter, *Sparrows Point: Making Steel—The Rise and Ruin of American Industrial Might* (New York: Summit Books, 1988), 296–299.

5. For the historical background, see generally National Industrial Conference Board, *Works Councils in the United States* (Boston: National Industrial Conference Board, 1919), 4–12; Carroll French, "The Shop Committee in the United States," *Johns Hopkins University Studies in Historical and Political Science*, 41 (1923), 15–32; Ernest Burton, *Employee Representation* (Baltimore: Williams & Wilkins, 1926), 25–44; U.S. Department of Labor, Bureau of Labor Statistics, *Characteristics of Company Unions, 1935*, Bulletin No. 634, June 1937 (Washington, D.C.: Government Printing Office, 1938), 7–28.

6. For a detailed account of the incident, see Barron Beshoar, *Out of the Depths: The Story of John R. Lawson, a Labor Leader* (Denver: Colorado Labor Historical Society and Denver Trades and Labor Assembly, 1942), 166–179.

7. Ben Selekman and Mary Van Kleek, *Employes' Representation in Coal Mines: A Study of the Industrial Representation Plan of the Colorado Fuel and Iron Company* (New York: Russell Sage, 1924), 27–28, 36. [Editor's note: "Employe" is a now-outdated spelling.].

8. George P. West, *Report on the Colorado Strike* (Washington, D.C.: Government Printing Office, 1915), 187.

9. French, "Shop Committee," 24–25.

10. Burton, *Employee Representation*, 30.

11. Robert Ozanne, *A Century of Labor-Management Relations at McCormick and International Harvester* (Madison: University of Wisconsin Press, 1967), 117.

12. David Brody, *Workers in Industrial America: Essays on the 20th Century Struggle* (New York: Oxford University Press, 1980), 58; see also Stuart Brandes, *American Welfare Capitalism, 1880–1940* (Chicago: University of Chicago Press, 1976), 119–134.

13. Sumner Slichter, "The Current Labor Policies of American Industries," *Quarterly Journal of Economics*, 42 (1929), 432.

14. For an excellent treatment of the point, see Neil J. Mitchell, *The Generous Corporation: A Political Analysis of Economic Power* (New Haven, Conn.: Yale University Press, 1989).

15. 29 U.S.C. 158(a)(2) (1976). In 29 U.S.C. 152(5), a labor organization is defined as "any organization . . . or any agency or employee representation committee or plan in which employees participate and which exists for the purpose, in whole or in part, of dealing with employees concerning grievances, labor disputes, wages, rates of pay, hours of employment, or conditions of work."

16. See, for example, *Airstream, Inc. v. NLRB*, 877 F.2d 1291 (6th Cir. 1989) (denying enforcement of Board's order and holding as a matter of law that employee committee was not a "labor organization" under the Act).

17. See, for example, Note, "Collective Bargaining as an Industrial System: An Argument Against Judicial Revision of Section 8(a)(2) of the National Labor Relations Act," *Harvard Law Review*, 96 (1983), 1662–1682; Note, "Participatory Management Under Sections 2(5) and 8(a)(2) of the National Labor Relations Act," *Michigan Law Review*, 83 (1985), 1736–1769; Thomas Kohler, "Models of Worker Participation: The Uncertain Significance of Section 8(a)(2)," *Boston College Law Review*, 27 (1986), 491–551; Note, "Rethinking the Adversarial Model in Labor Relations: An Argument for Repeal of Section 8(a)(2)," *Yale Law Journal*, 96 (1987), 2021–2050.

18. James A. Gross, "Conflicting Statutory Purposes: Another Look at Fifty Years of NLRB Law Making," *Industrial and Labor Relations Review*, 39 (1985), 10.

19. Ray Marshall, *Unheard Voices: Labor and Economic Policy in a Competitive World* (New York: Basic Books, 1987), 3. Marshall's thesis is supported in "The Payoff from Teamwork," *Business Week*, July 10, 1989, 56–62 (cover story). See also Commission on Workforce Quality and Labor Market Efficiency, *Investing in People: A Strategy to Address America's Workforce Crisis* (Washington, D.C.: U.S. Department of Labor, 1989), 33.

20. William Ouchi, *Theory Z: How American Business Can Meet the Japanese Challenge* (New York: Avon, 1981), 36.

21. Charles Heckscher, *The New Unionism: Employee Involvement in the Changing Corporation* (New York: Basic Books, 1988).

22. *Wall Street Journal*, January 12, 1989, p. A1, and A7.

23. S. C. Gwynne, "The Right Stuff," *Time*, October 29, 1990, 76 (cover story).

24. See, for example, Guillermo Grenier, *Inhuman Relations: Quality Circles and Anti-Unionism in American Industry* (Philadelphia: Temple University Press, 1988); Rick Fantasia, Dan Clawson, and Gregory Graham, "A Critical View of Worker Participation in American Industry," *Work and Occupations*, 15 (1988), 468–488.

25. Donald Wells, *Empty Promises: The Quality of Working Life* (New York: Monthly Review Press, 1987); Mike Parker, *Inside the Circle: A Union Guide to QWL* (Boston: South End Press, 1985); Mike Parker, "New Industrial Relations Myth and Shop Floor Reality: The 'Team Concept' in the U.S. Auto Industry," paper presented to the Conference on Industrial Democracy, Woodrow Wilson International Center for Scholars, Washington, D.C., March 28–30, 1988; Mike Parker and Jane Slaughter, *Choosing Sides: Unions and the Team Concept* (Boston: South End Press, 1988).

26. *Wall Street Journal*, June 19, 1989, A2.

27. Stephen P. Robbins, "The Theory Z Organization from a Power-Control Perspective," *California Management Review*, 25 (1983), 67 (emphasis deleted).

28. See, for example, Michael Goldfield, *The Decline of Organized Labor in the United States* (Chicago: University of Chicago Press, 1987); Thomas Kochan, Harry Katz, and Robert McKersie, *The Transformation of American Industrial Relations* (New York: Basic Books, 1986); Richard Freeman and Morris Kleiner, "Employer Behavior in the Face of Union Organizing Drives," *Industrial & Labor Relations Review*, 43 (1990), 351–365.

29. The economic and constitutional underpinnings of the Act are embodied in its declaration of policy, which institutionalizes the process of collective bargaining in this country:

It is hereby declared to be the policy of the United States to eliminate the causes of certain substantial obstructions to the free flow of commerce and to mitigate and eliminate these obstructions when they have occurred by encouraging the practice and procedure of collective bargaining and by protecting the exercise by workers of full freedom of association, self-organization, and designation of representatives of their own choosing, for the purpose of negotiating the terms and conditions of their employment or other mutual aid or protection.

29 U.S.C. § 158(1).

30. U.S. Department of Labor, Bureau of Labor-Management Relations and Cooperative Programs, *U.S. Labor Law and the Future of Labor-Management Cooperation* (Washington, D.C.: BLMR No. 104, 1988), 2.

CHAPTER 2

From Employee Representation to Trade Unionism

ORIGINS AND DEVELOPMENT OF REPRESENTATION PLANS

By the 1920s, the concept of "industrial democracy" was generally familiar in the American workplace. Prompted by numerous successful examples of labor-management cooperation during World War I, labor experts urged that such efforts be continued to create a new postwar industrial system. One authority described the industrial relations environment with characteristic optimism:

The more intelligent and liberal industrial executives, labor leaders, publicists and statesmen, because of the remarkable achievements of industry during the war arising from the unprecedented spirit of cooperation which prevailed between employers and employees, hoped, in part, at least, to see this spirit carried over into the normal times of peace.[1]

But, in fact, industrial democracy already had an impressive pedigree dating from the previous century, and the ideal is deeply embedded in American labor history.[2]

One scholar suggests that "shop committees existed as early as 1833 and the 'shop council' was put forward as an antidote to the labor strife of 1886," but, he added, "no important American company adopted employee representation until almost the turn of the century."[3] In a more recent study, David Montgomery notes that the Straiton & Storm company, a cigar manufacturer, had developed an elaborate employee representation plan for its cigarmakers in the late 1870s.[4] As described by George Storm in his testimony before a Senate Committee, the Straiton & Storm plan incorporated participatory techniques that are common to most subsequent efforts at workplace democracy.[5] Storm also cogently presented the managerial rationale for establishing such plans.

In 1883, Straiton & Storm was the largest manufacturer of cigars in the United States, and possibly the largest in the world. The company employed some 2,200 workers and produced 250,000 cigars per day, which were distributed throughout the United States and exported to several countries. George Storm was committed to the proposition that American government rested on the will of the people, and, he argued, it was important to recognize that American wage earners stood on the same political footing as American capitalists. Economic inequality, however, led to organizations of workers and eventually to strikes. Employers exacerbated labor conflict by exploiting workers as "an article of merchandise, which, having been bargained for and secured at a price satisfactory to the buyer, [the capitalist] may then take such means as seem to him best to dispose of the article at its highest value and profit to himself without giving the article any further consideration." The inherent conflict between labor and capital prompted Straiton & Storm to devise a system of arbitration for resolving workplace disputes.

Storm explained to the Committee that his company had instituted a board of arbitration in 1879, which consisted of four delegates elected by employees, four company representatives appointed by management, and a neutral chosen from another branch of the company. Selection of delegates, Storm recalled, aroused a "very great interest," and workers discussed "the merits of their candidates with as much warmth as probably would be found in a political contest." By majority decision to which the company invariably adhered, the arbitration board adjusted any matters of wages or working conditions that were in dispute. Storm praised the plan as a means of eliminating labor-management conflict within the firm:

By the method here adopted, and the certainty that any difficulty that arises will be adjusted, and believing than any such difficulty will be settled upon a fair basis, it has enabled us to use all our energies in the natural pursuit of our business, without giving the question of labor half of our time, or being constantly troubled with the nightmare that perhaps there may be a strike to-morrow morning; hence, I believe we have been more prosperous and our business has been more satisfactory than it was prior to the existence of this board.

Significantly, Storm did not oppose workers' affiliation with trade unions; most of his employees, he believed, belonged to one of the unions associated with the industry. Unionism was simply irrelevant to the company: "We reserve to ourselves, according to compact with [the men], and as long as it exists, the right to adjust our difficulties in our own way." Further, Straiton & Storm remained unaffected by the numerous strikes and lockouts taking place in the trade at the time, because the arbitration procedure removed the incentive to strike. As Storm observed, "we have never suffered from [a strike] since we had this board of arbitration; prior to that, we did." Trade union leaders, according to Storm, viewed the company's program "with great misgivings, and had tried, at various times, to make it odious, either to the work-people or to ourselves." Such efforts were to no avail, he added: "It has taken such a firm hold on the minds of our people that I do not think, at present, anything could shake it."[6]

The Straiton & Storm plan thus exhibited in elaborate detail the major characteristics of participation schemes. It was predicated on political equality as a justification for enfranchisement in the workplace; it assumed a common interest between workers and employers, and it was designed to reduce the level of adversarialism within the firm. Although the plan was initiated by management, Storm emphasized that its success depended on the company's willingness to yield a meaningful increment of power to the employees' elected delegates. Not all employers were capable of the requisite degree of honesty in dealings with their employees, Storm cautioned, and in such cases, attempts at workplace democracy were futile. He contemptuously dismissed managers who used participation as a subterfuge to deceive workers:

I have had employers come to me to inquire about this method of arbitration, and how it worked, and after taking all the trouble to explain it to them, they would say in a sly manner, "Well, I suppose you have it all your own way, don't you?" These people are unfit to have arbitration—they are tricksters. In speaking of arbitration, we must, therefore, leave all such people out of account.[7]

Another early, and more widely known, attempt to provide a system of worker participation occurred at William Filene's Sons, a retail clothing establishment in Boston. In 1898, William Filene organized the Filene Cooperative Association and delegated authority to employees to maintain certain welfare programs, such as the lunchroom and entertainment funds. The experiment was sufficiently successful that in 1903, under the leadership of Edward A. and A. Lincoln Filene, the Association was granted a constitution. Eventually, the Filenes created a representation structure known as the Co-operative Association Council and, in 1901, an Arbitration Board was empowered to resolve disputes between employees and management. The Arbitration Board had authority "to act as a final court of appeal in all cases of controversy between the company and an employe and between one employe and another." In one case, for example, an elevator operator discharged for insubordination appealed to the Board and was reinstated with a two-week suspension.[8]

The philosophy of the Association was straightforwardly aimed at enhancing service and profitability. "Sharing both management and ownership embodied the conviction that only by enlarging the scope of employes' responsibility and by endowing them with power commensurate with that responsibility could they give their best to the business."[9] Edward Filene, in any event, believed that "industrial democracy, under which employees will have an adequate voice in the policies of industry and an adequate stake in the profits of industry," had become inevitable. Not only because industrial democracy was "theoretically right," Filene said, but because the nation had committed itself "to political democracy, because we have given to the masses of employees who far outnumber the employers a political vote with which they can get anything and everything they find themselves unable to get by industrial methods." For the immediate future, consequently, managers had an obligation to "be as autocratic as necessary and as democratic as possible" in maintaining a profitable operation while educating workers for participation in the democratic processes that would attend the coming industrial transformation.[10] Nor did the Filenes oppose trade union membership as an interference with their program of worker participation, and in one instance, the Filene management accommodated union members who offered to resign from their unions in order to secure all the benefits of the Filene Co-operative Association. For a period of time, union members were denied bonuses and vacations, but they were eventually afforded full status in the Association and were urged to remain in good standing in the union.[11]

As a third example of the early plans, H. F. Porter instituted a "factory committee" in 1904 at the Nernst Lamp Company in Pittsburgh. Porter is sometimes credited with the "pioneer installation" of a shop committee in the United States, although his system did not confer any delegated authority to the committee.[12] The committee, which consisted of representatives from the clerical force, the factory operatives, and the foremen, served largely as vehicle of communication for matters of concern to employees. A secondary function was to administer the "suggestion system" that Porter installed as a part of the committee's purpose. That feature, Porter noted, was extremely beneficial to both workers and the company:

As soon as the opportunity was offered, and each operative found that it would be not only perfectly safe to offer a suggestion which would even at first glance deprive him or her of a livelihood, but that such a suggestion would lead to instant remuneration and to more profitable occupation, there soon blossomed in an apparently barren field a rich crop of ideas.

Porter criticized managers of the time for having lost the "close touch" between owner and worker characteristic of the older methods of employment. To elicit the intelligence and "spontaneous helpfulness" of employees, Porter urged a broad program of welfare in the workplace, and the Nernst plan incorporated procedures that dealt with employee education, safety and health, and cultural activities such as the "Musical and Dramatic Association." Those methods, according to Porter, "furnished an incentive on the part of the employees to give to the employer the best there was in them, and not only during working hours but at all times, the forces of personal interest, enthusiasm, and individual capacity were directed toward the welfare of the company." Regarding the influence of the Nernst plan, Porter explained that the company resisted invitations to advertise its techniques "on the principle that one should not advertise the fact that he is simply doing what is right." But in any event, workers learned of the superior conditions at the company, "and the list of applications for positions by the very best class of employees from other factories, not only in the neighborhood but at a distance, was a long one." There was, of course, a financial incentive for employers to follow the Nernst methods: "It was the intelligent and vital force of this organism that put the company on a paying basis, testifying to the efficiency in the industrial world of the ethical laws that 'right makes might.' "[13]

Beginning in the early 1910s, popularizers of worker participation such as John Leitch extolled industrial democracy as a panacea for labor unrest and low production. Leitch claimed that 50 percent of American industrial capacity was lost due to strikes and labor disputes; he also claimed that labor-management conflict could be eliminated by proper organizational techniques and offered his experience at the Packard Piano Company in 1912 an illustration. Following an unsuccessful strike, the company experienced declining productivity, poor quality, and lower profits. Packard subsequently employed Leitch as an industrial consultant. By instituting a regular series of plant meetings and a sharing arrangement for increased savings, Leitch realized a 5.5 percent savings in production costs within one month. Similar economies were realized over a period of several years. As for the "union troubles" at the company, "they got lost in the shuffle." Leitch argued that trade unionism and industrial democracy were compatible with one another because workers were able to freely choose between the systems. When the Garment Makers' began an organizing drive at the Printz-Biederman Company in Cleveland, for example, the employee representatives adopted a resolution opposing any interference by an "outside organization" and tendered to the company the employees' "most earnest and sincere support."[14]

Leitch's plan was based on the model of the U.S. government, and his version of industrial democracy was defined as "the organization of any factory or other business institution into a little democratic state, with a representative government which shall have both its legislative and executive phases." In addition to a House of Representatives, elected by workers, and a Senate composed of appointed members from the ranks of foremen, Leitch provided for a Cabinet consisting of the executive officers of the company with the president as chairman. The Cabinet was not elective and possessed a power to veto the "legislation" emanating from the shop floor.[15] In practice, then, the Leitch proposal differed significantly from the actual practices of the American government; nevertheless, "because of the superficial resemblance to the American governmental structure and procedure, the Leitch plan captivated the imagination of not a few employers and wage earners."[16] The most important application of the Leitch plan was at Goodyear Tire & Rubber Company in 1919. Paul Litchfield, the company official responsible for initiating the plan, perceived the labor problem of the postwar era to be the discovery of "a remedy for stopping the spread of Bolshevism." That particularly virulent "industrial disease" was generated by conflict between wage earners and capitalists, both of whom had legitimate claims on the products of the enterprise. To reconcile those claims, Litchfield proposed an "Industrial Republic" based on the federal constitution and initiated the scheme at the Akron plant on July 3, 1919.[17]

A small number of other employers introduced plans in the prewar period, including those at the American Rolling Mill Company, Nelson Valve Company, Hart, Schaffner & Marx, White Motor Company, and Philadelphia Rapid Transit Company. In some instances, the plans were a direct consequence of "labor difficulties" experienced by management.[18] But the Rockefeller plan at the Colorado Fuel & Iron Company marks a transition from the early, tentative phases of industrial democracy to a massive project of corporate reorganization directed toward the eradication of trade union sentiment within the firm.

Employee representation was the centerpiece of Rockefeller's strategy of control within the organization and his quest for legitimacy in American public opinion. His scheme of industrial democracy enabled Rockefeller to transform himself from an object of virulent criticism to a social reformer of the first rank. More important, the Rockefeller experience presaged a generalized movement in American business during the Progressive era and offered crucial guidance in the formation of the new business ideology that "expanded business priorities to include social responsibility and sought publicly to establish the notion of a 'good corporation.'"[19] The events at CF&I, consequently, illustrate both the magnitude of the problem that confronted Rockefeller and his enormous personal contribution to its favorable outcome. With Rockefeller's imprimatur, a new era of participation commenced.

THE LUDLOW MASSACRE AND THE BROTHERHOOD OF MAN

In the summer of 1913, the United Mine Workers of America requested a conference with the coal operators of southern Colorado to discuss working conditions in the mines. Consistent with their practice, the operators refused all union overtures, insisting that they would maintain the "open shop." The UMWA scheduled a convention in Trinidad, Colorado, on September 8 and invited the operators to attend for a discussion of wages, hours, and working conditions in the mines. Having had no response, the UMWA set a strike date of Tuesday, September 23, and formulated a list of demands. Those demands included recognition of the union, wage increases corresponding to the scales then in effect in Wyoming, elected checkweighmen, the right to trade with any merchant, an eight-hour working day, and enforcement of the mining laws of the state of Colorado.[20] The mine operators, led by J. F. Welborn and L. M. Bowers of CF&I, rejected all demands and, most emphatically, the proposal for union recognition. When the strike commenced as scheduled, the miners were forced to vacate the company premises. In the words of Mother Jones, who was present at the scene:

I have never witnessed in any State of this great Union the brutal and horrible pictures as I saw yesterday as I went to Ludlow. Here was a lot of poor wretches on that wagon; their life earnings were piled on that wagon. There was a mother with a babe in her arms; it was cold, and the sleet was coming down; and as I looked at that picture I fairly trembled for the future of the world.[21]

With sporadic incidents of violence, the strike continued throughout the winter and spring of the following year. Governor Ammons sent the Colorado Militia to the area in early October, ostensibly with the mission of maintaining order. The militia actively began to support the interests of the coal operators, and it soon became populated with mine guards, drifters, and outlaws. Lt. Karl Linderfelt, who was extremely unpopular with the miners, commanded the notorious Company "B." On April 20, Linderfelt ordered the miners at Ludlow to deliver a particular individual into the soldiers' custody. The miners responded that the person was not in the camp, and shortly thereafter shots were exchanged. The soldiers overran and burned the colony, killing two women and eleven children who had hidden beneath the floor of a tent.

During the battle, Linderfelt captured Louis Tikas, the leader of the Ludlow colonists. Linderfelt struck Tikas on the head with a rifle, inflicting a serious wound that may have caused Tikas' death.[22] Linderfelt testified that when he was notified of Tikas' capture, "I got right up from my position and went right over there, and I said to Louis Tikas, I said, 'I thought you were going to stop this,' and he told me—he called me a name that no man will take and I struck him with my gun."[23] Later, according to Linderfelt, Tikas was shot while trying to escape. Pearl Jolly, a miner's wife, offered a somewhat different version of the event:

After they took him [Tikas] prisoner, they couldn't decide for a little while how they wanted to kill him. Some contended to shoot him; some contended that he should be hanged. Finally, Lieut. Linderfelt went up and hit him over the head with a rifle, broke the butt of the gun over his head, and then made the remark he had spoiled a good gun on him.

They stepped on his face. We have a photograph. I don't believe we have it here, but it shows plain the prints of the heel in his face. After he fell, he was shot four times in the back.[24]

The brutality of the Ludlow incident provoked a tremendous public outcry against the coal operators and against Rockefeller personally; according to Rockefeller's biographer, "the name of Rockefeller was denounced from one end of the country to the other."[25] Rockefeller hired public relations expert Ivy Lee to counteract the adverse publicity. Lee's task was to present the point of view of the mine operators, and, acting in close cooperation with the operators' committee, he prepared and distributed 40,000 copies of a bulletin describing the strike.[26] Lee accepted the facts given to him by the operators and made no independent effort to determine the authenticity of the statements, which, in one instance, resulted in a particularly distorted picture of the salaries paid to United Mine Workers officials. The CF&I corporation paid all costs of publication and distribution of the bulletin.

Concerning his general strategy, Lee compiled a list of "the names of Members of Congress, of members of State legislatures, of the leading newspapers of the country, of the leading officers of the American Federation of Labor, of all the officers I could obtain of the United Mine Workers of America, of all the other important labor leaders in the country, as well as a good many others." Lee went on to explain the point of the massive distribution of the pamphlet:

The idea was, and it was Mr. Rockefeller's idea, that the truth as it was understood by him, and as it was understood by the operators, was sound; that we ought to make it known to the public; that if it was not sound, any publicity for it would clear it up; and we wanted everybody, the labor leaders, the press, and everybody else to get our point of view.[27]

Lee's program was a impressive success. But it was only one relatively transitory phase of Rockefeller's rehabilitative project; the second, and more enduring, aspect was the plan of employee representation.

On August 1, 1914, Rockefeller wrote to Mackenzie King, the former Canadian Secretary of Labor and an expert in industrial relations, concerning the situation in Colorado. Rockefeller noted that some 2,000 strikers remained in the tent colonies and were a "constant menace to peace and are only held in subjection by the presence of the Federal troops." Permanent stability could be achieved, Rockefeller said, only if two conditions were satisfied. First, the UMWA would have to abandon the strike, which was not "likely to happen in the near future." Second, according to Rockefeller, peace would be assured by the company's "developing some organization in the mining camps which will assure to the employees the opportunity for collective bargaining, for easy and constant conferences with reference to any matters of difference or grievance which may come up, and any other advantages which may be derived from membership in the union." Reminding King that the two men had previously discussed such an idea when King visited Rockefeller's home, Rockefeller concluded by requesting King to draft "an outline of such an organization" for Rockefeller's consideration.[28]

King replied to Rockefeller on August 6. In a long and prescient letter, King surveyed current labor conditions and speculated on the effects of the world war. He suggested that unions would cease organizing activities and concentrate on preserving their gains. "Recognition simply for the sake of recognition is going to be seen to be less pressing as an immediate end than that of maintaining standards already existing, and unions may rightly come to regard as their friends and allies companies and corporations large enough and fair enough to desire to maintain these standards of their own accord." Consequently, King argued, unions that fought for the "shadow of recognition" would be simply "wasting resources." King perceived an alternative between the "the extreme of individual agreements on one side and an agreement involving recognition of unions of national and international character on the other"; that alternative was

the straight acceptance of the principle of collective bargaining between capital and labor immediately concerned in any certain industry or group of industries, and the construction of machinery which will afford opportunity of easy and constant conferences between employers and employed with reference to matters of concern to both, such machinery to be avowedly constructed as a means on the one hand of preventing labor from being exploited, and on the other of insuring that cordial cooperation which is likely to further industrial efficiency.

King cautioned that if such a principle were adopted, "the machinery to be adopted should aim primarily at securing a maximum of publicity, with a minimum of interference, in all that pertains to conditions of employment."[29]

Rockefeller forwarded King's proposal to Welborn and Bowers, who were staunchly opposed to the plan. Bowers, for example, wrote Rockefeller that "this matter should not be taken up at the present time." Bowers assured Rockefeller that the strike "was not entered into or called by or approved of by our miners, but vigorously opposed by them, including the few labor-union miners long in our employ." He pointed out that it would be inconsistent to form a committee, for the innovation "would discount every utterance we have made and insisted upon, that there were no differences whatever and the strike was not forced because of any grievances or differences." Moreover, Bowers knew that the UMWA would accept a joint operator-miner committee structure even without union recognition and would seize the opportunity to "shout it over the world that they had won the strike." Other operators would not accept the plan, and "the socialistic papers would charge us with dodging and hiding behind this eleventh-hour scheme to save our faces." Bowers emphasized that "to move an inch from our stand at the time that defeat seems certain for the enemy would be decidedly unwise, in my opinion."[30]

From a similar perspective, Welborn added his arguments in a letter to Rockefeller on August 20. Welborn said that the King plan "would weaken us with our men . . . and would, in the minds of the public, be an admission on our part that a weakness, the existence of which we had previously denied, was being corrected." Concerning King's proposed visit to Colorado, Welborn suggested that it would be unnecessary because there was no demand by the miners for a board of arbitration. "Whatever demand there may be of that character comes from the uninformed public and is an opinion, rather than a demand, based on misinformation as to conditions surrounding the Colorado strikes."[31]

Acquiescing to the views of Bowers and Welborn, Rockefeller agreed that it would not be desirable to pursue the representation plan at that time. But on September 5, 1914, President Wilson personally intervened in the dispute. Wilson wrote to each of the coal operators, pointing out that federal troops had assumed the considerable burden of maintaining order in the state and urging them to accept a plan of conciliation to resolve the affair. The Wilson plan proposed a three-year agreement, during the life of which the UMWA would neither demand recognition nor picket mine sites. The operators would in turn agree to comply with the mining laws of Colorado, to rehire any strikers who had not violated the law, and to provide a grievance procedure subject to final resolution by a commission appointed by the president. All other disputes, individual and collective, that affected wages and working conditions would be submitted to the impartial commission. The UMWA, meeting in a special convention, accepted the plan; the operators rejected it as an interference with their rights to manage the operation.[32]

Rockefeller's legal advisor, Starr Murphy, wrote Welborn on September 8 concerning Wilson's proposal. Murphy cautioned that the president's action had produced a "delicate situation" that Welborn was to handle in a "careful and diplomatic way . . . avoiding on the one hand any entanglement with the labor union and on the other an attitude which would arouse a hostile public opinion." Shortly thereafter, Murphy informed Welborn that Wilson's plan was receiving strong public support and it seemed apparent that "public opinion will demand either the acceptance of the President's proposition or some constructive suggestion from the operators." In any event, "a mere refusal to do anything would be disastrous."[33] On September 18, with the assistance of Ivy Lee, Welborn wrote to President Wilson declining his proposal. But, Welborn told the president, we are now developing an even more comprehensive plan, embodying the results of our practical experience, which will, we feel confident, result in a closer understanding between ourselves and our men. This plan contemplates not only provision for the redress of grievances, but for a continuous effort to promote the welfare and the good will of our employes.

In fact, Welborn had no such plan and wrote Murphy on the following day mentioning the eventuality of "its being necessary to propose some plan to take the place of that presented to us by the President."[34]

Murphy replied to Welborn on October 5, indicating that criticism of Rockefeller continued and suggesting the formation of a mine committee to provide a medium of communication between the employees and the operators. Such a procedure, Murphy believed, "would take the place of the objectionable Grievance Committee referred to in the plan which has been adopted by the President." Murphy stressed the importance of prompt action to dampen public antagonism toward the owners:

Most of the adverse criticism arising from the operators' refusal to accept the President's plan in its entirety is based upon their apparent unwillingness to give the men any opportunity for an expression of opinion. I am afraid this criticism cannot be met by anything except some organized means of such expression. While we ourselves may be perfectly sincere in our statement that at present the men have an opportunity to present their views to the higher officials, it is difficult to convince the public of that fact, and consequently public opinion is hostile.

Murphy summed up the need for prompt action to protect the Rockefeller reputation: "This public opinion is an important factor in the situation and has got to be reckoned with."[35]

In answer, Welborn agreed that Murphy's strategy might be to the advantage of the company. Welborn wrote that he had already considered a plan "of getting at the complaints of the various men," and would extend the procedure to all the mines. He repeated, however, that the formation of a committee should still be avoided, because "that would come too near one of the demands of the miners' organization . . . and is expressed through their so-called truce proposal presented by the President." Rather, Welborn suggested that three "safe" men be appointed by the mine management to consult on matters of health and safety. Welborn insisted that the committees be composed "as to make it appear that they all represent the same interest," thereby conveying the impression that the committees were not adversarial in nature. Above all, he said, "every step should be made with very great care, so as to avoid impressing the men with the feeling that we are alarmed or think that we ought to give them some representation which heretofore they have not had."[36]

Welborn's pallid conception of a grievance committee eventually gave way to the more robust plan of representation that was formally implemented in December 1914. On the point of Welborn's conversion, Rockefeller was closely questioned by Chairman Walsh during the Commission hearings. Walsh asked Rockefeller what brought Welborn to change his mind concerning the two very different proposals, and Rockefeller answered: "I hope that the more suggestions were made to him [Welborn], the more he began to see the views of others were worthy of consideration." Rockefeller denied that the plan was drawn up by King and forced on Welborn; he did admit that there was a "radical difference" between Welborn's initial plan and the plan that was adopted. Pressed as to Welborn's motives, Rockefeller suggested that Welborn had never actually made up his mind on the matter.[37] In any event, Welborn made a public announcement on December 17 that he had employed a mining expert named David Griffiths to adopt "a method (more systematic than heretofore in use) by which our workmen could reach the higher officers of the company on matters in which they were concerned."[38]

Given the above statements, it is clear that CF&I officials were not actuated simply by the altruistic desire to provide industrial democracy for their miners. Their consistent position, indeed, was that a representation plan was unnecessary and an admission of weakness. Commenting on the final plan, West concludes that it was "conceived and executed by men who were determined that no element of real collective bargaining should enter into it." And, West pointed out, the plan significantly served the interests of the employer by legitimating the continued retention of all authority over the miners: "The effectiveness of such a plan lies wholly in its tendency to deceive the public and lull criticism, while permitting the Company to maintain its absolute power."[39]

Rockefeller's own behavior and beliefs, which were guided in large part by King's influence, were at best ambivalent. On the one hand, Rockefeller believed himself a humanitarian reformer who enjoyed a personal rapport with labor leaders. As he wrote in 1921, Rockefeller perceived no difference in his objectives and those of the trade unionists—"namely a fair deal for the working man"—and, consequently, he saw "no reason why we should distrust each other or work against each other, that the best results can only be obtained by our being tolerant, respecting each the other's sincerity of purpose."[40] One fundamental point eluded Rockefeller in his advocacy of employee representation, which was that such devices enabled management to retain undiminished control over its prerogatives. In fact, Rockefeller had little genuine interest in nurturing the democratic impulses of his workers. Rather, "his interest in employee representation can most charitably be characterized as one of industrial peace at any price, save unionization."[41]

Regardless of his motivation, Rockefeller undertook a publicity campaign that established his national reputation as an authority in labor affairs; in Irving Bernstein's cogent summary, "seldom has an industrial relations program been launched with such impressive staging and with such striking initial success."[42] Without previous announcement, Rockefeller and King arrived at the mining camps around Trinidad, Colorado, on September 19, 1915. Rockefeller's personal appeal in the camps was a matter of detailed, and highly laudatory, newspaper coverage.

On September 20, Rockefeller visited the Berwind camp and ate at the camp boarding house. He spoke to various miners about conditions at Berwind, including an Italian worker named Morelli. The *Denver Post* reported their conversation:

"Look here, Mr. Morelli," said Mr. Rockefeller, "I want to have a heart to heart talk with you. Just forget that I am a wealthy man and talk frankly to me as you would to any of your brother miners. I believe this thing of capital and labor fighting is all wrong. I am devoting the biggest part of my time to bringing about peace between labor and capital, and I want you to tell me what I can do to help matters in this camp."

Suitably impressed by his employer's concern, Morelli assured Rockefeller that there had been significant improvements in the operation of the mine and the treatment of the miners since the end of the strike.[43]

Rockefeller continued his tour of the camps for the next several days, scoring important publicity gains at each location. In the underground mine at Frederick, Rockefeller borrowed a miner's pick and dug coal for a short period. He then told the assembled miners: "We are all partners in a way. . . . Capital can't get along without you men, and you men can't get along without capital."[44] Among other activities, Rockefeller led a miner's parade in his honor and attended a dance at a camp schoolhouse, where he held the sleeping child of a Hungarian miner's wife for some hours and later danced with every willing woman present. Such incidents led the *Post* to praise Rockefeller for his personal demeanor: "You have acted so well your part, in so modest, unassuming and manly a way."[45]

Nor was laudatory media attention confined to the immediate geographical region; the *New York Times* also featured Rockefeller's activities in front-page coverage. On September 21, the *Times* headline reported that "Rockefeller Sees How Miners Lived," and the accompanying story described his visit to Berwind. Two days later, the *Times* again devoted prominent space to Rockefeller. In a skillful portrayal of welfare capitalism at its poignant best, the *Times* declared on page 1 that "Miner's Child in Colorado Tells the Financier How to Make Money." It described Rockefeller's visit to a school in Trinidad, where a twelve-year-old girl explained how her class had established a "store" for the purchase of school supplies. The *Times* continued: "The girl then branched off into a discussion of stocks and bonds. Mr. Rockefeller listened gravely as the child told of the things which make bond issues safe or unsafe."[46]

Rockefeller arrived in Denver on September 25. During the next four days, he devoted himself to the representation plan and the role of the UMWA in the new scheme of things. Rockefeller actually offered to meet with union leaders, but they rejected the representation plan as incompatible with trade union principles. In their view, the plan was "not a union and can never be recognized as such by the American labor movement, and it must be obvious that the great principle of free government and industrial democracy cannot be restored in the coal camps of southern Colorado thru [sic] the instrumentality of an organization so created and so controlled."[47] As the UMWA correctly perceived, Rockefeller had no intention of dealing on a formal basis with any union, and that point was made manifestly clear to contemporary observers in one particular incident. The Women's League of Denver requested a conference with Rockefeller to discuss labor conditions. Rockefeller met with them on September 28, assuring them that he would not make any public comment on their meeting. After the event, several women told reporters that they understood Rockefeller to say that he was willing to grant union recognition. Male reporters, most of whom had accompanied Rockefeller through the camps, were amazed by that revelation and urged Rockefeller to clarify his position. Rockefeller denied that the matter of union recognition had been discussed, but he did say that he had read to the League a portion of the testimony he had given to the Commission on Industrial Relations. The reporters thereupon were able to "straighten out" the confusion engendered by the Women's League and the members' lack of understanding on that crucial issue.

Rockefeller's position was reaffirmed the next day when he announced his representation plan to the press. One reporter wrote that Rockefeller "believes [the plan] will make unions unnecessary and strikes an impossibility." The essence of the plan was a personal relationship, by which was meant the exclusion of any outside parties. "It is now definitely known that the CF&I company will never recognize or in any way deal with the union. It hopes to do away with the union for all time by giving the men something in its place—something which Mr. Rockefeller seems sincerely to believe will be better for both labor and capital." The plan, the article concluded, was designed to create a "United Republic of Labor and Capital."[48] That interpretation of Rockefeller's objective was consistent with his earlier statement that industrial "freedom" was based on the right of every worker to determine "for himself whether he should join the union or not," a principle that was intolerable under the UMWA's demand for a closed shop.[49]

To formally introduce his new plan of industrial democracy at the mines, Rockefeller assembled company officers and employee representatives at Pueblo on October 2. He described his conception of the corporation as consisting of four parties: stockholders, directors, officers, and workers. Each party, Rockefeller said, had common interests in supporting the organization, and each was necessary to the corporation's continued success. He informed the audience that the CF&I common stockholders had not received dividends for fourteen years and cautioned them that "capital will not stay indefinitely where it does not get proper recognition and a reasonable return." If all parties did not work harmoniously to the full extent of their respective abilities, Rockefeller said, the entire corporation became unbalanced, and the consequences were detrimental to workers generally. Rockefeller emphatically cautioned his employees against the withholding of their labor: "And I think there is no one thing that threatens greater harm to the interests of the workingmen of this country than that pernicious, that wicked, that false doctrine, that a man should do just as little work in a day as he possibly can, and just as poor work as he possibly can, and hold on to his job."[50] The Colorado Industrial Plan, Rockefeller explained, was a means of protecting and safeguarding the mutual interest. He described the plan at length, indicating that he had spent "practically every daylight hour of this last week" preparing the plan with company officers. After describing the plan, he urged the representatives to recommend it to all workers in the camps and to vote on it within a few days.

On October 8, Rockefeller addressed the Denver Chamber of Commerce and elaborated on the scheme of representation. Reiterating earlier statements, Rockefeller emphasized that he was not opposed to labor organizations; it was as "just and proper," he said, "for labor to associate itself into organized groups for the advancement of its legitimate interests, as for capital to combine for the same object." Although combinations of labor might occasionally engage in practices that were "unlawful or unworthy," Rockefeller strongly believed in the principle of organization. A successful enterprise, however, could be developed only "by a fuller recognition of the common interest of employers and employed; and by an earnest effort to dispel distrust and hatred and to promote good-will."

To further the mutual interests of the CF&I miners and the company, Rockefeller continued, the board of directors had approved a plan of industrial democracy based on joint committees of employee and management representatives. The premise of the plan was that industrial peace and prosperity were beyond attainment "until labor and capital join hands and recognize that their interest is a common interest, that what hurts one hurts the other, that what develops the well-being and prosperity of one must of necessity develop the well-being and prosperity of the other."[51] Pursuing the economic premise in a later essay, Rockefeller argued that labor-management conflict proceeded from the conception "that the wealth of the world is absolutely limited, and that if one man gets more, another necessarily gets less." Accordingly, some employers believed themselves justified "in appropriating from the produce of industry all that remains after Labor has received the smallest amount which it can be induced or forced to accept," while other men believed that "Labor is the producer of all wealth, hence is entitled to the entire product, and that whatever is taken by Capital is stolen from Labor." Rockefeller maintained that such a pessimistic assessment "loses sight of the fact that the riches available to man are practically without limit, that the world's wealth is constantly being developed and undergoing mutation, and that to promote this process both Labor and Capital are indispensable."[52]

Miners voted overwhelmingly to support the Colorado Industrial Plan. UMWA officials, however, with some corroboration from employees, asserted that the company had forced the plan on workers. For example, different-colored ballots were used, creating a suspicion that their purpose was "so that the local superintendents would know how each miner voted." In one camp where the plan was defeated, a rumor circulated that the mine was to be closed. Employees petitioned management for a second election, and a majority voted in support of the plan. Many viewed the case as an example of employer pressure, and even though such speculations were based on circumstantial evidence, they nevertheless demonstrated "the state of mind of the miners that they should have such strong faith in an illusion."[53]

Despite its purported aspirations toward democracy, the Industrial Plan imposed severe limitations on the powers of workers to alter organizational practices. Employees had no genuine voice in the formulation of decisions concerning wages or basic managerial policies, for such matters were reserved to the company. The plan explicitly provided that "officials of the company may decide any question without consulting committees or employes' representatives." In addition, without a national organization such as the UMWA, CF&I employees obviously could have little meaningful influence over industry-wide conditions. The company precluded collective, class-oriented activities by confining workers to local representation, an advantage that was evident to other employers. "Local rather than national organization of employes is exactly what is desired by many employers; and some of these welcome employes' representation because they see only that phase of it which limits its activities to employes within a single company, and they believe it offers an escape from their difficulties with a trade union." Therefore, while the Plan produced "better living conditions and better relationships between managerial officials and miners," it had not become an " 'industrial constitution' for the company or for the industry, or a partnership for labor."[54]

The central proposition advanced in support of the Rockefeller Plan was the idea that labor and capital shared mutual, rather than ultimately conflicting, interests. Rockefeller maintained that the distribution of wealth between labor and capital did not produce an adversarial relationship; to the contrary, he said, there were "ample riches" available to workers and employers alike. Skeptics such as George West doubted that Rockefeller, King, or CF&I officials could expound that doctrine in good faith: "This notion that the interests of the employer and employee are common when applied to distribution of product is a fallacy that can hardly be advanced with sincerity by a man of intelligence."[55] Despite West's dismissal of the "harmony of interests" thesis, it was influential during the period and provided the conceptual backbone of the National Civic Federation (NCF), which was formed in 1900 to deal with topics of public policy. Particularly, labor members of the NCF promoted the trade agreement as a means of reconciling industrial conflict between workers and employers.[56]

In any event, whether Rockefeller's professed convictions were genuine or were merely a convenient ideological gloss on the representation plan, the plan neither permitted employees a voice in the distribution of profits nor a significant increment of power in the operations of the company. The importance of the Rockefeller achievement was not its benefit to miners in Colorado. To the contrary, the beneficiaries of the plan were employers in the steel industry and elsewhere who used it as a model for circumventing governmental interference in their firms during World War I and, in the years immediately following the Armistice, for eviscerating the increases in membership and renewed economic strength unions had acquired during the conflict.

FROM THE SHOP COMMITTEE TO THE OPEN SHOP

The American participation in World War I and the labor upheavals of 1919 significantly altered the industrial relations environment. Employers entered the postwar era determined to retrench the gains made by the labor movement, which had nearly doubled its membership during the years 1915–20, rising "from 2.8 million in 1916 to a peak of 5.0 million in 1920."[57] An important source of labor's enhanced stature was attributable to the wartime regulatory activities of the Wilson administration. In major sectors of the economy, government agencies initiated systems of collective bargaining through shop committees, lending further stature to the concept of employee representation. To forestall such intervention, and thereafter to reestablish the full measure of their power in the workplace, managers relied on the representation plans as the centerpiece of their employee relations strategies.

In April 1918, President Wilson created the War Labor Board (WLB) to supervise labor relations in war industries and to maintain industrial production during the war. The WLB consisted of five representatives of management chosen by the National Industrial Conference Board, five representatives of labor chosen by the American Federation of Labor, and two representatives of the public chosen by the management and labor representatives. By proclamation, President Wilson authorized the WLB "to settle by mediation and conciliation controversies arising between employers and workers in fields of production necessary for the effective conduct of the war, or in other fields of national activity, delays and obstructions which might, in the opinion of the national board, affect detrimentally such production." Wilson adopted the recommendations that had been developed by an earlier joint labor-management War Labor Conference Board, including the principles that workers had rights to organize and bargain collectively, that existing conditions in union shops should be maintained, and that there should be no strikes or lockouts during the war. Designed in part as a conciliatory body, the WLB in practice functioned primarily to adjudicate disputes, and in sixteen months of its existence, it heard 1,251 separate controversies.[58]

To further collective bargaining practices, the WLB frequently mandated labor-management negotiations in establishments where there was no prior trade union relationship. Such awards were problematic, because the parties were unfamiliar with techniques of collective bargaining. "The shop committee," as Caroll French notes, "was already at hand to be used in the solution of the problem," and the War Labor Board actively promoted committees as a substitute for collective bargaining. In more than 125 awards, the WLB provided for employee representation, which it often considered as "of more importance than the immediate adjustment of grievances."[59]

Under the stimulus of the War Labor Board and related agencies, representation plans flourished in 1918–19. The National Industrial Conference Board reported in 1919 that of 225 plans surveyed, 120 were created through the auspices of the federal government and 105 were voluntarily instituted by employers.[60] The number of shop committees continued to increase in the postwar period. One important reason was that the representation plan had "come to appeal to those employers who see in it a most welcome substitute for collective bargaining though the trade union."[61] That aspect of employee representation was made palpably evident in the Industrial Conference of 1919.

At President Wilson's request, representatives of employers, labor, and the public met in Washington in October 1919 "for the purpose of reaching, if possible, some common ground of agreement and action with regard to the future conduct of industry."[62] The conferees, however, encountered an immediate and insuperable obstacle to consensus, which was the right of employees to engage in collective bargaining. By October 21, many of the delegates had concluded that further proceedings would be of no value. President Wilson appealed to the group to make a further effort at agreement. At that point, the labor delegation proposed a resolution stating that "the right of wage earners to organize without discrimination, to bargain collectively, to be represented by representatives of their own choosing in negotiations and adjustments with employers in respect to wages, hours of labor, and relations and conditions of employment is recognized." The public delegates supported the resolution, but it was rejected by the employer group. Bernard Baruch, for the body, notified Wilson that the conference had failed to agree on the issue of collective bargaining and was therefore adjourning. Baruch added that neither the conference nor any group opposed the principle of collective bargaining. "The difficulty that arose and the issue upon which the conference failed to agree was not upon the principle involved but upon the method of making it effective."[63] Notwithstanding Baruch's diplomatic assessment, the underlying dispute in fact centered on the very existence of trade unionism.

The employer delegates believed that the increasingly powerful labor movement posed a threat to fundamental rights of property and entrepreneurial control and were convinced that it was "the duty of employers not to limit their actions to the refusal to deal with unions but to destroy the movement itself."[64] A key element in management's drive for the "open shop" was the employee representation system, in which collective action was confined to a single location and "organization and loyalty was shop-centered, rather than class oriented." The business delegation urged the conference to recommend employee representation "as a way to kill unionism with kindness while maintaining labor in its proper place and the employer in his position of rightful control." Coupled with such a limited mechanism of adjusting grievances, the business representatives sketched a broad scheme of welfare policies intended to arrive at "an enlightened and benevolent capitalism."[65] Accordingly, the rupture between labor and business at the Industrial Conference evidenced a profound, irreconcilable clash of values and philosophy and signaled the great offensive against labor that occurred in early years of the 1920s.[66] The massive "welfare" programs of the 1920s were designed to reduce turnover, increase productivity, and to ensure "smooth labor waters, untroubled by strikes and agitation which threatened the power and authority of the employer." Importantly, "employee representation was the main weapon of the welfare arsenal in the businessman's thrust toward this goal, and in most instances he held on to it longer than to any other form of welfare capitalism."[67]

Many contemporary industrial relations experts viewed the growth of employee representation as a positive force in the relations between labor and capital. William Leiserson, for example, noted in 1928 that "perhaps the most significant contribution of Personnel Management . . . has been its development of employee representation machinery for managing economic and governmental problems as distinguished from the purely personnel problems." Leiserson believed it significant that the managers of "great capitalistic enterprises" would find it desirable to speak of industrial democracy, regardless of their motivations in doing so. The plans often inured to the benefit of employees—so much so, in fact, that workers sometimes expressed a preference for company unions over trade union representation. Moreover, like Rockefeller, Leiserson viewed the principles and successes of representation as a repudiation of antiquated theories of conflict:

To use a political analogy, Employee Representation means that management has substituted constitution for autocratic government in industry, and it has thereby swung to the left in the direction of collective bargaining, trade unionism, and industrial democracy. The organized labor movement of the country, on the other hand, in promulgating its new wage policy and in its approval of scientific management has swung to the right in the direction of the program of the personnel managers.

For that reason, labor and capital might join in cooperative efforts "where the best of both are combined."[68] Other personnel specialists likewise applauded the new era of mutual harmony with its demise of the "inevitable conflict theory"[69] and an end to the "state of siege or trench warfare" that characterized "militant labor and negative capital."[70]

But one of Leiserson's fellow academics, the noted economist Frank Taussig, expressed reservations about the ease with which employee representation systems appeared to meliorate class issues. To speak only of the "common interest" of participants in an enterprise, Taussig said, was simplistic. "In this sort of talk there is usually an absurd glozing of the inescapable conflict on the terms for dividing the joint product." Representation schemes had the effect of promoting the notion of common interest, but, Taussig added, "they do not constitute industrial democracy, and do not ever have as their goal anything like democracy." The reality of representation plans was that they were vertical organizations, remaining under the control of the employer. In the event of disputes over wages and working conditions, workers were "hampered not only by the traditions of place and power and discipline, but by the simple fact that they are dependent on the employer for their job." At best, the plans constituted a "beneficent despotism" and were established "in not a few cases for the very reason that they do weaken the bargaining power of the employees."[71]

Taussig's cautionary observations—as against Leiserson's unalloyed enthusiasm—with respect to the managerial objectives underlying representation plans are substantiated in a revealing memorandum from H. F. Brown, a vice-president of the E. I. du Pont de Nemours Company to President Ireneé du Pont. Brown wrote that he had attended a dinner in New York City on April 2, 1919. Present at the event were the presidents, vice-presidents, or chairmen of the boards of the following companies: General Electric, E. I. du Pont, General Motors, Westinghouse Air Brake, Westinghouse Electric, Goodyear Tire & Rubber, Bethlehem Steel, Irving National Bank, Standard Oil of Indiana, Standard Oil of New Jersey, and International Harvester. The assembled guests heard a lecture by journalist Pomeroy Burton on labor conditions in Great Britain. Burton's address, which detailed the adversarialism and working class radicalism afflicting British industrial relations, so perturbed the members of the audience that J. J. Raskob introduced a resolution to form an employer committee to study labor unrest. The executives, Brown continued, accepted Raskob's suggestion, and four meetings of the "New York Conference" were subsequently held. At the initial meeting, "it was decided that the question of employees' representation was fundamental and the most important for consideration and conclusion."[72]

Of particular concern to the Conference study group was a discernible trend in the Wilson administration favoring the growth of trade union bargaining. Major V. Merle-Smith, an expert on European labor relations, reported to the Conference on his recent experiences at the diplomatic summit in Paris. Brown's memorandum summarized Merle-Smith's remarks and their implications for members of the Conference:

He has just come from Paris and was greatly impressed with the necessity for giving immediate attention in the United States to labor problems. He told us that 65% of all the strikes which have taken place in Europe during and since the war have been not on account of wage demands, but have been of a communist or syndicalist origin. It is not chiefly wages the workmen want, but a new order of social and economic relations. He stated his fear that President Wilson and his advisors might come back to the United States imbued with the idea that the safety of America from Bolshevism lay in a much more complete unionization of industry; that the labor question and labor problems might be made a political issue; that the Government or some other party coming into power might bring pressure to bear upon industry to recognize trade unions and the American Federation of Labor. After hearing Major Merle-Smith, the Conference decided that it was important to draw up a statement of reasons why the Joint Conference Plan of industrial employees' representation is better adapted to American industrial conditions than the so-called "Whitley" or "National Industrial Council Plan" of England.[73]

The reasons for preferring the Joint Conference Plan—as devised by Rockefeller and King and used at Colorado Fuel & Iron and Standard Oil of New Jersey—over the British method had to do above all with the issue of unionism.

In an Appendix D attached to the du Pont memorandum, Brown explained the advantages of the Joint Conference Plan. First, Brown noted, "the English Plan is built upon the principle of two opposing interests, Capital and Labor, organized separately. But the Joint Conference Plan assures unity of interest and cooperation on the part of all directly concerned." Second, "the English Plan presupposes unionized conditions which prevail in England, but which do not prevail in America, where only a minority of workers are unionized. It would be distinctly un-American to force here such unionization as the English Plan requires." A third reason for the superiority of the nonunion system of representation was the alignment of interests in the enterprise. "The English Plan introduces into labor discussions representatives of outside organizations who cannot have as their primary interest the good of the particular company concerned, since they are not associated with it either as managers or employees; the Joint Conference Plan brings into discussion with the management representatives who are employees themselves, and hence are vitally interested in the company's success."[74]

Concluding his memorandum, Brown reiterated the importance of employee representation and the purposes it served:

The New York Conference advocates strongly the adoption of some plan of employees' representation by all corporations as the first and most important step in safeguarding their own interests by securing a loyal, contented and efficient group of employees. . . . I am convinced that the duPont Co. should adopt without delay a plan of employees' representation similar to that in use by the Standard Oil Co. of New Jersey. This is a Plan of the utmost simplicity and consequently may be put into operation with the minimum probability of antagonization [sic] and suspicion on the part of employees.[75]

Brown documented the point in an Appendix F to the memorandum, which is a newspaper report describing the transformation in labor relations occurring at Standard Oil's Bayonne plant between 1917 and 1919, largely as a result of the company's representation plan.[76] Not only did the plan produce better employee-employer relations, it also led to a significant increase in productivity and profits. The attachment reinforces the point that major American employers were sensitive to the threat of worker mobilization and reacted to it with organizational forms that protected them against collective action and furthered their self-interest.

For its part, organized labor was largely unreceptive to the principle of employee representation as a form of collective bargaining. At the American Federation of Labor (AFL) Convention in 1919, delegates John Owens and Henry Raisse, at the request of workers in the iron and steel industry, introduced Resolution No. 201 opposing company unions. In its preamble, the resolution declared that many steel corporations had introduced systems similar to the Rockefeller plan and which were presented as a "great improvement over the trade unions." But in practice, those systems precluded free choice of representatives and meaningful bargaining. Committeemen were routinely intimidated and no outside assistance was tolerated. The company union, accordingly, was a complete failure: "With hardly a pretense of organization, unaffiliated with other groups of workers in the same industry, destitute of funds, and unfitted to use the strike weapon, it is totally unable to enforce its will, should it by a miracle have one favorable to the workers." The resolution condemned representation plans as "a delusion and a snare set up by the companies for the express purpose of deluding the workers into the belief that they have some protection and thus have no need for trade union organization."[77] The AFL continued its hostility to representation plans through the 1920s.[78] Although the labor-management environment was characterized by some degree of cooperation during the period, employers implacably pursued goals of increased control over production and the elimination of a collective union voice for workers.[79]

The number of employee representation plans reached a peak for the decade in 1926, when 432 companies reported having such plans. The expansion of employee coverage is demonstrated by comparison of the years 1919 and 1928; in the former year, 403,765 employees fell under the representation plans, and in 1928, there were 1,547,766.[80] According to the calculations of Harry Millis and Royal Montgomery based on National Industrial Conference Board data, the relationship between representation plans and trade unionism during those years was marked by a rapid relative growth of the company plans. In 1919, plan membership amounted to only 9.8 percent of the total trade union membership. But nine years later, the 1,547,766 members of company unions were measured against 3,144,300 trade union members, for a new ratio of 44.5 percent.[81] With the single exception of 1927, in fact, membership in trade unions declined steadily from the economic contraction of 1921 until the end of 1933; and at that point, labor was in its worst relative position since 1910.[82]

During the period 1928–32, membership in company unions declined from 1,547,766 to 1,263,194. Because larger firms tended to retain their plans, however, the number of employees covered by representation plans was only 7.9 percent less in 1932 than in 1926.[83] As a consequence of, and in reaction to, the collective bargaining policy embodied in the National Industrial Recovery Act of 1933, proportional growth of the company unions surged ahead of the rapid increase in trade union membership over the next several years. In 1932, company union membership was 40.1 percent of trade union membership; by 1935, it was 59.5 percent.[84]

The steel industry illustrates with particular clarity the dynamics of employee representation and the important continuities that can be traced in twentieth-century management thought. Conceived as an antigovernment, antiunion strategy by Rockefeller and King in 1914, representation plans were so deployed by the Midvale and Bethlehem steel companies in 1918. Following Roosevelt's New Deal economic programs, steel companies led the struggle to define labor policies in such a manner as to preserve a central role for the company programs. Their efforts were so successful that company-dominated employee organizations became the fundamental issue in the Wagner Act debates and the focal point of Senator Wagner's legislative agenda.

THE FEDERAL GOVERNMENT AND THE STEEL INDUSTRY: TOWARD A DEFINITION OF COLLECTIVE BARGAINING

The first system of employee representation in the steel industry was devised in 1918 by William Dickson, vice-president of the Midvale Steel

Company, and an outspoken advocate of labor reform. Dickson was a major figure in the development of progressive labor policies in the industry between 1901 and 1923, often in spite of the resistance of his superiors at U.S. Steel and later at Midvale.[85] Yet even Dickson's reasons for creating a representation plan were less the product of idealism than of threatened governmental action by the War Labor Board and an impending union drive at Midvale.

In April 1918 the International Association of Machinists (IAM) began organizing Midvale employees. The union presented a contract to Midvale officials on April 30, which the company rejected. A strike began in June, and union official William Kelton notified the WLB that more than 3,500 employees were involved in the stoppage.[86] A. C. Dinkey, president of Midvale, disputed that figure. Dinkey telegraphed W. Jett Lauck, secretary of the WLB, on July 2 and informed him that employees had been returning to work over the past weeks. Dinkey concluded with his personal assessment of the situation: "In my judgment this strike was inaugurated for the purpose of compelling us to recognize the union. I believe the trouble is about over. In view of all the circumstances we are unwilling to submit the matter for consideration to your board under conditions which you have named."[87]

Kelton persevered in his petition to the Board and the government applied greater pressure on Midvale to institute a means of dealing with employee grievances. Secretary of the Navy Josephus Daniels sent a strongly worded telegram to Midvale officials on September 13 stating that he was "surprised and somewhat disturbed" that the company had refused to cooperate with the National War Labor Board by submitting the labor dispute to arbitration, and he mentioned that the Midvale workers had returned to their jobs only because of the WLB intervention. Daniels urged the company to "inform the Taft-Walsh Board immediately of your entire willingness to submit your side of the case" and emphasized that "the matter is urgent and serious."[88]

Dickson regarded the Daniels telegram as a unique opportunity for labor reform and was extremely energetic in promoting a program of industrial democracy. On September 18, Dickson met with Judge Elbert Gary, the president of the American Iron & Steel Institute and the most influential individual in the steel industry. Dickson explained to Gary that federal officials had urged Midvale to comply with a recommendation of the War Labor Board that Midvale engage in collective bargaining with the Machinists. The government action, Dickson said, was a violation of President Wilson's policy of maintaining the relative positions of labor and capital during the war, and it indicated the "beginning of a well-organized campaign to force the Unionization of all our plants." Should the industry not react promptly on a united front, Dickson cautioned, it would soon be "completely dominated by irresponsible labor leaders," to the detriment of the country as a whole. Dickson concluded his presentation to Gary with a proposal for defusing the union organizing effort.

In this connection, our company now has under consideration and will probably adopt, a system of collective bargaining with its employees, along somewhat the same lines as that adopted some years ago by the Colorado Fuel and Iron Company, and we believe that the adoption of such a plan will furnish a complete answer to objections which have been raised as to the present system.[89]

Dickson was familiar with the CF&I plan, having conferred some time earlier with officials of that company and having reviewed their plan in detail. Indeed, according to Eggert, Dickson "not only consulted with officials of Rockefeller's Colorado Fuel & Iron Company about their plan of employee representation, he also borrowed freely from it, paraphrasing its language and adjusting its specific provisions to the situation at Midvale."[90]

As Dickson predicted in the conversation with Gary, Midvale quickly acted to implement the representation plan. Dickson submitted a draft to the Midvale superintendents on September 19, and the company's directors promptly endorsed it. Several days later, Dickson met with the elected employee representatives to provide them with a final version of the plan. He commended the new system of collective dealing to them as "marking a distinct epoch in the history of American business," and asserted that all other steel companies would soon follow Midvale's lead. The delegates unanimously voted to adopt the company's proposal.[91]

Dickson's strategy of using employee representation to thwart the IAM drive and foreclose a WLB order to bargain with the union was a complete success. At the WLB's hearing on the matter held in early November, Dickson testified that the plan had been conceived in April 1918 and was simply given its final form in September. Frank Mulholland, attorney for the IAM, described the representation plan as a creature of management, dominated by nonsalaried foremen acting as representatives, for whom workers had been forced to vote. Mulholland's incisive cross-examination revealed both the true motives of Midvale management and Dickson's equivocation regarding the plan's origins. Mulholland asked if workers might be justified in their suspicion that the company had adopted its plan primarily to avoid an order from the WLB Dickson replied:

Such a supposition on the part of the employes who had lost confidence in the management might be natural. I can only answer that by stating that the evidence which has been brought before you this morning shows, I think, conclusively that the matter had been under consideration for months, prior to any difficulty between the company and its employes arose.

When Mulholland asked directly about Midvale's antiunion designs, Dickson was somewhat more candid:

Q: Have you not purposely, intentionally, adopted this plan, in order to try to initiate your ideal, or accomplish your ideal [of labor-management cooperation], without dealing . . . through organized labor?

A: Yes, without dealing with organized labor as it is at present administered; kindly underline those last words.[92]

In March 1919 the WLB sent Examiner John O'Brien to investigate and report on conditions at Midvale. O'Brien concluded that the election of employee representatives to the Shop Committee had been fairly conducted and that the union's claim of supervisory domination was unfounded because the alleged foremen were actually working "gang leaders." O'Brien's superior, E. B. Woods, cautioned O'Brien that the investigation should be scrupulously fair in order to vindicate the Midvale scheme and the concept of employee representation. "I am so much interested in the success of this enterprise at Midvale," Wood wrote, "that I should be extremely sorry if there appeared any prospect, even though a remote one, of a situation developing there which could be pointed to by Union officials here [in Washington], or elsewhere, as an indication that the Union men do not get a square deal under systems of collective bargaining, other than the Union agreement."[93] In his official report, O'Brien assured the WLB that the Midvale system was admirably suited to the ends of collective bargaining: "I would respectfully recommend that the War Labor Board should not disturb the present Shop Committee, which is an exceptionally efficient one."[94] Dickson's version of industrial democracy was officially sanctioned.

Almost simultaneously with the implementation of Dickson's plan at Midvale, Bethlehem Steel Company had voluntarily introduced ERPs at its Steelton, Lebanon, and Sparrows Point, Maryland, works in October 1918; those specific facilities did not fall under the purview of the War Labor Board. The main Bethlehem plant at Bethlehem, Pennsylvania, however, was subject to the regulation of the WLB, and Bethlehem officials reacted to the WLB's pressure by pursuing alternatives to a union relationship. Acting on a complaint by machinists and electrical workers, the WLB determined in July 1918 that the dissatisfaction of the Bethlehem employees had a detrimental effect on the war effort, that the conflict between workers and management at the plant was of "unquestionable significance" to the WLB, and that a major cause of unrest was the absence of "any method of collective bargaining." In its findings and order of July 31, the WLB afforded employees a "direct voice in determining their working conditions," provided a method of bargaining and a means of conference between employees and employer, and permitted the "prompt adjustment of all differences."[95]

Even though the Machinists were instrumental in securing the WLB's award, the award did not require union recognition as part of the committee system. Accordingly, Bethlehem took steps to ensure that trade unions would play only a minimal role in the collective bargaining process.

The antiunion tactics relied on by Bethlehem management to counteract the WLB's intervention and to confine its influence were the immediate product of Rockefeller's and King's collaboration, with Midvale serving as a conduit. Dickson, as noted, was familiar with and greatly influenced by the CF&I plan. Charles Schwab, chairman of Bethlehem, summoned Dickson to a conference in early 1918, and industrial relations at both companies thereafter followed identical paths. Having experienced an IAM drive and a WLB investigation, both companies by autumn "had set up employee representation plans in order to escape recognizing or dealing with regular unions."[96] Not content only with Dickson's counsel, Bethlehem also secured the talents of Rockefeller's two most impressive players. In the summer of 1918, Bethlehem President Eugene Grace contacted Mackenzie King, who subsequently drafted several memoranda outlining a plan and the method of its implementation. Although Grace denied that the WLB was a factor in King's employment, the evidence suggests that "King's primary purpose was to shield the company from the War Labor Board. It also indicates the lengths to which [King] was prepared to go to help the company accomplish this end."[97] Grace further relied on Schwab's—and formerly Rockefeller's—publicity agent, the indefatigable Ivy Lee, to promote the Bethlehem plan. Lee worked diligently to attain favorable publicity for the endeavor in the *New York Times* and the trade journals, and between November 1918 and February 1919 the company's plan won "reluctant acquiescence" from the WLB as an acceptable substitute for the WLB's conference committee system.[98] *Iron Age* published a copy of the Bethlehem plan in October 1918 and predicted that "it will be studied with interest not only by steel manufacturers but by other employers in [related industries]." The influence of the WLB was evident in Bethlehem's policy toward union membership, for the plan "expressly concedes the right of employees to belong to unions."[99]

In turn, the Bethlehem Plan proved to be an essential link between the antiunion strategies of the postwar period and the representation plans of the early 1930s. Robert R. R. Brooks found that by the end of 1934, the number of plans in steel had increased from 7 to 93, and the percentage of workers covered by company plans had correspondingly expanded from approximately 20 percent to more than 90 percent. Further, he said, "the great bulk of the industry, including United States Steel, followed the Bethlehem [ERP]. Most of the plans were put into effect in June 1933, and were almost universally initiated and sponsored by management."[100] The thrust of those plans was directed against the New Deal legislation intended to promote collective bargaining, when American capitalism once again confronted a crisis of governmental interference in the relations between worker and manager.

President Franklin D. Roosevelt signed the National Industrial Recovery Act (NIRA) into law on June 16, 1933. Section 7(a) of the Act provided that employees had the right to "organize and bargain collectively through representatives of their own choosing," free from coercion by the employer. No employee, as a condition of employment, would be forced to join any company union, or "to refrain from joining, organizing, or assisting a labor organization of his own choosing."[101] By mid-1934, the majority of employers in steel had adopted or reinstituted employee representation plans, generally taking the position advanced in 1918 before the WLB that such plans were a legitimate method of labor-management dealing and satisfied the government's interest in collective bargaining procedures.

In a pamphlet published by the Iron and Steel Institute, the Institute attacked the "public misconception" that the industry was opposed to collective bargaining. To the contrary, they asserted, steel companies stood "squarely in favor of the right and the practice of collective bargaining with its employees." The critical issue, however, "involve[d] the form of such bargaining." The Institute opposed labor unions on the ground the unions claimed an "exclusive right to represent the employees of the Industry, despite the fact that their membership in the groups does not, and never has embraced more than a negligible minority of employees." The steel industry, in contrast, favored organizations limited to employees at a particular work site.

Relying on the data collected by the National Industrial Conference Board, the Institute claimed that in 3,314 companies employing 2,585,740 employees, 45 percent were covered by representation plans, as contrasted with 9.3 percent of employees bargaining through labor unions. The term "company union," according to the Conference Board, was appropriate to signify a method of collective bargaining, but "the implication . . . that management controls the affairs and decisions of the employee organization is absolutely unwarranted." An essential feature of a successful ERP was that "employees be given the right of independent meetings, elections and conclusions." Drawing a comparison to the American Federation of Labor Plan, the Institute pointed out that ERPs were superior in a number of respects. They were constructed upon the theory that harmony, confidence, and understanding could be developed in the work relationship; the AFL, however, advocated the theory that "the interests of capital and labor are inevitably antagonistic—that there must be, in the nature of things, a perpetual conflict between employer and employees." Such a view exacerbated class differences and promoted "bitterness and hostility, foster[ed] suspicion and friction, and [drove] a wedge between men and management." ERPs had the further advantage of protecting individual rights, accommodating local conditions, and improving the employees' understanding of the employer's business operation. Last, and of particular importance to the Institute, the representation plans satisfied both the letter and the spirit of section 7(a) of the NIRA. Having implemented its own system of collective bargaining, the steel industry insisted that no further protection of its employees was necessary. "Today collective bargaining is an established and a legal fact. It needs no walking delegates to assure it; no labor politicians to demand it."[102]

The proliferation of ERPs in the steel industry spearheaded a national campaign. Company unions were actively promoted by other employers as early as July 1933, with the encouragement and support of the steel companies. The National Association of Manufacturers (NAM) undertook a fund-raising campaign to promote ERPs, and it raised a total of $7,000, approximately one-half of which was contributed by the Iron and Steel Institute. Part of those funds were expended on the study conducted by the National Industrial Conference Board that figured so prominently in the Institute's report, and additional amounts were given to the Mandeville Press Bureau, which distributed press releases favorable to the plans. As a congressional investigate committee concluded, the intimate relationship between the public relations experts and the industrialists was not generally known to the public.

The evidence is unmistakable that in the promotion of employee representation plans, the [NAM] employed the National Industrial Conference Board to accumulate data for which they paid the cost, and used the Mandeville Press Bureau to disseminate publicity throughout the country in favor of such plans. Neither editors nor the reading public knew that the "fact-finding and statistical organizations"—the National Industrial Conference Board—and the Mandeville Press Bureau, were both acting for the National Association of Manufacturers.[103]

In addition to the publicity campaign, a number of regional conferences were arranged for the promotion of ERPs; the specific thrust of that activity was to convince employers who did not have plans to adopt them in their best interests as employers. Although the NAM was the originating force behind the conferences, its role remained hidden. The American Management Association was the active sponsor of the meetings and solicited more funds to provide further promotional events. To contemporary observers, the underlying purpose of the new ERPs was clear. "By the fall of 1933," one observer noted, " 'company unionism' had assumed the character of a nation-wide counter offensive against trade unionism."[104] Substantiating that point, a Bureau of Labor Statistics study conducted in 1935 revealed that 41.6 percent of the employers surveyed had instituted ERPs because trade unions were threatening organization in the locality.[105]

The competing interpretations of section 7(a) concerning trade union representation and the company representation plans soon became problematic. In August 1933, President Roosevelt authorized the creation of a National Labor Board (NLB), chaired by Senator Robert Wagner, to mediate disputes and issue decisions under the Act; and in a case involving textile workers in Reading, Pennsylvania, the NLB achieved a "conspicuous success" when it negotiated a settlement based on a secret election to determine the matter of representation.[106] The NLB's theory of collective bargaining was grounded on Board-sponsored elections and the principle of majority rule, which held that the organization chosen by a majority of workers was entitled to represent all workers in a unit. Consistent with its emerging doctrine, "the Board rejected the principle of proportional representation because that principle had never established itself in American political life and because collective bargaining traditionally meant that one and only one labor organization should negotiate a contract on behalf of a given group of workers."[107] Of a total of 183 elections conducted by the NLB between August 1933 and July 1934, covering 546 units and 103,714 voters, more than 69 percent of the workers voted for trade union representation, while 28.5 percent favored employee representation plans, and 2.1 percent voted for no representation or other organizations.[108] But despite Wagner's vigorous efforts to transform the NLB into a "supreme court of labor relations" and its impressive load of 1,818 cases, the NLB's view of collective bargaining did not prevail within the Roosevelt administration.[109]

General Hugh Johnson and Donald Richberg, respectively the administrator and general counsel of the National Recovery Administration, refused to accept the concept of exclusive representation. They believed that workers might choose a plurality of representatives, each one of which had the right to bargain on behalf of their constituents. Thus, there was "no necessary conflict, under the law, between the trade union and the company union. Both might exist side by side among the same labor groups."[110] Roosevelt initially supported the NLB and the majority rule concept; but, within months, he had reversed his position in order to resolve a major strike in the automobile industry. The consequences of Roosevelt's decision were significant. According to one analysis of the NIRA, "settlement of the auto strike on the basis of the Johnson-Richberg principle of minority representation sounded the death-knell for the NLB."[111] Moreover, the NLB faced both intensified employer opposition to its orders and an inability to enforce compliance through the Department of Justice, which was responsible for NLB litigation. The related themes of employer intransigence toward organized labor, the centrality of company unions to employer strategies, and the legal vulnerability of the NIRA are exemplified by the Justice Department's unsuccessful attempt to secure judicial approval of section 7(a). Appropriately enough, the first court test of NLB authority involved a company union in the steel industry, and the litigation provides an excellent case study of the emergence of a legal ideology favoring managerial programs of employee participation over the rights of trade unions.

JUDICIAL DEVELOPMENTS: WEIRTON STEEL AND THE NIRA

Ernest Weir, the founder of Weirton Steel, embodied important values of American capitalism, and his struggle with Wagner and the National Labor Board helped to focus the attention of employers on crucial labor law issues. In the contest at Weir, labor was represented by a rank and file steelworker named Billy Long, who claimed to speak for a majority of Weir's employees. Long maintained that workers desired representation by an AFL affiliate. The government, through its administrative arm, attempted to enforce the established interpretations of the NIRA regarding secret ballot elections and exclusive representation. The conflict was eventually resolved by a judicial decision that reflected a managerialist view of the industrial world.

Unlike many other employers in the steel industry, Weir had no experience with employee representation prior to 1933, preferring to deal with employees on an individual basis. Enactment of the NIRA prompted Weir to investigate systems of collective bargaining, and he contacted Eugene Grace of Bethlehem Steel for guidance. The Bethlehem Plan proved so attractive that Weir, after minor modification of the document, printed and distributed 15,000 copies to his workers. That same day, June 22, 1933, Weirton President John Williams posted an official notice stating that "the Employees' Representation Plan will be adopted by the Weirton Steel Company." In the elections held on June 30, employees selected 49 representatives. Judge Nields of the federal district court of Delaware, where the NLB brought its suit for enforcement, found that "in round numbers 85 percent of the employees eligible to vote participated in the June election," and any evidence of the employer's coercion or interference with the elections "was trifling and not worthy of mention." During early summer, Judge Nields wrote that "harmonious relations prevailed" at Weirton, but within a short time "the seeds of discord were planted. Organized labor took notice of the Weirton situation."[112]

Specifically, in July 1933 the Amalgamated Association of Iron, Steel, and Tin Workers sent an organizer named Romanogli to the Clarksburg area, and he began soliciting Weir's employees to join the union. Within three months, the union organization consisted of Blue Eagle Lodge No. 32 at Clarksburg, five lodges at Weirton, and one at Steubenville, Ohio. Led by Billy Long, workers at the Weirton tin plate operation struck for recognition on September 24. Pickets at the mill forced a shutdown of operations there, and the strike spread to Clarksburg and Steubenville. Long made a demand for union recognition, to which Weir himself responded in an open letter to employees. Weir explained that the company adhered to the policies set forth in the NIRA, including the provisions for collective bargaining. While the company did not discriminate against workers belonging to the Amalgamated, neither would it tolerate compulsory membership in any organization. Weir noted that a substantial majority of employees had voted in the selection of employee representatives, and he insisted the company's obligation was to maintain that form of dealing:

Our duty under the NRA is clear. We must recognize the committees which have been selected and cannot be expected to negotiate with any other committee which happens to present itself. Under the NRA, our employees are free to select committees of their own choosing, whether made up of employees or not, but once the committees have been selected, we must recognize those committees. If the Company begins the practice of negotiating with any committee that presents itself, it will not be complying with the provisions of the Code which it has signed and its covenants with the President, and it is apparent that great confusion might result if several committees present themselves to negotiate with us.[113]

Thus, Weir insisted on the principle of exclusive majority representation for the company union, while other employers were eviscerating the NIRA by repudiating the same concept—both positions supported as insuring workers' freedom of choice.

On October 10, having persistently rejected the union's demand for recognition, Weir opened the mills and commenced operations. At that point, Long and other union members petitioned the National Labor Board for assistance, and Senator Wagner sent a telegram to Weir requesting reinstatement of the strikers and submission of the dispute to the NLB for mediation. Weir replied that "there is nothing now properly before the National Labor Board for decision relating to our strike." Weir added that "in a desire to cooperate in the President's Recovery Program," he would appear before the NLB to make a statement.[114]

The NLB hearing took place on October 16, 1933. Senator Wagner was present as chair, with Weir speaking for the company and Long speaking for the employees. Reverend Francis Haas, a Board member, also attended the hearing and participated in all negotiations regarding settlement of the dispute. The eventual outcome of the NLB hearing was a negotiated memorandum providing that an election would be held during the second week of December under NLB supervision and with "the procedure and method of election to be prescribed by the Board." As the election date approached, Wagner notified the company of the rules that would govern the election. The proposed regulations, transmitted to Weirton on December 9, prompted a letter from Weir to Wagner in which Weir claimed that "these rules are not in accordance with the agreement which we made with you on October 16." Weir noted that the employee representatives had modified the plan to permit the election of nonemployees so as "to conform to the provisions of the N.R.A.," but no other changes had been suggested at the hearing. The NLB's proposal, however, amounted to "a radical change in substance in the form of a plan now in force at Weirton and not of mere procedure, and we have no right to consent to [NLB modification]." Because of the various attempted alterations in the plan and the lateness of the NLB's documents, Weir maintained that the company had no alternative: "Under the circumstances, we must consider any arrangement with you terminated, and the election will proceed in accordance with the rules adopted by the employes' organization."[115]

The Board believed that Weir's conduct was in plain violation of the NIRA. Reverend Haas strongly disagreed with Weir's interpretation of the settlement and the company's course of action. Having participated in the formulation and drafting of the agreement, Haas stated by sworn affidavit that "throughout the discussion it was the clear understanding that the election would provide the employees with a full and unrestricted opportunity to select their representatives and to choose any form of self-organization they might desire." No restrictions were to be placed on employee freedom of choice, for, in fact, evidence at the hearing established that "the provisions of the plan permitted the Weirton Company to control the plan, precluded any independence of action on the part of employees and prevented any effective collective bargaining. The dissatisfaction of the employees with the plan had been one of the causes of the strike." Moreover, company officials clearly understood that the plan of representation would be challenged in the election and that all matters of substances were left to the NLB's discretion. The very purpose of the election, Haas insisted, was to allow employees an unfettered choice between Amalgamated representation or the company plan, and any contrary argument was baseless. In Haas's words:

The main question at issue was whether the workers were represented by the Employee Representation Plan or by the Amalgamated Union and its officials. There obviously was no need for any special agreement permitting the striking employees to participate in the company union election as they already had that right independent of any agreement. The construction which the [company] seeks to place on the agreement makes it entirely meaningless. To intimate that in conversation Senator Wagner and I made statements in such plain contradiction of the evident meaning and purpose of the agreement is to ascribe to us either duplicity and deceitfulness or a willingness to participate in a futile proceeding.[116]

Despite NLB opposition, the Weirton employee representatives proceeded with the election under their own auspices. In the balloting on December 11, a majority of Weirton employees selected representatives from among their fellow employees. The NLB determined that Weir's repudiation of the Board's authority warranted enforcement litigation, and it decided to use the case as a test of section 7(a). According to a file memorandum of January 11, 1934, there was "convincing evidence" compiled by NLB and Justice Department investigators to prove that Weirton had interfered with the rights of its employees to organize and bargain through their own representatives. The unlawful acts included not only the abrogation of the settlement agreement, but numerous other offenses as well:

It cannot be too strongly emphasized that the case against the Weirton Steel Company does not consist merely of its repudiation of the agreement with the National Labor Board or its refusal to permit the National Labor Board to conduct the election of December 15th. The evidence covers a wide range of offenses and there would be ample justification for proceeding in the courts against the company for a violation of Section 7, even though the agreement with the National Labor Board had never been repudiated.

Among other violations, the memorandum continued, Weirton Steel had formed a company union that interfered with the self-organization of employees because employees were given no choice whether to accept or reject the plan. Further, the investigation revealed the "most varied proof" of the company's active coercion of employees, including discharges and threats of discharge, threats of plant closures, gifts of food and drink to employees, and extra compensation paid to the employee representatives.[117] For those reasons, NLB field investigators urged litigation in order to enforce the Board's authority.

In the ensuing trial, the factual and legal issues were resolved adversely to the NLB. Judge Nields observed that a total of 9,336 employees were given ballots, and 6,813 valid ballots were counted. "The result of this election," said the court, "is conclusive evidence that an overwhelming majority of the employees approved of the employee representation plan then in effect." Contrary to the Amalgamated's allegations that workers were coerced and intimated during the election, such allegations were not "sustained by any proof of acts or words of any member of the management."[118]

The court also found the employee representation plan to be an effective and satisfactory means of labor-management relations. Between the inception of the plan and October 1, 1934, the employee committees processed 1,040 cases, the majority of which dealt with wage grievances, followed by working conditions and safety. A total of 697 cases were settled in favor of employees and 124 in favor of management, with the remainder withdrawn or pending. At one point, the representatives demanded, and received, a 10 percent general wage increase.[119]

Such facts implicitly repudiated the government's expert witnesses, including no less an authority than John R. Commons, who asserted that company unions could not engage in genuine collective bargaining. In an affidavit submitted to the court, Commons said that there was a "substantial unanimity of opinion among economists and others who have disinterestedly studied labor relations as to the reasons for conflict between company unionism and trade unionism." Basically, Commons pointed out, "a company union is an organization of employees fostered by the employers for the purpose of controlling the employees' organization." The Weirton plan resembled many other company unions, and because management was a party to the creation of the plan, it did not constitute employee self-organization. Even more destructive of employee free choice, the plan reserved a management veto over any decisions; thus, representatives were forced to accept the ultimate authority of management. Commons concluded that the plan was a company-dominated entity that could not act as an agent of collective bargaining because of its many failings:

[I]t gives to the employer a veto power in any change in the Plan, even in the designation of whom may be chosen to be representatives; it does not provide for any collective action; it gives such a veto power to the management on the wishes of the representatives that it can be only described as economic coercion rather than bargaining; and it does not provide for the free election of representatives.[120]

But Commons' theories made little impression on Judge Nields.

Based on his view of the facts, Nields rejected the government's request for injunctive relief. The Weirton plan, he ruled, did not constitute a violation of the terms of the NIRA providing for collective bargaining; it was neither dominated by the company nor unlawfully influenced employees in their rights under the statute. Indeed, Nields added, harmonious relations between workers and managers was an "essential feature of the [manufacturing] enterprise. If satisfactory, the court will not disturb it." Nields emphatically rejected the idea of class conflict as a corollary of employment:

It is said this relation involves the problem of the economic balance of the power of labor against the power of capital. The theory of a balance of power or of balancing opposing powers is based upon the assumption of an inevitable and necessary diversity of interest. This is the traditional old world theory. It is not the Twentieth Century American theory of that relation as dependent upon mutual interest, understanding and good will. This modern theory is embodied in the Weirton plan of employee organization.[121]

Consequently, the plan was a lawful and effective means of collective bargaining that "in all respects" complied with the provisions of section 7(a) of the NIRA. Despite the court's Panglossian description of the Weirton ERP and the "modern theory" of industrial organization, the debate concerning Weirton was far from concluded, and the arguments in the case were reiterated in the legislative history of the Wagner Act.

In addition, even though the *Weirton* case was generally concerned with the legitimacy of employee representation under section 7(a), Judge Nields' opinion proceeded to hold the NIRA unconstitutional as beyond the scope of federal power. The government argued that the statute was based on federal control over interstate commerce. That argument, the judge concluded, was inconsistent with established judicial precedent: "In a number of cases the Supreme Court has declared that the commerce clause of the Constitution cannot be construed to bring within the regulatory power of Congress the entire industrial life of the nation." The company's plants were involved in production only; raw materials transported in interstate commerce to the facilities were transformed into entirely new goods. Any interstate commerce connection between the materials of production and the finished items was overly tenuous. "If defendant's manufacturing plants and manufacturing operations are to be regarded as instruments for the interstate movement of goods, it follows that practically all of the manufacturing industry of the United States would be brought within the control of the federal government."[122]

To summarize, the *Weirton Steel* case reflected all of the major weaknesses of the NIRA and its implementation. The NLB had no legal authority to impose its decisions on employers, and, in any event, there was a significant divergence of interpretation regarding collective bargaining under section 7(a). Employers insisted that company unions satisfied their legal obligations regarding collective bargaining, and they also maintained that exclusive majority representation effectively created the "closed shop" to which they were opposed. Judge Nields' ruling threw the weight of the federal judiciary against Wagner's effort to fashion a national labor policy out of the ambiguous rights guaranteed in section 7(a). Meanwhile, however, Wagner persisted in his goal of a legislative solution to the problems encountered by the NLB.

On March 1, 1934, Wagner introduced into the Senate his Labor Disputes Act (S. 2926). The legislation was designed to resolve the major issues raised during the NLB's brief existence.[123] Company unions were dealt with in sections 5(3) and (4) of the bill, which prohibited employers from initiating or influencing the formation, governance, or functioning of a labor organization, or contributing financial support to it.[124] The congressional prohibition on company unions reflected a national labor policy based on assumptions about the institutional nature of collective bargaining. That is, according to the emerging view, "questions involving wages, hours, and working conditions had to be dealt with on an industry- or nationwide basis if settlements conducive to general economic conditions were to result"; and, by design, any organization limited to bargaining at one plant or firm could not effectively act on labor's behalf in the national economic arena.[125] Administration of the law was to be entrusted to a National Labor Board granted broad power to issue unfair labor practice complaints, conduct hearings, fashion remedies, and petition federal courts for judicial enforcement of its orders.[126]

The Labor Disputes Bill was debated throughout the legislative session. Confronted with "industry's unqualified opposition," lack of presidential support, and debilitating amendments, Senator Wagner withdrew the bill in mid-1934.[127] Wagner explained that in doing so, he was "following the leadership of the President," who believed that "a temporary measure ought to be passed to relieve an emergency situation," but Wagner assured the Senate that he would continue the struggle for a statute the following year, "when the country will have become sufficiently educated as to the need for it."[128] Subsequently, in June 1934, Congress approved Public Resolution No. 44, which authorized the president to create labor boards to investigate labor disputes and conduct elections for determination of collective bargaining representation.[129] By executive order of June 29, 1934, Roosevelt created the first or "old" National Labor Relations Board (NLRB). Consisting of chairman Lloyd Garrison and members Harry A. Millis and Edwin S. Smith, the NLRB mandate was to implement section 7(a) of the NIRA.[130] In carrying out that mandate, the NLRB preserved and elaborated the "common law" of labor relations originating with the NLB.[131]

In February 1935, Senator Wagner renewed his effort to enact a collective bargaining law. S.1958, the National Labor Relations (Wagner) Act, embodied Wagner's experience with the NLB and incorporated previous legislative concepts. The proposed bill strengthened the powers of the NLRB, set forth a constitutional basis for the law, severed all ties between the NLRB and the Department of Labor, and provided in express terms for exclusive representation by the majority representative. Despite the initial opposition of employers, the Act proceeded through the Senate and the House with relatively little debate, passing in the Senate on May 16, by a vote of 63 to 12.[132] On May 27, the Supreme Court announced its decision in the *Schechter Poultry* case invalidating the NIRA.[133] Because the *Schechter* opinion was widely viewed as an insuperable constitutional impediment to the pending legislation, in the words of one contemporary observer, "the opposition [to the NLRA] just folded up. There was no reason for them to go on record and to go through a bruising battle on the floor."[134]

President Roosevelt signed the National Labor Relations Act on July 5, 1935. The law had little immediate effect on employers, however, who were assured by respectable authorities that the Act "unnecessarily and arbitrarily infringes upon the individual liberties of the employer and the employee, and is therefore invalid."[135] In fact, the employers' "bitter opposition to the law made it impossible for the NLRB to function as Congress intended until the act was sustained by the Supreme Court [in 1937]."[136] Notwithstanding employer resistance, workers translated the abstract rights conferred upon them by the Act into reality. In 1934, union membership stood at 3,088,000 members, or 11.9 percent of the nonagricultural work force; by 1937, there were 7,001,000 members comprising 22.6 percent of the nonagricultural work force.[137] The remarkable surge of union activism was not attributable to the legal protections afforded workers between July 1935 and April 1937, but rather it occurred despite the lack of them. In his analysis of the early years of the Wagner Act, Karl Klare emphasized the importance of workers' mobilization as a means of securing collective bargaining rights:

It is of transcendent importance . . . to appreciate that the Wagner Act did not fully become "the law" when Congress passed it in 1935, or even when the Supreme Court ruled it constitutional in 1937, although obviously these legal events enhanced the legitimacy of the labor movement. The Act "became law" only when employers were forced to obey its command by the imaginative, courageous, and concerted efforts of countless unheralded workers. This was one of the rare instances in which the common people, often heedless of the advice of their own leaders, seized control of their destinies and genuinely altered the course of American history.

The "crucial breakthroughs," Klare adds, were the General Motors–United Auto Workers Agreement and U.S. Steel's recognition of the Steel Workers Organizing Committee.[138]

For almost two decades, the steel industry had relied on participation plans as a technique of union avoidance. Those plans were created in response to external threats from unions and the federal government. Whatever benefits the plans offered to employees—and, as William Dickson energetically argued, they could contribute to the improvement of working life—were incidental and secondary to the preservation of managerial power. In 1936 SWOC discovered that, ironically, the employee representation plans were the vulnerable point at which to concentrate its organizational campaign. SWOC's success in subverting the plans offers helpful insights for the future reform of our labor law. If the objectives of employee freedom of choice and self-determination in the workplace are to have meaningful content, workers must have, at a minimum, a viable and accessible alternative to programs unilaterally imposed by employers.

THE ERPS AND THE STEEL WORKERS ORGANIZING COMMITTEE

When John L. Lewis and other dissident labor leaders founded the CIO in November 1935 to undertake mass industrial unionization, one problem that immediately confronted them was the lack of an institutional base in the steel industry. Historically, the Amalgamated Associated of Iron, Steel and Tin Workers had assumed jurisdiction over union activities in steel, and while "the CIO knew that it could not organize steel through the Amalgamated, . . . neither was it willing, at a time when its future ties to the AFL were uncertain, simply to ignore the jurisdictional rights of the Amalgamated."[139] Lewis' solution was an agreement in June 1936 between the CIO and Amalgamated, pursuant to which the Steel Workers Organizing Committee was granted authority "to handle all matters relative to the organizing campaign, other than the issuance of charters." The CIO, in return, contributed an organizing fund of $500,000.[140] Lewis appointed Philip Murray, a UMW vice-president, as chairman of SWOC.[141] On June 17, SWOC held its first official meeting; among those present was Clinton Golden, whom Lewis had named as SWOC regional director for the Pittsburgh area. Golden previously had been director of the National Labor Relations Board's 6th Region and was instrumental in persuading leaders of the Amalgamated to accept Lewis's offer of support.[142] That afternoon, SWOC issued a public announcement declaring:

The objective of the Committee is to establish a permanent organization for collective bargaining in the steel industry. . . . Once a substantial proportion of the steel workers have signified their desire to enjoy the benefits of collective bargaining through a genuine labor union, we shall approach steel management and request that they observe the public policy of the United States by peacefully negotiating a collective bargaining agreement.

Four days later, SWOC held a mass rally on the banks of the Youghiogheny River near McKeesport, Pennsylvania. Murray and Golden addressed the assembled steel and coal workers, and Murray pledged: "The drive to unionize the steel industry will continue if it takes 10 years!"[143]

SWOC's approach focused in the first place on the employee representation plans. In a memorandum of September 11 to his subregional directors, Murray discussed the subject of "certain recent significant and healthy developments in the direction of independent thinking and action among employee (company union) representatives of certain subsidiaries of the U.S. Steel Corp., and particularly the Carnegie-Illinois Steel Co." Murray said that the representatives had formed a joint Chicago-Pittsburgh Council on August 25 and had held a second meeting in Pittsburgh on September 9. On that date, they had requested a conference with officials of U.S. Steel, but the company had refused. Consequently, the representatives were planning a series of subregional conferences in the Pittsburgh and Chicago areas, the ultimate objective of which was a national convention attended by delegates of all company facilities. Murray then set out a strategy for the field organizers:

In view of the foregoing, I want you to devote more of your time to the work of contacting the employee representatives in your territory. It is important that you establish a personal, and where-ever possible, a friendly contact with them either as individuals or as groups. Explain this program to them—interest them in it and then enlist their active volunteer support in getting as many of the employees whom they represent in the mills to sign up as possible. Endeavor to get them interested in attending one of the three sub-regional conferences which will be held in the near future.

I want to know as a result of your personal contacts just which of the employee representatives in your territory are in sympathy with this program. I want you to send me their names and addresses and tell me something about them. Likewise, I want to know which of the employee representatives in your territory are actively opposing independent action by their groups.

Murray cautioned the organizers to proceed with care and to avoid taking "uncalled for and unnecessary chances" so as to minimize the risk of discharge for union sympathizers. Murray said that as a result of his contacts with the representatives, he was convinced "that hundreds of them are willing and anxious to cooperate with us in this campaign." To assist the organizers, Murray concluded, he was assigning Harold Ruttenberg and John Mullen "to concentrate on this work."[144]

The key in-plant organizer for SWOC in the Pittsburgh region was Elmer Maloy. Maloy was employed at the Duquesne plant of Carnegie-Illinois, where, he recalled, Arthur Young had developed a plan and appointed the first group of representatives in May 1934. Disenchanted with the operation of the plan and its lack of effectiveness, Maloy had decided in early 1935 to run for the position of representative. His election was a mandate for the emerging progressive faction among the representatives.

All the walks were painted with my check number and name, the water tower, clear up for 50 feet in the air, and down in the open hearth and all the buildings and everything. Everybody knew that Maloy was running, there was no question about that. Well, I got twice as many votes as the two old representatives.

Maloy was appointed to the rules committee of the representation plan, and he immediately became aware of the limitations of the ERP relative to managerial control. At his first committee meeting, Maloy proposed to amend the rules governing the ERP. One of the employer's representatives supported the motion and suggested that it be put to a vote. The ubiquitous Arthur Young, by then the director of labor relations at U.S. Steel, informed the committee that no changes would be made. Maloy recalled Young's statement to the group. "You're not going to change any rules in this plant. If you change one rule in this plant, you can change them all. And when any changes are made, I'll make them." Young's declaration was hardly surprising to Maloy; in fact, he had anticipated such a response and later remembered: "Well, then, that was one of the things that we wanted to prove, that [the] ERP didn't mean a damn thing."[145]

In the Chicago region, George Patterson had succeeded in organizing an independent association numbering some 3,000 employees from the South Works of Carnegie-Illinois. Under his leadership, rank and file steelworks formed the Associated Employees union in September 1936. Patterson, meanwhile, continued to act a chairman of the Calumet Council of Employee Representatives. Throughout the early part of 1936, Patterson remained in contact with Lewis, who advised Patterson that if he "just kept [his] shirttail in [the union] would be there." On July 16, 1936, Patterson formally delivered his organization to Murray and accepted a SWOC charter.[146]

In the last four months of 1936, the representatives met on a number of occasions. The most important of those meetings was held on December 20, 1936, at the Fort Pitt Hotel in Pittsburgh. More than 250 delegates from 42 plants were in attendance, and on this occasion, they formally declared their support for the CIO. The delegates' first order of business was unanimously to elect Maloy as chairman. Various speakers then criticized the Employee Representation Plan. Mr. Ramsay of Bethlehem described the plan "as a whip held over the men by a dominant management." Mr. Garrity of the Edgar Thompson works "called on the proponents of the plan to defend it. No person present made any defense of the plan." The delegates' views of employee representation were ultimately embodied in Resolution No. 1, notable for its energy and candor:

Whereas; The management in the steel industry finances, controls, dominates, and intimidates the company union, and ... the company union is a device of the management to prevent bona fide industrial organization of the steel workers, and ... the Federal Congress and President of United States have outlawed company unions financed or dominated by employers, and ... the company union is powerless to win substantial gains from the management, and ... the company union is simply a committee of men from different departments in the mill and is denied the right to hold meetings of the men, issue membership cards, or collect dues ... therefore, BE IT NOW RESOLVED: That the progressive representatives here assembled condemn the company union as a farce, a sham, an insult to the intelligence of steel workers, and a Rip Van Winkle form of collective bargaining where the company union representatives try to bargain and the management actually does the collecting.

Following a speech by Philip Murray and a ten-minute recess, the delegates adopted a number of resolutions, including Resolution No. 1. To provide a new organizational structure, the respective district councils of Pittsburgh, Youngstown-Cleveland, and the Eastern District merged together into a Regional Council that was to be known as the C.I.O. Representatives Council. Maloy was elected president of that body, and three vice-presidents were chosen from each district. The delegates also adopted a Declaration of Principles, which reiterated the link between unionization and the employee representation plan. The first principle adopted by the Council was that "all steel workers be organized into a National Industrial Union." The remaining three principles translated the general objective into a specific strategy. The elected employee representatives within the plants were to "use their influence to enroll the steel workers into the Steel Workers Organizing Committee's campaign." With respect to the workers' view of the ERPs, the Council proposed that "all steel workers be thoroughly informed by employee representatives who know from experience that the company union is a device of the management and totally unable to win any major concessions for the steel workers." Last, the Council agreed that "C.I.O. employee representatives remain inside the company unions for reasons obvious to all."[147]

Despite its overwhelming success, the SWOC domination of the company unions was not unopposed. An articulate and vocal minority of representatives, headed by "Colonel" Fred Bohne, persistently argued against trade union affiliation. In a revealing portrait, SWOC District Director Elmer Cope astutely analyzed Bohne's character and attachment to the principle of company unionism.

Cope and another SWOC staff member, Tommy Evans, visited Bohne at his home on October 19. Cope remarked first on Bohne's age—"at least sixty"—and second on Bohne's "obvious sincerity and crusading spirit." Bohne's beliefs were a curious mixture of populism and company loyalty:

It is his contention that he has always been in favor of industrial unions and that he would do nothing to stand in the way of seeing a strong union develop. He believes, and with sincerity, that the company union can be developed into an effective collective bargaining instrument for the workers in steel. When I pressed him for his views regarding our movement he simply stated that he believed that by gradually extending the powers and scope of the representative bodies they could be welded into the kind of thing we are after. He visualized one big employee representative organization which would eventually embrace the workers throughout the steel industry. He even went so far as to suggest that perhaps in due time we would find ourselves united.

Unpersuaded by Bohne's arguments, Cope noted that if Bohne "really is sincere he is having a pipe dream." Nevertheless, the force of Bohne's opposition could not be discounted: "He's a pretty slick article and the company certainly knows what it is doing when it caters to him. Of course, his influence must be destroyed." Cope suggested that the pro-SWOC representatives, such as Maloy, "will have to be pretty careful and pretty shrewd if they are to swing him our way or to discredit him." Above all, Cope thought, the organizing activity would have to be carried out "in such a way as not to solidify the representatives around him."[148]

Near the end of 1936, a Defense Committee was formed by Carnegie-Illinois employees sympathetic to the ERP. During its short existence, the Defense Committee held several meetings, retained its own legal counsel to represent members in NLRB hearings, and produced a short antiunion publication.[149] The committee also contacted company president Benjamin Fairless to inform him of its activities and received his enthusiastic endorsement. Fairless wrote: "I can assure you that the writer and his associates will cooperate in every possible way with your Committee as it is our firm conviction that the Plan of Employee Representation in effect in the Plants of the Corporation is the best Plan for collective bargaining so far devised."[150]

In a leaflet addressed to "our fellow employees of the Carnegie-Illinois Steel Corp," the Defense Committee attacked the trade union campaign and its leadership. Members of the Committee were "convinced without a shadow of a doubt that with very little expense to us, without a closed shop and WITHOUT STRIKES, we can secure with our own organization more than we can attain with Mr. Lewis' CIO." According to the Defense Committee, Lewis enjoyed an annual income of "two and one-half million dollars per year" from the United Mine Workers, and he was the "sole and final authority" regarding disbursement of that money. The Committee also rejected charges that the ERPs were dominated and coerced by management. "This not only is a rank falsehood, but we resent being pictured as a bunch of chuckle-headed stool-pigeons." The leaflet concluded with a plea for unity that echoes Rockefeller's declarations two decades earlier: "The employer and employees must work together for their common good. There must be a spirit of co-operation and brotherhood if both are to progress materially and socially. They must cease to regard each other as enemies, and recognize themselves as joint trustees of one of the most important elements of our national life."[151] Despite the Defense Committee's show of opposition, the struggle for unionization at U.S. Steel was over within months.

On January 9, 1937, John L. Lewis met with Myron Taylor, chairman of the board of U.S. Steel, to discuss recognition of SWOC. Taylor contacted the heads of the subsidiary operations to ask if they would sign a labor contract in accordance with current practices under the ERPs. Shortly thereafter, the board of directors agreed that Benjamin Fairless of Carnegie-Illinois should negotiate the preliminary agreement with Philip Murray, and on March 2, Fairless and Murray "set their signatures to the most important single document in the history of the American labor movement."[152]

The controversy among workers at U.S. Steel regarding trade unionism versus employee representation illustrates the various dimensions of the issue. Such fundamental concerns as freedom, coercion, autonomy, and power are articulated in the opposing views of company unions. Those same issues are embedded in the legislative history of the Wagner Act and demonstrate the deeply divisive nature of participation schemes. At a basic level, the dialogue between Bohne, Maloy, and other steelworkers reproduces basic debates about democracy under capitalist conditions of production. Supporters of employee representation assumed that if employees chose those organizational forms through the exercise of "free choice," then their choice should be upheld. Knowledgeable and persuasive critics, such as Senator Wagner, perceived inherent coercion and lack of choice in such arrangements, and the legislative record abounds with penetrating criticisms of employer-sponsored participation programs.

Importantly, the meaning of section 8(a)(2) of the National Labor Relations Act has been shaped not only by congressional debate, but also by more than fifty years of administrative and judicial interpretation. The text of the statute, relatively straightforward in its proscription of managerial interference with the collective activities of workers, often yields to the manipulation of the NLRB, courts, and even to the views of legal commentators. Legal discourse produces its own structures of attitudes and values. Thus, workers may be persuaded that the legal principles set forth in the NLRA adequately protect their rights and fairly accommodate their legitimate claims to a voice in the enterprise. But more realistically, judicial lawmaking often promotes the managerial perspective at the expense of workers' interests. Chapter 3 traces the development of a labor law vision that propounds ideals of democratic choice, mutual cooperation, and adjustment of conflict through nonadversarial procedures. Underlying the legal doctrine, however, are suspect propositions regarding the nature of managerial power in the workplace.

NOTES

1. W. Jett Lauck, *Political and Industrial Democracy, 1776–1926* (New York: Funk & Wagnalls, 1926), 17.

2. For a historical summary, see Milton Derber, *The American Idea of Industrial Democracy, 1865–1965* (Urbana: University of Illinois Press, 1970).

3. Stuart Brandes, *American Welfare Capitalism, 1880–1940* (Chicago: University of Chicago Press, 1976), 121.

4. David Montgomery, *The Fall of the House of Labor: The Workplace, the State and American Labor Activism, 1865–1925* (Cambridge: Cambridge University Press, 1987), 350.

5. U.S. Congress, *Report of the Committee of the Senate Upon Labor Capitol*, vol. II (Washington, D.C.: 1885), 803–819 (testimony of George Storm).

6. *Report*, 805–806, 810, 815–818.

7. *Report*, 806.

8. Mary La Dame, *The Filene Store: A Study of Employes' Relation to Management in a Retail Store* (New York: Russell Sage Foundation, 1930), 261, 237–258.

9. La Dame, *Filene Store*, 72.

10. Edward A. Filene, *The Way Out: A Forecast of Coming Changes in American Business and Industry* (Garden City, N.Y.: Doubleday, 1925), 170, 160.

11. La Dame, *The Filene Store*, 134–138.

12. Caroll French, "The Shop Committee in the United States," *Johns Hopkins University Studies in Historical and Political Science*, 41 (1923), 15.

13. H. F. Porter, "The Higher Law in the Industrial World," *The Engineering Magazine*, 29 (1905), 648, 655.

14. John Leitch, *Man to Man: The Story of Industrial Democracy* (New York: B. C. Forbes, 1919), 62, 191–192.

15. Leitch, *Man to Man*, 140–146.

16. John R. Commons, *History of Labor in the United States, 1896–1932*, vol. III [Don Lescohier, *Working Conditions*] (New York: Macmillan, 1935), 339.

17. Paul W. Litchfield, *The Industrial Republic: A Study in Industrial Economics* (Boston: Little, Brown, 1920); and also Paul Litchfield, *The Industrial Republic: Reflections of an Industrial Lieutenant* (Garden City, N.Y.: Doubleday, 1946). For a "revisionist" treatment claiming that the antiunion bias of the Goodyear plan, and others, has been exaggerated, see Daniel Nelson, "The Company Union Movement, 1900–1937: A Reexamination," *Business History Review*, 56 (1982), 335–357. Nelson has since revised his revisionism. In his description of union avoidance strategies in the 1930s, Nelson characterizes the Goodyear corporation as "one of the best-known practitioners of the belligerent and sophisticated versions of persistent antiunionism between 1933 and 1941." The key component of Goodyear's strategy was "an advanced and innovative program of welfare capitalism, capped by one of the most effective company unions in American history, the Industrial Assembly." Daniel Nelson, "Managers and Nonunion Workers in the Rubber Industry: Union Avoidance Strategies in the 1930s," *Industrial and Labor Relations Review*, 43 (1989), 43–44.

18. For treatments of the period, see generally, National Industrial Conference Board, *Works Councils in the United States* (Boston: National Industrial Conference Board, 1919), 4–6; Ernest Burton, *Employee Representation* (Baltimore: Williams & Wilkins, 1926), 25–44; Commons, *History of Labor*, 337–339.

19. Neil Mitchell, *The Generous Corporation: A Political Analysis of Economic Power* (New Haven, Conn.: Yale University Press, 1989), 7.

20. George West, *Report on the Colorado Strike* (Washington, D.C.: Government Printing Office, 1915), 15–85.

21. "Address of Mother Jones at Starkville, Colorado, September 24, 1913," in Commission on Industrial Relations (CIR), *Final Report and Testimony*, 64th Cong., 1st Sess., 1915–16 (Washington, D.C.: Government Printing Office, 1916), 9, 7254 (hereafter CIR, *Final Report*). For other descriptions, see Barron Beshoar, *Out of the Depths: The Story of John R. Lawson, A Labor Leader* (Denver: Colorado Labor Historical Society and Denver Trades and Labor Assembly, 1942); West, *Report*; Samuel Yellen, *American Labor Struggles, 1877–1934* (New York: Monad Press, 1974), 205–250; George S. McGovern and Leonard F. Guttridge, *The Great Coalfield War* (Boston: Houghton Mifflin, 1972).

22. Ben Beshoar, a physician, testified at Tikas' inquest that he was uncertain whether gunshots or the blow to Tikas' head resulted in death. West, *Report*, 129. The military presented its official story in Report of the Commanding General [John Chase] to the Governor, *The Military Occupation of the Coal Strike Zone of Colorado by the Colorado National Guard, 1913–14* (Denver: Smith-Brooks Printing Co., 1914).

23. CIR, *Final Report*, 7, 6895.

24. CIR, *Final Report*, 7, 6351.

25. Raymond Fosdick, *John D. Rockefeller, Jr.: A Portrait* (New York: Harper & Brothers, 1953), 151. For an example of the attacks on Rockefeller, see Walter

Fink, *The Ludlow Massacre* (Denver: [Policy Committee, District 15, United Mine Workers of America], 1914).

26. For a treatment of Lee's association with Rockefeller, see H. M. Gitelman, *Legacy of the Ludlow Massacre; A Chapter in American Industrial Relations* (Philadelphia: University of Pennsylvania Press, 1988), 28–37.

27. CIR, *Final Report*, 8, 7903.

28. CIR, *Final Report*, 9, 8440.

29. CIR, *Final Report*, 8, 7844–7845.

30. Letter to Rockefeller, August 16, 1914, quoted in CIR, *Final Report*, 9, 8441–8442.

31. Quoted in West, *Report*, 172.

32. West, *Report*, 98.

33. Quoted in West, *Report*, 98–99.

34. Quoted in West, *Report*, 174–175.

35. Quoted in West, *Report*, 176–177.

36. Quoted in West, *Report*, 177–178.

37. CIR, *Final Report*, 8, 7839–7840.

38. CIR, *Final Report*, 9, 8446.

39. West, *Report*, 186.

40. Rockefeller to E. A. Van Valkenburg, June 28, 1921, quoted in Gitelman, *Legacy*, 337.

41. Gitelman, *Legacy*, 337.

42. Irving Bernstein, *The Lean Years: A History of the American Worker, 1920–1933* (Boston: Houghton Mifflin, 1960), 160.

43. *Denver Post*, September 20, 1915, 1, 3.

44. *Denver Post*, September 21, 1915, 3.

45. *Denver Post*, September 24, 1915, 1, 3.

46. *New York Times*, September 23, 1915, at 1, col. 7.

47. *Denver Post*, September 25, 1915, 2.

48. *Denver Post*, September 30, 1915, 1, 2.

49. CIR, *Final Report*, 8, 7838.

50. John D. Rockefeller, Jr., "To the Employes, " in *The Colorado Industrial Plan* ([New York: n.p.], 1916), 39, 42.

51. "To the People of Colorado," Address to the Chamber of Commerce, Denver, Colorado, October 8, 1915, reprinted in John D. Rockefeller, Jr., *The Personal Relation in Industry* (New York: Boni and Liveright, 1923), 113, 115, 117.

52. "Labor and Capital—Partners," in ibid., 39–40.

53. Ben Selekman and Mary Van Kleeck, *Employes' Representation in Coal Mines: A Study of the Industrial Representation Plan of the Colorado Fuel and Iron Company* (New York: Russell Sage, 1924), 291.

54. Selekman and Van Kleek, *Employes' Representation*, 386, 389–390, 398.

55. West, *Report*, 189.

56. Bruno Ramirez, *When Workers Fight: The Politics of Industrial Relations in the Progressive Era, 1898–1916* (Westport, Conn.: Greenwood Press, 1978), 77–82.

57. David Gordon, Richard Edwards, and Michael Reich, *Segmented Work, Divided Workers: The Historical Transformation of Labor in the United States* (New York: Cambridge University Press, 1982), 154–155.

58. U.S. Department of Labor, Bureau of Labor Statistics, *National War Labor*

Board: A History of its Formation and Activities, Together with Its Awards and the Documents of Importance in the Record of Its Development, Bulletin No. 287 (Washington, D.C.: Government Printing Office, 1922), 34, 16. The two public members of the National War Labor Board were Frank Walsh and William Howard Taft; the entity was thus sometimes identified as the "Taft-Walsh Board."

59. French, "Shop Committee," 24, 25.

60. National Industrial Conference Board, *Works Councils in the United States* (Boston: National Industrial Conference Board, 1919), 13.

61. French, "Shop Committee," 30.

62. Letter from President Woodrow Wilson to Samuel Gompers, September 3, 1919, quoted in U.S. Department of Labor, *Reports of the Department of Labor, 1919* (Washington, D.C.: Government Printing Office, 1920), 20. Wilson sent the same text to the other invitees.

63. Department of Labor, *Reports, 1919*, 23–24.

64. Haggai Hurvitz, "Ideology and Industrial Conflict: President Wilson's First Industrial Conference of October 1919," *Labor History* 18 (1977), 521. See also Charles Russell, "Collective Bargaining in the President's First Industrial Conference," *Annals, American Academy of Political and Social Science*, 90 (1920), 63–65. A member of the commission, Russell asked the chair of the employer's group to draft a resolution acceptable to that group. "They came back," he said, "with a resolution, which it was perfectly obvious to every intelligent being was a resolution that could not possibly be accepted either by labor or the public group, because it was, in effect, a denial of the fundamental and primitive principles of collective bargaining."

65. Hurvitz, "Ideology and Industrial Conflict," 522–523; see also Paul H. Douglas, "Shop Committees: Substitute for, or Supplement to, Trades-Unions?" *Journal of Political Economy*, 29 (1921), 91.

66. See, generally, Robert Dunn, *The Americanization of Labor: The Employers' Offensive Against the Trade Unions* (New York: International Publishers, 1927).

67. Brandes, *American Welfare Capitalism*, 134.

68. William Leiserson, "Contributions of Personnel Management to Improved Labor Conditions," *Wertheim Lectures on Industrial Relations, 1928* (Cambridge, Mass.: Harvard University Press, 1929), 154, 158.

69. Burton, *Employee Representation*, 60–64.

70. John Calder, *Modern Industrial Relations: Policy and Practice* (New York: Longmans, Green, 1924), 159.

71. Frank W. Taussig, "The Opposition of Interest between Employer and Employee: Difficulties and Remedies," *Wertheim Lectures*, 214, 216, 219–220.

72. Memorandum from H. F. Brown to Ireneé du Pont, May 16, 1919. Records of E. I. du Pont de Nemours & Co., Administrative Papers, Acc. 1662, Box 27, "Employee Representation," Hagley Museum and Library, Wilmington, Delaware. The "New York Conference" became better known as the "Special Conference Committee (SCC)," and continued its activities into the 1930s. Du Pont's labor policies and the company's relationship with the SCC are analyzed in John C. Rumm, "The Du Pont Company and the Special Conference Committee, 1919–1939: A Study in Comparative Labor Relations," unpublished paper presented at the Duquesne History Forum, October 1983. The authors are grateful to Mr. Rumm for his generous assistance in matters relating to du Pont.

73. Brown, "Memorandum," 9.

74. Brown, "Memorandum," 42.

75. Brown, "Memorandum," 10.

76. Brown, "Memorandum," 53–58.

77. *Report of Proceedings of the Thirty-Ninth Annual Convention of the American Federation of Labor* (Washington, D.C.: Law Reporter Printing Co., 1919), 249–250.

78. Burton, *Employee Representation*, 64–65. See also Robert W. Dunn, *Company Unions: Employers' "Industrial Democracy"* (New York: Vanguard Press, 1927), 175–183 ("Labor's Case against the Company Union").

79. Compare Sanford M. Jacoby, "Union-Management Cooperation in the United States: Lessons from the 1920s," *Industrial & Labor Relations Review*, 37 (1983), 18–33, with Bryan Palmer, "Class, Conception and Conflict: The Thrust for Efficiency, Managerial Views of Labor and the Working Class Rebellion, 1903–22," *Review of Radical Political Economics*, 7 (1975), 31–48, and also William Lazonick, "Organizational Capabilities in American Industry: The Rise and Decline of Managerial Capitalism," *Business and Economic History*, Second Series, 19 (1990), 35–54.

80. National Industrial Conference Board (NICB), *Collective Bargaining Through Employee Representation* (New York: National Industrial Conference Board, 1933), 15–17, Tables 1 and 2.

81. Harry Millis and Royal Montgomery, *Organized Labor* (New York: McGraw-Hill, 1945), 837 (Table 16).

82. Leo Wolman, *Ebb and Flow in Trade Unionism* (New York: National Bureau of Economic Research, 1936), 33–34.

83. NICB, *Collective Bargaining*, 16.

84. Millis and Montgomery, *Organized Labor*, 841 (Table 17).

85. For a study of Dickson's life and career, see Gerald G. Eggert, *Steelmasters and Labor Reform, 1886–1923* (Pittsburgh: University of Pittsburgh Press, 1981). The abysmal working conditions in the steel industry, particularly at U.S. Steel, are described in Commission of Inquiry, Interchurch World Movement, *Report on the Steel Strike of 1919* (New York: Harcourt, Brace, and Howe, 1920).

86. "Report of Examiners of the Labor Controversy at the Midvale Steel and Ordnance Co., Philadelphia, Pa.," July 4, 1918, National War Labor Board (NWLB) Case Files, 1918–1919, Docket No. 129, Record Group 2, National Archives, Suitland, Maryland.

87. A. C. Dinkey to W. Jett Lauck, July 2, 1918, in ibid.

88. Josephus Daniels to Midvale Steel and Ordnance Co., Sept. 13, 1918, in "Report of Examiners."

89. William B. Dickson Papers, Box 5, Folder 5, Labor Archives, The Pennsylvania State University. The Dickson collection includes fragments of an unpublished memoir. Chapter X of that document is devoted to employee representation.

90. Eggert, *Steelmasters*, 115.

91. "Minutes of Conference," Dickson Papers, Box 5.

92. "Transcript of Hearing, Midvale Steel & Ordnance Co.," 423, NWLB Case Files.

93. E. B. Woods to John O'Brien, March 19, 1919, NWLB Case Files.

94. "Report of Administrative Examiner," March 22, 1919, NWLB Case Files.

95. Department of Labor, *National War Labor Board*, 138–139, 143.

96. Eggert, *Steelmasters*, 109.

97. Gitelman, *Legacy*, 254.

98. Mark Reutter, *Sparrows Point: Making Steel—The Rise and Ruin of American Industrial Might* (New York: Summit Books, 1988), 152–153.

99. *Iron Age*, 102 (1918), 1020–1022.

100. Robert R. Brooks, *As Steel Goes ...: Unionism in a Basic Industry* (New Haven, Conn.: Yale University Press, 1940), 79.

101. 48 U.S. Stat. 195 (1933).

102. American Iron and Steel Institute, *Collective Bargaining in the Steel Industry* (New York: American Iron and Steel Institute, 1934), 3, 5, 7–8, 14.

103. Report of the Committee on Education and Labor, *Violations of Free Speech and Rights of Labor* (Washington, D.C.: Government Printing Office, 1939), 76th Cong., Part 6, at 90–91.

104. Leverett S. Lyon et al., *The National Recovery Administration: An Analysis and Appraisal* (Washington, D.C.: Brookings Institution, 1935), 490.

105. U.S. Department of Labor, Bureau of Labor Statistics, *Characteristics of Company Unions*, Bulletin No. 634 (Washington, D.C.: Government Printing Office, 1935).

106. See Irving Bernstein, *The New Deal Collective Bargaining Policy* (Berkeley: University of California Press, 1950), 58–59.

107. Lyon, *National Recovery Administration*, 473.

108. Alfred Bernheim and Dorothy Van Doren, *Labor and the Government: An Investigation of the Role of the Government in Labor Relations* (New York: Twentieth Century Fund/McGraw-Hill, 1935), 95, Table 1; and see also Emily C. Brown, "Selection of Employees' Representatives," *Monthly Labor Review*, 40 (1935), 1–18.

109. For an account of Wagner's work on the NLB, see J. Joseph Huthmacher, *Senator Robert F. Wagner and the Rise of Urban Liberalism* (New York: Atheneum, 1968), 160–163.

110. Lyon, *National Recovery Administration*, 463.

111. Peter Irons, *The New Deal Lawyers* (Princeton, N.J.: Princeton University Press, 1982), 212.

112. *United States v. Weirton Steel Co.*, 10 F.Supp. 55 (D.C. D. Del. 1935), 62–63.

113. Quoted in *Weirton Steel*, 68, f.n. 3.

114. *Weirton Steel*, 70.

115. E. T. Weir to Senator Robert Wagner, December 11, 1933, in Weirton Steel, Transcripts, Briefs and Exhibits, 1933–35. National Labor Board, Executive Secretary, 1933–34. Record Group 25, National Archives, Suitland, Maryland.

116. Affidavit of Reverend Francis J. Haas, *United States v. Weirton Steel Co.*, copy in Weirton Steel, Transcripts, 2–3.

117. Memorandum, Weirton Steel Case, January 11, 1934, in Weirton Steel, Transcripts, 2–3.

118. *Weirton Steel*, 75–76.

119. *Weirton Steel*, 85.

120. Affidavit of John R. Commons, 1, 5, January 3, 1934, *United States v. Weirton Steel Co.*, in Weirton Steel, Transcripts.

121. *Weirton Steel*, 86.

122. *Weirton Steel*, 87, 90.

123. See, generally, James Gross, *The Making of the National Labor Relations Board:*

A Study in Economics, Politics and the Law (Albany: SUNY Press, 1974), 64–72; Bernstein, *New Deal Collective Bargaining*, 57–75.

124. National Labor Relations Board, *Legislative History of the National Labor Relations Act, 1935*, vol. I (Washington, D.C.: Government Printing Office, 1985), 3.

125. Christopher Tomlins, *The State and the Unions: Labor Relations, Law, and the Organized Labor Movement in America, 1880–1960* (New York: Cambridge University Press, 1985), 122–123.

126. Sections 201–205, *Legislative History*, NLRA, vol. I, 4–9.

127. For the circumstances surrounding the demise of the Labor Disputes Act, see Bernstein, *New Deal Collective Bargaining*, 57–75.

128. *Legislative History*, NLRA, vol. I, 1241–1242.

129. The resolution is reprinted in *Legislative History*, I, 1255B–1256.

130. The text of the order is published in National Labor Relations Board, *Decisions of the National Labor Relations Board, July 9, 1934–December 1934* [vol. I] (Washington, D.C.: Government Printing Office, 1935), vii–ix. For a further treatment of the first NLRB, see Gross, *Making of the NLRB*, 73–88.

131. Bernstein, *New Deal Collective Bargaining*, 84–88.

132. For a good description of the political forces leading to enactment of the NLRA, see David Plotke, "The Wagner Act, Again: Politics and Labor, 1935–37," *Studies in American Political Development*, 3 (1989), 105–156.

133. *Schechter Poultry Corp. v. United States*, 295 U.S. 495 (1935).

134. Statement of Philip Levy, member of the NLRB staff in 1935, quoted in Irons, *New Deal Lawyers*, 231.

135. National Lawyers Committee of the American Liberty League, *Report on the Constitutionality of the National Labor Relations Act* (Pittsburgh: Smith Bros. Co., 1935), vi.

136. Gross, *Making of the NLRB*, 3.

137. Michael Goldfield, *The Decline of Organized Labor in the United States* (Chicago: University of Chicago Press, 1987), 10, Table 1.

138. Karl Klare, "Judicial Deradicalization of the Wagner Act and the Origins of Modern Legal Consciousness, 1937–1941," *Minnesota Law Review*, 62 (1978), 266.

139. David Brody, "The Origins of Modern Steel Unionism: The SWOC Era," in Paul Clark, Peter Gottlieb, and Donald Kennedy, eds., *Forging a Union of Steel: Philip Murray, SWOC, and the United Steelworkers*, (Ithaca, N.Y.: ILR Press, 1987), 20.

140. Vincent Sweeney, *The United Steelworkers of America: Twenty Years Later, 1936–1956* ([Pittsburgh: United Steelworkers of America], 1956), 11.

141. On the relationship between Murray and Lewis, see, generally, Melvyn Dubofsky, "Labor's Odd Couple: Philip Murray and John L. Lewis," in Clark et al., *Forging a Union of Steel*, 40–44.

142. Thomas R. Brooks, *Clint: A Biography of a Labor Intellectual, Clinton S. Golden* (New York: Atheneum, 1978), 154–157.

143. Sweeney, *United Steelworkers*, 12, 14.

144. Philip Murray, Chairman, to Sub-Regional Directors, September 11, 1936, in Harold J. Ruttenberg Papers, Box 3, Folder 14. Labor Archives, The Pennsylvania State University.

145. Transcript of Oral Interview [Elmer Maloy], November 7, 1967, 11–12. Labor Archives, The Pennsylvania State University.

146. Transcript of Oral Interview [George Patterson], October 1967, 1–22. Labor Archives, The Pennsylvania State University. See also Robert Brooks, *As Steel Goes*, 86–89.

147. "District Representatives Council" [Minutes of the Meeting, December 20, 1936], in Ruttenberg Papers, Box 4, Folder 6.

148. Elmer Cope to Harold Ruttenberg, October 20, 1936, in Ruttenberg Papers, Box 3, Folder 19.

149. Press Release, January 14, 1937, Editorial Bureau of Defense Committee of Employee Representatives, and Minutes of Meeting, January 18, 1937, in Ruttenberg Papers, Box 4, Folder 6.

150. B. F. Fairless to Owen Jones et al., January 9, 1937, in Ruttenberg Papers, Box 4, Folder 6.

151. Defense Committee, "To Our Fellow Employees of the Carnegie-Illinois Steel Corp.," 1936, in Ruttenberg Papers, Box 4, Folder 6.

152. Robert Brooks, *As Steel Goes*, 108.

CHAPTER 3

The Legal Context of Worker Participation

THE WAGNER ACT

From early on, Senator Wagner was adamant concerning the dangers that the company unions posed for a system of genuine collective bargaining, and, in an important sense, employer control of workers' organizations became the predominant theme of the congressional debates about Wagner's legislation. In March 1934, shortly after the introduction of the Labor Disputes Act, Wagner published an article in the *New York Times* asserting that the company union "runs antithetical to the very core of the new-deal philosophy." Employer-dominated organizations of employees had increased substantially between 1932 and 1934, Wagner said, pointing out that the number of employees covered by company unions rose from 432,000 in the former year to 1,164,000 in the latter, for an increase of 169 percent. Wagner attributed high levels of industrial conflict to the existence of the company unions and perceived two undesirable consequences if their deployment was not checked. "One is that the employer will have to maintain his dominance by force, and thus swing us directly into industrial fascism and the destruction of our most-cherished American ideals; the other is that employees will revolt, with wide-spread violence and unpredictable conclusions."

Wagner based his arguments against the company unions on two distinct grounds. The first line of attack was an institutional one, which asserted that a system of bargaining confined to a single plant or employer could not adequately strengthen the position of workers in an industrial economy. Conceding that the company union often improved personal relations between employer and employee on a local level, Wagner insisted nevertheless that "it has failed dismally to standardize or improve wage levels, for the wage question is a general one whose sweep embraces whole industries, or States, or even the Nation." Plant-level bargaining denied the worker expert assistance with problems of industrial relations and perpetuated a relation of subservience between the representatives and the employer with whom they dealt. Company unions, then, were an impediment to the formation of durable structures for the conduct of bargaining.[1] Echoing Wagner, NLRB Member Edwin Smith emphasized in an apt metaphor that Congress desired legislation that would enable labor to extend its negotiating power, and "for any such fundamental economic purpose the company union is indeed a broken reed."[2]

Second, with respect to the needs of individual workers and their freedom of choice, Wagner explained that the Labor Disputes Act did not preclude competition between trade unions and company unions "in an open field." At the same time, he added, the right to choose representatives freely was "a mockery when the presence of a company union firmly entrenched in a plant enables an employer to exercise a compelling force over the collective activities of his workers. Freedom must begin with the removal of obstacles to its exercise."[3] Underlying this aspect of Wagner's critique of company unions are crucial assumptions about power in industrial society. Those assumptions were explored in Wagner's candid exchange with Senator Millard Tydings of Maryland on June 16, 1934, the day on which Wagner withdrew his bill in favor of Roosevelt's joint resolution.

In a discussion concerning certain amendments offered by Senator La Follette, Tydings referred to "a very significant letter" sent to him on behalf of workers at the Bethlehem plant at Sparrows Point. The letter was written by Charles Weaver, chairman of the employee representatives committee, who urged Tydings to oppose any legislation resulting in a closed union shop. "The plan of employees' representation has been functioning at this plant for 17 years," Weaver wrote, "and furnishes us with a highly satisfactory method for the settlement of the various problems arising in our employment relations." Weaver perceived that "the entire labor situation appears to be greatly clouded by misinformation, and if the absolute truth were told by everybody concerned in the present labor controversy, our plan of employees' representation would need no defense." Tydings claimed that the letter "speaks for itself" and "expresses the untrammeled and actual sentiment of the employees of that plant who in normal times number about 12,000 to 14,000."[4]

Wagner did not permit Tydings' characterization of the labor bill as "an invasion of the liberty of the worker" to pass unchallenged. "May I briefly explain to the Senate," Wagner inquired, "the plan which the Senator from Maryland says protects the freedom of the worker, while he claims that the legislation we propose is intended to deprive the worker of his just freedom?" Wagner then provided the senators with an example based on testimony before his committee:

Here is an actual case. I am giving evidence now; I am standing at my machine, working. The foreman walks over to me and says, "Here is your constitution." He goes along throughout the entire shop and says to each worker," "Here is your constitution." The worker takes the constitution and put[s] it in his pocket. He has no alternative. Refusal means the loss of his job. That is the way a company-dominated union is organized.

Wagner also observed that the Bethlehem corporation, to which Tydings referred, "has had a representative plan for many years, but it has nevertheless possessed the characteristics of the newer [post-NIRA] ones."[5]

Tydings objected that he merely wanted to insure that workers desiring the representation plan should not be "coerced into taking a plan they do not want," and asked Wagner if he knew "of any way to prevent any employee from coercing another employee to join or not join a union." In reply, Wagner pointed out that "there is no possibility that the same coercive power can be exercised by one employee against another that can be exercised by the employer against the employee." When Tydings once again insisted that he was representing a sizable group of constituents who feared that "they will be compelled or coerced to join a union which they do not want to join," Wagner angrily dismissed Tydings' criticisms. "Here is all there is to it," Wagner told the Senate. "We are extending the right to the workers to elect any individual or organization they choose, instead of being restricted. How is that compelling anybody to do anything? The charge of compulsion is a gross misrepresentation that has circled the country."[6] Yet in fact, Wagner's goal of individual free choice was conceptually at odds with the governmental encouragement of independent collective bargaining relationships throughout American industry toward the end of a more equitable distribution of wealth. Opponents of Wagner's bill, in their attacks, emphasized the common interests of workers and employers in industrial society and condemned the adversarialism and class antagonism implicit in the proposed legislation.

Among the more prominent defenders of the representation plans was Arthur Young, the architect of the plans in the steel industry and a knowledgeable exponent of the ideology of participation. Testifying before the Committee on Education and Labor in April 1934, Young began by rebuking a previous witness who had disparaged Rockefeller's Colorado plan as a "subterfuge." Young vindicated his former employer by insisting that "no one who has ever dealt with Mr. Rockefeller could ever question his absolute sincerity of purpose and act." In the U.S. Steel subsidiaries, Young continued, ERPs were introduced with the overwhelming support of employees, who would attest to the benefits of the plans. "There is no resentment on their part, no suspicion of hidden coercion or intimidation or subterfuge, because the initiation of these endeavors finds its fruit in a mutually satisfactory agreement on policies." More rhetorically, Young likened the "development of sound and harmonious relationships between men and management to the working out of a sound and harmonious relationship in marriage between man and his wife. Both depend upon a mutual conviction that their interests in life are largely in common, at least to the extent that they should form an alliance." Young concluded his testimony with an allusion to the precepts of the "Carpenter of Nazareth" as a guide to industrial conduct: "Gentlemen, I say to you in all the sincerity at my command, the works council plan is likewise a supplement to the Golden Rule." Like Rockefeller some two decades earlier, Young drew upon a broad Christian ethic and the ideals of communal harmony fostered by cooperative relationships.[7]

Employers in steel were also highly visible during the hearings. Joseph Larkin, vice-president of Bethlehem Steel, presented the case for employee representation as a means of "having the employee and employer sit down together in a friendly and constructive atmosphere and, with a first-hand practical knowledge of their problems, work out a fair and equitable solution." The cooperative approach was "the strength of employee representation as contrasted with other forms of collective bargaining which seek to organize employees and employers into separate camps with drawn battle lines." Larkin perceived that the Labor Disputes Act aimed at a specific form of organization for workers: "My general criticism of the Wagner bill is not so much that it supports unionization as that it will in operation result in enforced unionization for every kind and condition of collective bargaining."[8]

For the U.S. Steel Corporation, Raoul Desvernine presented a brief opposing the Act. He argued that collective bargaining was already in place at U.S. Steel, where "approximately 129,798 eligible employees" were employed, and more than 83 percent of them had voted for the adoption of representation plans. Desvernine noted: "There has been comment that these plans are objectionable because we, in the first instance, had something to do with suggesting their form." Regardless, he asserted: "As long as the plans are voluntarily chosen by the employees and the plans are working effectively and satisfactorily to the employees, it is submitted that how the plans originated is immaterial." Embedded at the core of the proposed law, in Desvernine's view, was a flawed conception of the employment relationship. "The trouble with the whole bill is that it is designed to prevent any cooperation between an employer and his employees. It is designed to throw them into controversy and dealings at arms' length instead of setting forth certain basic rights of employees and imposing penalties for violation of those rights of employees." Desvernine also served as chairman of the National Lawyers Committee, which drafted and published a memorandum advising employers that the NLRA was constitutionally invalid.[9]

A number of workers also appeared before the Committee and supported the employee representation plans over the Wagner bill. John Collins, who worked in a filling station in New York City, said he represented some 1,000 employees of Sobol Bros., a Standard Oil subsidiary. Workers at Sobol Bros. had recently chosen to continue their representation plan by a margin of 816 to 76, Collins testified, and he regarded that vote as a mandate to oppose the pending legislation. Particularly, Collins feared that the bill would prohibit plans such as the one at Sobol Bros. The following dialogue then took place between Chairman Walsh and Collins:

The CHAIRMAN: I think I can assure you, young man, that this committee, so far as I know the sentiment of it, does not intend to recommend any legislation that will outlaw any union that the employees themselves desire to set up for the purpose of engaging in collective bargaining with their employers, provided that union is independent of domination and control by the employers.

Mr. COLLINS: Yes, sir; but the bill itself says, even if the company should initiate or participate in it, that that would be considered an unfair labor practice, and while the company does participate in it and has initiated it, nevertheless, we have substantially collective bargaining, and the others are just modes rather than the essence of collective bargaining.

Walsh was sufficiently impressed by the distinction that he informed Collins, "you ought to be a lawyer instead of a service-station man." Collins had, indeed, cogently posed the dilemma of an employee representation plan which, although initiated, participated in, and supported by the employer, was freely chosen by employees as a bargaining vehicle. Senator Wagner personally assured Collins "that if this is the kind of an organization that the employees want, that is what I am for 100 percent." Wagner then went on to capture the paradox of the law in a single sentence: "All I am trying to do, and I think, you believe me when I say that, is to make the worker a free man to join any organization that he wishes to join and, at the same time, to have genuine collective bargaining."[10] But whether it is feasible to permit a worker to join any organization, including one created and dominated by the employer, and simultaneously to promote "genuine collective bargaining," remains the crux of section 8(a)(2), and the tension between the aggressive promotion of collective bargaining under the aegis of powerful trade unions and an extreme solicitude for the preferences of the individual worker is amply evident in the legislative history. That same tension appears in the evolving interpretations of the statute.

ADMINISTRATIVE AND JUDICIAL INTERPRETATIONS: SECTION 7(a) AND SECTION 8(2)

By September 1933 the National Labor Board had embarked on the creation of a common law of labor relations emanating from the abstract guarantees of section 7(a). The venture necessarily involved the NLB in determining the validity of company unions in connection with employees' right "to organize and bargain collectively through representatives of their own choosing." The questions that arose included whether the term "representatives" could be limited to fellow employees, whether "representatives" encompassed an outside institution such as a trade union, and whether a company union could be selected by employees as its representative.[11] In a series of cases, the NLB forged a definition of "representative" that was incorporated into the National Labor Relations Act and embodied in the early decisions of both the old National Labor Relations Board and its Wagner Act successor.

First, the NLB ruled that an employer could not restrict the choice of a representative to one of the employer's employees. In *Berkeley Woolen Mills*, the NLB stated that, contrary to the employer's position, section 7(a) could not be construed to require that representatives must be selected only from the employer's current work force. "To give the code the interpretation sought by the company would nullify the employees' right to organize as they choose, for, in effect, it would limit each employees' organization to the individual plant, and would prevent the employees of a plant from joining any organization already in existence."[12] Likewise, the choice of representatives was not confined to individual persons, but might include a trade union organization as an entity. In *Hall Baking Co.*, the NLB expressly held that the union had authority to contract in its organizational capacity, and the employer could not insist on dealing with union officers only as individuals.[13]

The most problematic issue in the selection of representatives concerned the representative status of company unions. If a representation plan was initiated or maintained by the employer, if workers were not permitted to accept or reject the plan, or if they were denied the opportunity to vote for an outside union, the NLB typically rejected the plan as a legitimate method of collective bargaining. Conversely, if none of the three conditions was present, the plan was an expression of the employees' free choice. "The Board would then regard it as authorized to function with all the powers and rights inherent in a representative. No new elections were required." It followed under NLB doctrine that an employee representation plan in itself was not unlawful, nor did its mere existence create a presumption of employer coercion or interference. "When it could be demonstrated that an employee representation plan was the free choice of the employees, the Board invariably upheld the validity of such a plan." The employee representatives would then be entitled to engage in collective bargaining on behalf of their fellow employees.[14]

In the consolidated cases of *Federal Knitting Mills*, for example, the NLB vacated the Cleveland Regional Labor Board's direction of an election.[15] At an NLB hearing on January 17, 1934, conducted by Board member Leo Wolman, the attorney for the Interstate Knitting Mill contended that a second election was not necessary. When Wolman asked why the employer objected to the simple expedient of holding an election, the attorney offered several cogent arguments. First, counsel stated, the company president—a Mr. Heinze—did not object to an election, but he did resent the implication that he had violated the law. "He takes great pride in the fact that he has complied with the NRA. His name is one of the first on the board in the public square in Cleveland as having volunteered to comply with the President's code." An unsupported charge of employee coercion was "a stigma that no man wants to take, lying down."[16] In addition, the company had entered into a one-year agreement covering wages and working conditions with the employee representatives, and that agreement presented an important issue of contractual obligation. As the attorney inquired of Wolman, "Let us say that new representatives are elected, and they are not pleased with this contract, and want a new contract. What becomes of our contract?" Wolman was unable to offer a satisfactory response to the question, which hinged on the crucial point of employee self-determination as opposed to the formalities of contract.[17] Most importantly, and as the NLB subsequently determined, there was no proof that employees had been coerced in their selection of representatives, including the alternative of an outside union. "Since," the NLB concluded, "there was no showing of any interference, restraint or coercion, and since the workers were afforded an unrestricted choice of representatives in each plant, we believe that the complaint of the union has not been sustained."[18]

The first, or "old," National Labor Relations Board generally continued the basic principles formulated by the NLB. In *Danbury & Bethel Fur Co.*,[19] the employer instituted a company union in July 1934, shortly after the settlement of a strike. The United Hat Fur Workers petitioned for an election, which the Board conducted in August. The work force consisted of 106 employees; of that number, 26 voted in the Board election and 19 favored union representation. Finding that the employer had coerced the employees into supporting the company union and boycotting the Board election, the Board ordered the company to refrain from "aiding or encouraging" the company union, "and from dealing with it for collective bargaining purposes." Further, the Board ordered the company to recognize and deal with the United Hat Fur Workers Union; that remedy was appropriate, the Board reasoned, because the evidence showed that the union represented a majority of workers prior to the strike, and "unless other influences intervened, the United would no doubt have continued to represent a majority of the company's employees after the strike's termination."[20]

A different result was reached in the *Firestone Tire and Rubber Co.* case.[21] There, the company argued that its Employees Conference Plan was supported by a majority of employees and, consequently, that the United Rubber Workers' petition for an election should be dismissed. Applying the NLB principles, the Board determined that a genuine issue of representation existed and rejected the company's contention than an election was unnecessary. Among other conclusions, the Board determined that the company played an active role

in the drafting, adoption and financing of the Employees Conference Plan; that the Plan has never been put to a vote of the employees for acceptance or rejection; that the employees have never had an opportunity of voting on whether they wanted to be represented as provided in the Plan or by Local #18321, of which a large number of Firestone employees are members.

Similarly, denying the union's motion that the Plan be declared "illegal," the Board concluded that the Plan was entitled to a place on the ballot, despite the employer's active support. The Board's rationale was grounded on employee freedom of choice:

Since the election is to determine a choice of representatives for collective bargaining, we may, in extreme cases, be justified in refusing a place on the ballot to an organization or plan of representation which by its very terms is incapable of serving as a collective bargaining agency. This, however, we should rarely have occasion to do, since ordinarily the choice, good or bad, is for the employees to make.[22]

Allowing the unrestrained choice of representatives, whether "good or bad," was thus one of the Board's basic principles. But that fundamental premise was contradicted by another, and equally important, feature of the Wagner Act.

The old Board's most controversial decision was issued in *Houde Engineering Corp.*, which held that the representative selected by a majority of voters was the exclusive representative of all employees within the bargaining unit.[23] In the *Houde* opinion, the Board articulated a theory of collective bargaining that rested not on employee freedom of choice, but on national economic prerequisites. Custom and precedent, the Board said, demanded that the NIRA's conception of collective bargaining be interpreted as "that long-observed process whereby negotiations are conducted for the purpose of arriving at collective agreements governing terms of employment for some specified period." The emphasis on labor contracts was inseparably linked with the statutory purposes of the NIRA, starting from the proposition that "the fundamental aim of the Act was to restore prosperity by increasing purchasing power." To that end,

industry was to be stabilized by permitting employers to combine together, immune, to a large extent, from the restrictions of the anti-trust laws, for the purpose of eliminating cut-throat competition, waste, and the grosser evils of unplanned production. At the same time, hours were to be reduced, wages increased, and reemployment effected on the largest possible scale. These vital readjustments could not be brought about by the law alone. Close and continuing cooperation between management and labor was e[s]sential in working out the readjustments and in seeing to it that the gains which industry might derive from its new powers to control production and prices would be equitably shared with the wage earners, and thus serve to increase purchasing power.

Within the redistributive framework, "collective bargaining and the collective agreements resulting therefrom would be an essential part of this process." Negotiated labor contracts were at the core of the NIRA policy, first, as a means of stabilizing conditions of employment, and second, to insure that those conditions would eventually become "reasonably uniform within each particular industry."[24] Accordingly, the employer was ordered to bargain only with the majority representative and to cease any further dealings with the company union.

In its first published decision, the Wagner Act NLRB adopted an interpretation of section 8(2), which conflated the institutionally based approach of *Houde Engineering* with the free-choice policy rationale of *Firestone Tire* and, by doing so, initiated a radical departure from the flexible approach of the NLB and the old NLRB. The Pennsylvania Greyhound Lines instituted an Employees Association in July 1933. Management designed the Association and imposed it on workers without their consent. Through a committee system and a "memorandum of understanding," employees might appeal disciplinary action and complaints about working conditions; there was no mechanism for collective negotiations. Based on that evidence, the Board concluded that the employer dominated and controlled the Association, which fell within the statutory definition of a labor organization. "It was planned by the management, initiated and sponsored by it, and foisted upon the employees who had never requested it. The initial elections were conducted by the management, its organization chartered by the management and its By-Laws written by the management. Its functions were described and given to it by the management." Thus, the Board reasoned, "There can be but one way of remedying the unlawful conduct in this case and that is a complete withdrawal of all recognition from the Association as representative of the employees, in addition to the order requiring cessation of such domination, interference and support." The employer's influence had so completely permeated the Association's structure, only the disestablishment of the Association would protect "genuine employee organization."[25]

The Board's reasoning and remedy in *Pennsylvania Greyhound* were approved by the U.S. Supreme Court.[26] Conceding that it had created and dominated the Association, the company argued that disestablishment was too severe a remedy, and the Third Circuit ruled in the employer's favor on that point.[27] The Supreme Court disagreed, noting that the "company union [was] so organized that it is incapable of functioning as a bargaining representative of employees." It had no power to convene meetings, to assemble its membership, or to make changes in its by-laws. "In view of all the circumstances the Board could have thought that continued recognition of the Association would serve as a means of thwarting the policy of collective bargaining by enabling the employer to induce adherence of employees to the Association in the mistaken belief that it was truly representative and afforded an agency for collective bargaining, and thus to prevent self-organization."[28] The Board and the Supreme Court, accordingly, took the position that representation schemes initiated or dominated by the employer could be inherently destructive of free employee choice. That view of the law soon crystallized.

In *Newport News Shipbuilding & Drydock Co.*,[29] the Board disestablished a representation plan that, with various revisions, had been in existence since 1927. After the *Jones & Laughlin* decision, the company proposed changes in the plan to bring it "within the letter as well as within the spirit of the Wagner Act." The changes included eliminating compensation for the employee representatives and the removal of management representatives from the committee structure. The Board held that "the provisions of the plan as revised, no less than the manner of its revision, indicate that it is still the creature of the [employer]." Because the character and structure of the plan had been determined by the company and could not be changed without the consent of the company, the company had unlawfully interfered with the employees' rights of organization. Accordingly, the Board ordered that the Employees Representative Committee be "completely disestablish[ed]."[30]

Denying the Board's petition for enforcement, the Fourth Circuit relied on "certain facts that were proved either by uncontradicted evidence or by stipulation of counsel." Those facts, the court said, "must be taken into consideration since they bear directly upon the inquiry whether or not the Employees' Representative Committee is capable of representing the employees in collective bargaining, free from domination or interference by the employer."[31] The court's review of the evidence showed that a substantial majority of employees had, on several occasions, indicated their support for the plan. On June 7, 1938, after the Board's trial examiner recommended disestablishment of the Committee, the employees held a referendum on the plan. A total of 4,078 workers voted in the election, and 3,455 voted to continue the plan. Further, the company had removed all provisions in the plan objectionable to the Board. For those reasons, the court concluded, the Board's finding that the Committee remained the "creature of the company" was not supported by the evidence. Nor, the opinion continued, did the order of disestablishment comport with the policies of the Act:

The National Labor Relations Act . . . was designed to deal with the actualities of industrial life in this country, and to promote peace in relations between employer and employees by securing to employees the right, too frequently denied in the past, to organize and bargain collectively, with complete freedom and independence through representatives of their own-choosing. The purpose of the Act will not be served by destroying an organization that is without doubt the chosen representative of the great majority of the employees, even though it may be thought that their decision to restrict their spokesmen to American born fellow workmen is unwise. To deny them this right is to ignore the express command of the statute.[32]

Therefore, the Committee was entitled to retain its status as the employees' representative.

Reversing the court of appeals, the Supreme Court adopted an interpretation of section 8(2) that abandoned the economic rationale for independent trade union representation in collective bargaining and indulged in a vapid excursus on the nature of freedom of choice. The Court conceded that the results of the referendum election were properly a part of the record. But despite that manifestation of employee desire, the Court went on, the Board's determination was not erroneous. "While the men are free to adopt any form of organization and representation whether purely local or connected with a national body, their purpose so to do may be obstructed by the existence and recognition by the management of an old plan or organization the original structure or operation of which was not in accordance with the provisions of the law." The Board's remedial power was appropriate if it effectuated the policies of the Act, and "one of these is that the employees shall be free to choose such form or organization as they wish." With respect to the conceptually troubling fact that employees had voted for the Committee in an election they themselves had sponsored and conducted, the Court simply stated that "the provisions of the statute preclude 'such a disposition of the case." The Board could find that "the purpose of the law could not be attained without complete disestablishment of the existing organization which has been dominated and controlled to a greater or less extent by the [employer]." And, under the statute, "it is immaterial that the plan had in fact not engendered, or indeed had obviated, serious labor disputes in the past, or that any company interference in the administration of the plan had been incidental rather than fundamental and with good motives."[33]

The result of the Board's aggressive posture toward representation plans, and the Supreme Court's expansive approval, was a *per se* doctrine of illegality. "Freedom of choice" was, by definition, impossible in the environment of the company union. Particular manifestations of employee desires were overridden by an institutional imperative no longer anchored in wealth redistribution, but predicated on a psychological assumption regarding the nature of power. The Board disregarded evidence of employee support for company unions for two reasons. "First, fear of retaliation may be the motivating force [behind such evidence]. Moreover, the most effective and subtle type of employer domination would result in a complete lack of awareness on the part of the employees that they are joining a union of the employer's choice."[34] Neither did illegality require a showing of the employer's unlawful intent under the Court's reasoning; an infringement of section 8(2) might be an "incidental" one arising out of a "good motive." Subjective dimensions of employee representation yielded to perceived "objective" configurations of power in the relations of labor and capital.

As a result, the dilemma posed by service-station attendant John Collins and many others was resolved adversely to the company organizations. Collins suggested that the law should accommodate participatory systems such as employee representation, but NLRA jurisprudence rejected intrafirm collective activities in favor of trade union recognition. Consistent with that legal doctrine, employers might conceivably have accepted trade unions as the legitimate and exclusive voice of workers and afforded them a meaningful role in the operation of the enterprise. Rather than doing so, however, American employers embarked upon a course of action designed to restore their diminished rights of control. The managerial offensive culminated in the Taft-Hartley amendments of 1947, which transformed the balance of power in union-management relations.[35] Accordingly, the postwar industrial relations environment was characterized by a retrenchment of union strength and militancy.

EMPLOYERS AND THE WAGNER ACT: A RESPONSE TO UNION POWER

In the decade 1937–47, organized labor increased in size from 7,001,000 to 14,146,000 members, and, calculated as a percentage of the nonagricultural work force, reached its historic peak in 1945 with a figure of 35.5 percent membership.[36] Immediately following World War II, there was a massive wave of strike activity prompted by wartime price controls and rising inflation. Continued employer attacks on the NLRA and its administration led to enactment of state laws regulating union activity and to renewed pressure for federal action modeled on those state laws. In their classic study of the Taft-Hartley legislation, Millis and Brown identified three basic arguments that business groups advanced to justify reform of the NLRA. First, organized labor "had too much power," and it exercised that power to the detriment of employers and consumers alike. Second, unions were insensitive to the rights of individual members and the public. Third, the Wagner Act unfair labor practices were directed only toward employers, and there was a need to restore equity to the national labor policy.[37]

Following the Supreme Court's 1937 decision in *Jones & Laughlin* upholding the constitutionality of the NLRA, American business had confronted the threat of unionization with various strategies ranging from "persistent antiunionism" of a belligerent or sophisticated nature, through a grudging "realism" regarding the formidable presence of unions, to a "progressive" policy of accommodating to unionism.[38] Included among the "persistent antiunionists" were the reactionary employers such as National Steel—headed by Ernest Weir—and Republic Steel, under the control of Thomas Girdler. The sophisticated antiunionists consisted primarily of the Special Conference Committee firms such as Goodyear Tire and Rubber, International Harvester, Standard Oil, and DuPont, who more covertly resisted the incursion of outside representation and attempted to guide "their long-established employee representation plans toward lasting independence."[39] The Realists composed "a majority of American center firms [who] were compelled to accept unionism as a fact, often after strong opposition"; they finally conceded the fact of unionism but attempted to counter union power in daily labor relations activities through "orderly, institutionalized confrontations."[40] Last, such notable "progressives" as U.S. Rubber and General Electric acceded to the union relationship, believing that "management's task was one of constructive accommodation to the new circumstances, not outright resistance."[41] But whatever their respective tactics, American managers did not waver in their philosophy regarding the prerogatives of power. With "one firm voice," they expressed the fundamental faith that "their power was founded essentially on property right, and that their chief responsibility was to maximize profitable production in the interests of shareholders before anybody else." That ideology affirmed for society and for themselves their status as the repository of power within the enterprise. While recognizing that other groups within the social structure asserted legitimate claims over corporate activities, business steadfastly opposed the interference of the state or of workers' groups in the managerial process. The result was an "enduring contradiction" in which the reality of labor strength conflicted with the managerial aspiration of total control over production and operation of the firm.[42] That contradiction, obviously, precluded the formal bestowal of greater decisionmaking power on workers through their union representatives.

The managerial ideology was particularly evident on the political front, and more than twenty major legislative proposals were introduced in the 76th Congress during 1939–40. The most significant legislation was sponsored by Representative Howard Smith of Virginia. Chair of a House Committee formed to investigate the activities of the National Labor Relations Board, Smith presented a bill that received the support of business and industry groups, as well as of the American Federation of Labor; it provided substantial restrictions on labor union activity by, among other things, diminishing the scope of collective bargaining, "equalizing" the law through union unfair labor practices, changing the composition of the Board, and modifying representation procedures. The Smith Bill passed the House in April 1940, but no action was taken in the Senate.[43] Although the Smith

Committee and its legislative efforts did not result in any change in the law prior to the war, those activities had considerable impact on the political environment faced by labor.

In the 1940 presidential election, John L. Lewis opposed Roosevelt's candidacy, threatening to resign as head of the CIO if Roosevelt won a third term. After Roosevelt's election, Lewis chose Philip Murray as his successor, anticipating that Murray would accept Lewis' guidance. Murray opted instead to support Roosevelt's policies.[44] Leaders of the CIO, such as Murray and Sidney Hillman, responded to the hostility of congressional conservatives and the attacks of the AFL by aligning themselves more closely with the Roosevelt administration and seeking its protection against anti-CIO factions. That alliance had important implications for labor's subsequent political fortunes.[45]

During the war, Murray demonstrated his loyalty to Roosevelt's policies of uninterrupted wartime production by condemning labor radicals who engaged in unauthorized strikes, particularly when the strikes were led by communist sympathizers.[46] Throughout the war, worker unrest was dealt with through the union bureaucracy and the intervention of the National War Labor Board. Created on January 12, 1942, by Executive Order No. 9017, the NWLB had broad authority to deal with labor-management relations during the war, including the power to impose labor agreements on parties subject to its jurisdiction.[47] The NWLB stabilized wages according to the formula announced in the Little Steel Case, the principle of which was to maintain real wages at the general level of January 1941. "Adjustment would be permitted to correct any impairment in the standard occurring between that date and the beginning of the stabilization program as a result of the rise in the cost of living. Thereafter any direct relationship between wages and prices was to be eliminated."[48] The NWLB also assumed the power to grant maintenance of membership clauses in collective bargaining agreements, requiring all members on a certain date and thereafter to continue as members in good standing. The principal ground for denying a maintenance of membership clause to a particular union was that the union was "irresponsible," which, in practice, "was largely confined to whether the no–strike pledge was adhered to."[49] Union security led to a substantial increase in union membership during the war, with most new members falling under the maintenance of membership clauses. "At the beginning of 1944," according to one study, "approximately 13.7 million workers, or almost 45 percent of all workers in private industry were employed under the terms of union agreements," and over 20 percent of those workers were covered by maintenance of membership agreements.[50]

But numerous unsanctioned work stoppages, governmental pressures by the National War Labor Board on union leaders, and the imperatives of public sentiment led to increasingly bureaucratized control over the union rank and file. In the auto industry, for example, a strong steward system enabled the United Auto Workers to exert considerable power over production through wildcat strikes. Growing sentiment against the no-strike pledge led to a referendum on the issue in 1945; and although supporters of the pledge won by a substantial margin, stoppages actually increased after the vote. As a result, "auto company executives launched a campaign to rewin much of the shop-floor authority they had held in the nonunion era."[51] The perceived erosion of managerial authority at GM, and the necessity of halting further union encroachment into operational matters, merely reflected an emerging tenet of capitalistic faith throughout the nation.

Indeed, the central "problem" of postwar labor relations, according to Neil Chamberlain's influential study, was the incursion of unions into the domain of management rights. Through contract negotiations dealing with such issues as promotion, hiring and firing, seniority, and production levels, unions had threatened to restrict the range of absolute managerial discretion and to mount an "invasion" of managerial functions. The reaction of employers was predictable. "There is no question where managements stand on the issue," Chamberlain said. "They are convinced that the unions are seeking such inroads, that the attempt holds grave dangers for our social economy, and that it must be halted."[52] That general belief was translated into an effective program of action commencing with Truman's National Labor–Management Conference, which was convened in November 1945.

On November 5, President Truman charged the Conference members with the urgent task of formulating a plan of mutual cooperation to end industrial strife in the postwar era. "Representatives of labor and management are meeting here at this conference table," Truman declared, "to discuss their common problems and to settle differences in the public interest." The development of an effective industrial policy was crucial to the country's transition to a peacetime economy. Government controls imposed during the war were soon to be removed, with the possibility of intensified industrial conflict. "Our country is worried about our industrial relations," the president warned. "It has a right to be. That worry is reflected in the Halls of Congress in the form of all kinds of proposed legislation." Nonetheless, he advised the conferees: "You have it in your power to stop that worry. I have supreme confidence in your ability to find a democratic way to compose industrial difficulties."[53] Like President Wilson's 1919 labor conference, however, Truman's effort to establish labor peace through cooperative efforts encountered managerial intransigence.

The point of contention between labor and management at the 1945 conference was most clearly reflected in the committee statements dealing with the topic of "management's right to manage." Management members of Committee II informed the executive committee that no agreement could be reached in the matter of management rights, due, in part, to the fact that labor members of the committee would not agree to a listing of any specific rights that were nonnegotiable. From labor's attitude, management members drew a bleak conclusion:

The only possible end of such a philosophy would be joint management of the enterprise. To this the management members naturally cannot agree. Management has functions that must not and cannot be compromised in the public interest. If labor disputes are to be minimized by "the genuine acceptance by organized labor of the functions and responsibilities of management to direct the operation of an enterprise," labor must agree that certain specific functions and responsibilities are not subject to collective bargaining.

Clarifying their views, management representatives went on to list specific items that "are clearly the functions and responsibility of management and are not subject to collective bargaining." Included were such prerogatives as the determination of products to be made, location and establishment of new units, determination of methods of production, complete authority over financial policies, determination of management organization, the right to establish job content, size of the work force, allocation and assignment of work, quality standards, and the maintenance of discipline. Although the list was not exhaustive, it was sufficiently illustrative, with labor's acceptance, "to define with reasonable accuracy an area of responsibility which must be left to management, if management is to function effectively in the interest of labor, the investor, and the consuming public alike."[54]

Labor members of the committee, including the CIO's Clinton Golden, issued their response to management's attempted demarcation of subjects of bargaining. While they recognized that the "functions and responsibilities of management must be preserved if business and industry is to be efficient, progressive, and provide more good jobs," they nevertheless concluded that it was "unwise to specify and classify" such functions, but suggested that those matters be dealt with through the "development of sound industrial relationships." The problem was not one of power, but rather of mutual trust and understanding in economic relationships as well as political ones.

In our American political democracy the tradition is well established that government operates best when it enjoys the confidence and consent of the governed. In the same American tradition both labor and management must come to a realization that both can function most effectively when each enjoys the confidence and has the consent of the other.[55]

But, for the first time in more than a decade, management was prepared to seize the initiative in reconstituting the social structure of industrial power. Economic concerns were of secondary importance at that historical moment, Clark Kerr pointed out, "partly because it was power which had been subject to diminution, and also because of its actual or potential relation to income, as well as for its own sake."[56] Labor's proposed reconversion program, which sought to institutionalize the significant degree of state activism brought about by the crisis of war production, was the first of labor's postwar defeats.

In their attempt to secure a more permanent and meaningful role for labor in America, Philip Murray and the CIO advocated an Industry Council Plan, which generally "contemplated the fusion of economic and political bargaining at the very highest levels of industry governance." The Plan was the basis of Murray's "corporatist vision," which sought to assure that labor would be granted "a voice in the production goals, investment decisions, and employment patterns of the nation's core industries."[57] As explained by SWOC staff members Golden and Ruttenberg, labor's goal was coordinated industrial planning on a national level implemented through a planning board. The philosophy supporting the program was "intrinsically democratic" in that it permitted the cooperation of the principal economic groups to "solve their mutually dependent problems instead of either neglecting them or leaving them to a centrally constituted governmental bureaucracy to try and solve." The heart of the proposal consisted of an equality of power guaranteed by the state: "The formula for democratic control of a national planning effort should include the participation of organized labor as a coequal with management, with the government acting as the arbiter between these two relatively independent groups in a free society."[58] Moreover, a precondition for industrial or political democracy— or for a cooperative relationship—was "full production and full employment, because anything short of this cannot satisfy the basic motives that originally impelled workers to organize their unions and implement political democracy by the extension of its methods to their economic life."[59]

Murray's plan for active state intervention coupled with joint union–management control over industrial strategy lacked the political and economic support to become a reality. One of the most contested reconversion issues dealt with the continuation of wartime wage and price controls. President Truman issued Executive Order No. 9599 on August 16, 1945, stating that wage increases granted through collective bargaining or voluntary action would be authorized only "upon the condition that such increases will not be used in whole or in part as the basis for seeking an increase in price ceilings."[60] A number of perplexing questions arose in connection with the accounting aspects of E.O. 9599, and, as a result, "great uncertainty prevailed as to the nature of the price disclaimer." After the issuance of other orders in October and December, many problems were resolved; unfortunately, by late autumn, "it was too late." The delay between Truman's initial reconversion efforts and the opening of the labor-management conference in November "allowed the industrial unrest and the conflicts over prices and wages to develop to explosive proportions. The occasion for establishing an immediate postwar political balance of labor, management and farmer was lost."[61] Murray's experience at the Conference clarifies precisely what was at stake.

At the first meeting of the Conference's Executive Committee, Murray introduced a resolution dealing with wage increases. Although wages were not an issue on the Conference agenda, he urged the delegates to adopt a proposal incorporating Truman's guidelines into the framework of collective bargaining. Murray's proposal was opposed by the management group, which submitted its own proposal recommending "that the Conference not consider national wage policies nor attempt to define formulas to implement existing policies." The proposals were referred to a subcommittee that drafted its own resolution declaring the Conference "to be not a wage conference" and urging labor and management "to seek a solution to wage problems through participation in genuine collective bargaining" before resorting to a strike or lockout.[62] Thus, Murray's preliminary attempt to forge a national labor policy met with failure.

What it could not achieve at the Labor-Management Conference, the CIO tried to attain through the strike weapon. In that regard, the United Auto Workers' 1946 strike at GM marked a turning point in the postwar evolution. Although the GM dispute involved union demands for a substantial wage increase, economics was not the main issue at stake. "The gain or loss of an additional cent per hour was chiefly important as a symbol of strength or weakness, and as a means of increasing strength or inflicting loss of strength."[63] The UAW, led by Vice-President Walter Reuther, pursued a bargaining strategy directly linked to Murray's support for the Truman wage-price program. Reuther demanded a 30 percent wage increase and coupled that demand with the condition that the pay increase be granted without an increase in prices; moreover, he insisted that the company disclose its financial records so that its ability to pay could be determined. Not surprisingly, "the corporation denied the right of labor to inspect the books or demand disclosure of private economic estimates, and claimed it was defending American industry from a threatening radical ideology."[64] Reuther's plan resulted in a 113-day strike. Although workers obtained a total increase in compensation exceeding 19.5 cents per hour, Reuther did not succeed in his attempt to regulate prices, and within two months after the strike had ended, GM was granted authority by the Office of Price Administration to increase its prices.[65]

On the political front, conditions immediately after the war were particularly conducive to the enactment of antiunion legislation. Although business interests had attempted to amend the Wagner Act from the time of its constitutionality, the postwar labor climate gave renewed impetus to the legislative efforts, and the basic criticisms of the Wagner Act were renewed: organized labor had gained too much power and was dominant over management, thereby skewing the economic system; unions were irresponsible organizations requiring a greater degree of regulation; and there was a need for "equity" and "equality" in our labor law.[66] The wave of strikes in 1946 following the collapse of wage-price controls reinforced negative political perceptions regarding unions, and labor strife became an issue in the 1946 elections, which resulted in a Republican majority in both the House and the Senate for the first time since 1930.

In his State of the Union Address in January 1947, President Truman proposed certain limited measures to deal with labor-management problems. But, one commentator notes, "it soon became obvious that Congress had stronger legislation in mind than the President had proposed."[67] Six months later, Congress produced the Taft-Hartley amendments. Truman viewed the bill as unfair, undemocratic, and unworkable; in his veto message, he said that the legislation "taken as a whole would reverse the basic direction of our national labor policy, inject the Government into private economic affairs on an unprecedented scale, and conflict with important principles of our democratic society."[68] Two days later, Congress overrode the president's veto. The resulting statute contained, among its other antilabor provisions, prohibitions against union unfair labor practices, greater rights for the individual employee as against the collective interest, protection of employer campaign speech, and authority for states to outlaw union security clauses.[69] Despite organized labor's efforts over the next several years to repeal the "slave labor law," labor's unwillingness to compromise resulted in a political stalemate, and Taft-Hartley remained intact.[70]

TAFT–HARTLEY AND COMPANY UNIONS

Sections 8(2) and 2(5) of the Wagner Act survived without change in the Taft-Hartley legislation. Congress' chief objective relative to section 8(2) was to redress the Board's apparent hostility to independent unions, and Congress accomplished that goal by amending sections 9(c) and 10(c) to provide for equality of treatment for the independents. In its application of section 8(2), the Board had been criticized for "harshness" toward genuinely independent unions unaffiliated with the AFL or CIO. Such independents were often a permutation of the older employee representation plans, and where the Board found that the employer continued to favor and encourage the independent union, it would be disestablished.[71] In contrast, if sufficient "cleavage" or "fracture" existed between the former company union and the new independent, the Board regarded the independent as a legitimate organization; and, in fact, "the record shows that many independents were accepted as bona fide and given the use of the Board's machinery of elections." Statistically, independent unions demonstrated considerable vigor. In the twelve years of the Wagner Act, they won 3,920 elections, appeared on the ballot in 89 percent of the elections in which they petitioned, and, in the final year of the Act, appeared in one-sixth of all elections and won 65 percent of those.[72]

Section 9(c)(2) of Taft-Hartley required the Board to apply the same rules of decision in questions of representation "irrespective of the identity of the persons filing the petition." It continued that "in no case shall the Board deny a labor organization a place on the ballot by reason of an order . . . not issued in conformity with section 10(c)." The latter provision, in turn, stated that in determining a violation of section 8(a)(2), the Board must apply the same rules of decision "whether or not the labor organization affected is affiliated with a labor organization national or international in scope."[73] Congress may have intended to "permit company-dominated unions on the ballot in Board elections," although the Board interpreted the provision to require stricter treatment of affiliates rather than more lenient treatment of nonaffiliates.[74] While declining to modify section 8(2) itself, Congress did discuss changes in the law affecting worker participation, and those proposals are particularly pertinent to later interpretations of the law.

In H.R. 3020, which was introduced on April 10, Representative Hartley proposed the addition of a new section 8(d)(3) to the Act. The language provided that the following would "not constitute or be evidence of" an employer's unfair labor practice:

(3) Forming or maintaining by an employer of a committee of employees and discussing with it matters of mutual interest, including grievances, wages, hours of employment, and other working conditions, if the Board has not certified or the employer has not recognized a representative as their representative under section 9.[75]

The accompanying House Report explained that the purpose of the modification was to create an exception to section 8(a)(2), which would enable "employers whose employees have not designated a bargaining representative to set up [labor-management] committees" and deal with subjects of collective bargaining where no certified union representative was present. The amendment did not authorize company unions, according to the report, because "the employer and the committee may discuss and reach decisions, but neither side may require the other to make an agreement, or to follow the procedure of collective bargaining set forth in section 2(11) [of H. R. 3020]."[76] The House Minority Report rejected that reasoning, arguing that "such a committee could only be the nucleus for a company-dominated organization." The thrust of section 8(d)(3) was only too evident to the minority:

Since a condition precedent to the employer's freedom to organize a company union is that no organization be certified or recognized, the proposal is designed as a protection to those employers whose employees have not as yet begun organizational activities. It is aimed directly at current organizing drives and will resurrect and legitimatize those employee-representation plans so familiar prior to the passage of the National Labor Relations Act.[77]

In the House debates, other legislators expressed strong opposition to section 8(d)(3). Representative Norton, for example, condemned the proposal as "the boldest invitation to company-union activity imaginable." Employers, she argued, would be placed on "both sides of the bargaining table" and control over the process of collective bargaining would, over a period of time, have devastating consequences for a democratic political system. "One of the surest ways of destroying democracy is first to destroy labor," Norton said. She continued with a heated warning to other members about the nature of the American political process: "One of the sure ways to destroy labor is to so weaken it that its unions become impotent. And the surest way to render its unions weak and servile is to turn them over to the employer. You are treating with American democracy in this measure and particularly in these provisions."[78]

Section 8(d)(3) was deleted from the Conference Report of June 3, which was approved in the House on June 4 and in the Senate on June 6. The deletion was not due to any opposition to the provision, but rather was justified on the grounds that change was unnecessary. According to the Report, "this provision is omitted from the conference agreement since the act by its terms permits individual employees and groups of employees to meet with the employer and section 9(a) of the conference agreement permits employers to answer their grievances."[79] Consequently, one view is that the law already tolerated what section 8(d)(3) explicitly would have authorized and, therefore, section 8(a)(2) did not require alteration to permit those practices; by that reasoning, our labor law contemplates a legislative continuity between Wagner and Taft-Hartley. But judicial and Board interpretations of the NLRA's provisions dealing with employee organizations reflect divergence and inconsistency rather than clarity and uniformity. The evolution of judicial precedent is central to the contemporary legal predicament.

EMERGENCE OF A "MODERN" VIEW OF SECTIONS 8(a)(2) AND 2(5)

Beginning in the 1950s, federal courts of appeal began to fashion a labor law doctrine that focused on employee free choice and emphasized the cooperative aspects of labor-management relations. That interpretation, which adopts a "nonadversarial" perspective of employment, encompasses two separate lines of evolution. The first development, which arises in connection with section 8(a)(2), is the distinction drawn between the employer's unlawful "support" or "domination" of a labor organization and permissible "cooperation." The second, more recent, doctrinal innovation deals with the definition of a labor organization under section 2(5).

The policy basis for cooperative labor relations was articulated in several early cases. In *NLRB v. Valentine Sugars, Inc.*,[80] for example, the Fifth Circuit denied a Board order requiring the employer to withdraw recognition from the Valentine Independent Union, which had negotiated contracts on behalf of the Valentine employees. The Board found that the Independent was unlawfully supported by the employer through such assistance as providing meeting rooms, meals, transportation, and payment for time spent in negotiations. Those activities, the court of appeals said, could not be characterized as unlawful under the statute: "The Act itself makes plain that it was not enacted to produce or encourage feelings or relations of hostility and enmity between employer and employee, but to assuage such feelings and change such relations." Actions of the employer that were "courteous and friendly, or even generous," were not proscribed by section 8(a)(2) absent proof of the "forbidden thing, trying by purchase or coercions to acquire for management a kept and dominated vote." Because the Board did not produce sufficient evidence showing company domination of the Independent, the court deferred to the employees' apparently free choice of representatives. The Independent "had been a really independent union which had given the employees adequate representation, and no complaint of it had ever been made." Further, "it had been chosen by [employees] in two elections despite the organizing efforts of the charging union in this case, and had been duly certified by the Board."[81]

The employee free-choice analysis implicit in *Valentine Sugars* was extended one year later in the leading decision of *Chicago Rawhide Manufacturing Co. v. NLRB*.[82] The Chicago Rawhide Company established a shop committee in 1950 to handle grievances and administer recreational programs. When the Fur and Leather Workers Union commenced an organizational drive in 1951, a majority of employees petitioned the employer for recognition of the committee, and in a subsequent Board election, employees rejected the Fur and Leather Workers Union by a vote of 229 to 49. The employer then recognized the in-plant committee and began bargaining with that entity. The Board found a violation of the Act, reasoning that "there are ample indications of Employer assistance and of potential if not actual control." But potential domination, the appeals court held, was not sufficient proof of an unfair labor practice: "The employer-employee relationship itself offers many possibilities for domination, which is one of the reasons for the original enactment of the Wagner Act, but *actual domination* must be shown before a violation is established." Nor was the employer's assistance unlawful, since it amounted only to "mere cooperation." Importantly, the employees had expressed an uncoerced choice of representatives, and that choice was determinative of the unfair labor practice issue. Quoting earlier precedent, the court stated that "the test of whether an employee organization is employer controlled is not an objective one but rather subjective from the standpoint of the employees."[83] The *Chicago Rawhide* theory of employee free choice recurs in numerous appellate cases denying enforcement of Board orders.

In *Hertzka and Knowles v. NLRB*,[84] employees voted to decertify their union representative. Following the election, management solicited suggestions for establishing a management–employee "dialogue," and the employees proposed a committee system composed of management and employee representatives. The Board found that the committees violated section 8(a)(2) and ordered their disestablishment. Denying enforcement, the Ninth Circuit asserted that the "literal prohibition" of the statute should be "tempered by the recognition of the objectives of the NLRA." The purpose of the Act as a whole, according to the court, was "fostering free choice." That statutory purpose was the source of the enlightened judicial view of labor relations: "Courts have emphasized that there is a line between cooperation, which the Act encourages, and actual interference or domination considered from the standpoint of the employees, which the Act condemns." Proof of a section 8(a)(2) violation, the court stated, "must rest on a showing that the employees' free choice, either in type of organization or in the assertion of demands, is stifled by the degree of employer involvement at issue." Although management was represented on the committees—a traditional indicator of domination under Board law—the Ninth Circuit dismissed that fact by noting that "the employees can easily outvote [the management member]." Most important, the court reasoned that "to condemn this organization would mark approval of a purely adversarial model of labor relations." Any "cooperative arrangement reflect[ing] a choice freely arrived at," and which was "a meaningful avenue for the expression of employee wishes," was "unobjectionable under the Act."[85]

A more recent example of the free-choice analysis is found in *NLRB v. Homemaker Shops, Inc.*,[86] in which the Sixth Circuit disagreed with the Board's finding of domination. Concluding that there was not substantial evidence supporting the Board's determination, the court reiterated the judicial standard emanating from the early 1950s. "Not all cooperation and assistance between management and a union is proscribed by the Labor Act. The test of whether there is unlawful domination or assistance by the employer is a subjective one, turning on whether the employees are in fact being deprived of their freedom of choice." The providing of financial support, likewise, was characterized as cooperation, and not unlawful assistance, on the ground that a "myopic view" of section 8(a)(2) would undermine the free-choice policy supporting the Act. Regarding contrary Supreme Court precedent, the Sixth Circuit dismissed that doctrine as antiquated and outmoded.

Whatever value a *per se* prohibition on employer support of unions may have had in early cases arising under the Labor Act, *e.g., Newport News Shipbuilding & Dry*

Dock Co. . . . , a rigid rule, requiring a "purely adversarial model of labor relations" [citing *Hertzka & Knowles*], runs contrary to more recent trends—the decline of the notorious "company unions," the change in public policy from nurturing the nascent labor movement to regulating and limiting management and labor excesses alike, and the change in employee attitudes toward employer-employee relations.

Consequently, to disestablish or withdraw recognition from the committee at issue "would be to take away the employees' freedom of choice much more surely than by anything management has done."[87]

As the above analysis illustrates, judicial doctrine has successfully circumvented the literal meaning of section 8(a)(2). The distinction between cooperation and unlawful forms of assistance, and its grounding in the freedom-of-choice policy dimension, permits substantial employer intrusion into collective affairs of workers. A similar tendency is evident in cases dealing with section 2(5), which defines a "labor organization."

In *NLRB v. Cabot Carbon Co.*[88] the Supreme Court interpreted section 2(5) broadly so as to encompass almost all forms of employee organization. In that case, the employer established a system of employee committees to further labor-management communications and to discuss problems of mutual concern. The committees routinely met with management and presented proposals encompassing basic aspects of the employment relationship; at no time, however, did the committee attempt to enter into a formal labor agreement with the company. Based on those facts, the trial examiner found, and the Board agreed, that the committee arrangement was a labor organization unlawfully dominated and assisted by the employer.[89] The Fifth Circuit denied enforcement, concluding that the organization did not fall within the statutory definition because it did not engage in bargaining and therefore was not "dealing with" the employer. Rather, the Court of Appeals said, Congress intended to permit employee committees "which provide a forum for discussion of matters of mutual interest, but which are not formal organizations, do not follow collective bargaining procedures (formally or informally), have no powers to bargain collectively, and take no action inconsistent with the terms of an existing collective bargaining agreement."[90]

According to the Supreme Court, however, nothing in the plain terms of the statute or its legislative history suggested that " 'dealing with' should be limited to and mean only 'bargaining with' " as the appellate court incorrectly concluded. By handling grievances, transmitting proposals and requests on a variety of employment matters, and by engaging in discussions with plant officials, the committees performed functions expressly contemplated by the Act. It was immaterial, the Court added, that "the proposals and requests amounted only to recommendations and that final decision remained with [the employer]," for that same principle applied to trade union negotiations.

Moreover, the Court said, section 2(5) had not been modified by the Taft-Hartley amendments of 1947. Although, as previously discussed, Representative Hartley had proposed the addition of a new section authorizing the creation of employee committees, his proposal was rejected because the conferees determined that other amendments to section 9 of the act and the existing language of the statute adequately protected an employee's right to confer with his employer. But neither section 9 nor any other provisions of the Act, the Court held, permitted an employer to "form or maintain an employee committee for the purpose of 'dealing with' the employer, on behalf of employees, concerning grievances."[91] Consequently, the court of appeals' opinion had the effect of incorporating the defeated Hartley proposal into the law.[92] Despite the Supreme Court's clear and unequivocal opinion in *Cabot Carbon*, one court of appeals has constructed an "enlightened" interpretation of section 2(5) using the policy rationale of the *Chicago Rawhide* line of precedent.

In *Streamway Division, Scott & Fetzer Co. v. NLRB*,[93] the employer devised a committee system for the purpose of establishing a closer relationship between management and workers. Each department selected an employee representative who was to serve for a specified period of time, meeting with management on a regular basis during working time. The election of representatives was also conducted during working time, and the employer furnished, distributed, and tallied the ballots. At the ensuing meetings, the representatives discussed a variety of work-related concerns, which management in turn addressed. On one occasion, for example, the representatives criticized the company's vacation policy, and it was thereafter modified according to the employees' suggestions. Based on those facts, an Administrative Law Judge (ALJ) determined that the plan violated section 8(a)(2) and ordered the employer to discontinue it. The Board adopted the ALJ's findings and conclusions.[94]

The Sixth Circuit denied enforcement of the Board's order. It agreed that the employer had dominated the entity, but it concluded that the committee arrangement was not a "labor organization" within the statutory meaning of the term. The determinative point, according to the court, was whether or not the representatives were "dealing with" the employer through the committees. Limiting the Supreme Court precedent to its particular facts, the court of appeals announced a more "modern" and "enlightened" rationale for its decision. In its view, cooperative relationships between labor and management were to be fostered and encouraged rather than constricted by a parsimonious interpretation of the law. "Not all management efforts to communicate with employees concerning company personnel policy are forbidden on pain of violating the Act," the court stated, for "an overly broad construction of the statute would be as destructive of the objects of the Act as ignoring the provision entirely." Interpretation of section 2(5) was guided by reference to "employee free choice," which by analogy to section 8(a)(2) doctrine became the touchstone of legality. In the court's words:

Just as the Act provides democratic machinery to protect the employees' choice to bargain collectively, so equally it protects the employees' right to forego those benefits, if in their judgment their interests are best served by this course. There has been no evidence of company hostility toward the union and no evidence that the Company itself interfered with any exercise of employee rights to bargain collectively, unless it might be said that an enlightened personnel policy led them to be content with the status quo. This was their choice.[95]

Thus, considerations of employer motivation and employee perceptions of free choice were to prevail in interpretations of section 2(5), despite the weak and unpersuasive reasoning supporting such a conclusion. As the authors of a leading labor law treatise point out, "characterizing meetings of a formally structured representation committee as 'individual' dealing is a feat of linguistic interpretation available only to those for whom an out-come rather than language is the standard."[96]

The judicial liberalization of section 8(a)(2) is advocated by some analysts and opposed by others. The objections to the judicial trend are cogently developed in a 1983 article in the *Harvard Law Review*, which argues that the structure of collective bargaining depends upon the institutional auton-omy of unions. To focus exclusively on "employee free choice" as the criterion of section 8(a)(2) violations "neglects the historical purposes of the Act. The Act was not designed solely, or even primarily, to preserve em-ployee free choice in the broadest sense of that term."[97] More accurately, the purpose of the statute is to promote a vigorous, arms-length bargaining relationship within a broader framework of conflict resolution. "Far from mandating a system of adversarial relations and class conflict, . . . the re-quirement that management and employees deal at arms length serves to confine industrial strife within relatively stable bounds." Further, the author contends, if the current economic environment warrants revision of our labor law, such revision should be undertaken by Congress rather than by the courts' dubious interpretations of the Act: "Major revision of a social compact such as the Act is a job for Congress, not for the courts."[98]

From the opposing perspective, other commentators have advocated con-tinued judicial flexibility in interpreting section 2(5) and section 8(a)(2).[99] Recognizing that "traditional analysis under sections 2(5) and 8(a)(2) leaves little, if any, opportunity for employers to initiate participatory management techniques in nonunion settings," one author argued that the Sixth Circuit's approach in *Scott & Fetzer* reflects the proper policy toward participatory activities.[100] The basis of the argument is that Congress intended, through the Labor Management Relations Act of 1947, "to expand opportunities for labor-management cooperation" while still prohibiting company unions. Thus, courts should draw a distinction under section 2(5) between those organizational forms that are merely participatory and those that are designed to be *representational*. Such a distinction, according to the author, "leaves intact a strong prohibition of traditional company unionism while at the same time allowing employers to experiment with more humane and cooperative modes of industrial relations so long as the employees raise no objections."[101]

As the foregoing commentary suggests, several significant issues emerge from section 8(a)(2) and 2(5) jurisprudence. Those issues constitute the framework for the formulation of public policies concerning unions and collective bargaining in the contemporary American economy. Accordingly, any program of legislative change must take certain basic considerations into account.

First, participatory programs are an important part of the organization of the modern American workplace. They obviously serve managerial needs, but managerial needs standing alone are not a sufficient justification for their existence. Rather, when important policy ends coincide with worker participation, such as improved productivity and increased democracy, participation should be encouraged. But if participation is a means of coercion, control, and interference with genuine employee freedom of choice, effective regulation is imperative. That fundamental tenet has been embedded in our labor law since section 7(a) of the National Industrial Recovery Act.

Second, the current effectiveness of our labor law in dealing with innovative work design is questionable. Board interpretations of section 8(a)(2) are at odds with important federal court decisions. Incompatible lines of doctrine create uncertainty, generating yet more litigation and ambiguity. No clear, universally applicable rules have emerged from more than fifty years of precedent; it is unlikely that continued adjudication can produce such rules in the immediate future. Indeed, the current discourse surrounding law and participation has not appreciably advanced the arguments found in the legislative history of the Wagner Act.

Third, and perhaps most important, a significant institutional issue is at stake: that is, should courts interpret the law according to their concepts of labor relations policy, or should Congress reform the NLRA to permit new forms of participation in the workplace? The judicial branch of government, by virtue of its antidemocratic nature, is an unsuitable forum for policy development, and experience demonstrates that judges have produced poor results through case adjudication of section 8(a)(2). Yet the possibility of political reform is also problematic. Organized labor is hardly in a position to advocate favorable changes successfully in labor law because employers now enjoy a substantial legal and political advantage under existing conditions. Incentives for change, accordingly, must be generated from a broad political base.

Chapters 4 and 5 present an argument for legal reform and a specific legislative program. The starting point is an analysis of participation in its contemporary setting. We examine the managerial interests driving involvement systems in today's workplace, focusing particularly on participation as a technique of control over employees; that point is documented through a case study of a specific program. We then address the impediments to statutory reform—primarily an entrenched set of beliefs in this country regarding the collective bargaining system and union power. Our contention is that unions urgently require legislative support in order to maintain a viable presence in our society, and contrary to a body of popular opinion, unions can contribute to the economic effectiveness and competitiveness of American industry and general social well-being. Last, we suggest a concise legislative agenda that has the singular merit of political acceptability.

NOTES

1. Reprinted in National Labor Relations Board, *Legislative History of the National Labor Relations Act*, 1935 [hereafter *Legislative History, NLRA*] (Washington: Government Printing Office, 1985), vol. I, 23–25.

2. *Legislative History, NLRA*, 1539–1540.

3. *Legislative History, NLRA*, 24–25.

4. *Legislative History, NLRA*, 1219–1220.

5. *Legislative History, NLRA*, 1234.

6. *Legislative History, NLRA*, 1235–1237. Wagner's biographer says of this exchange: "Wagner allowed his emotions to sway his words more than at any other time during his long senatorial career," and at one point in the debate, Wagner "fairly shouted across the desks at Tydings." Joseph Huthmacher, *Senator Robert Wagner and the Rise of Urban Liberalism* (New York: Atheneum, 1968), 170.

7. *Legislative History, NLRA*, 759, 764.

8. *Legislative History, NLRA*, 819. Larkin's testimony was given on April 5, 1934. On March 26, 1935, he appeared at the hearings on S. 1958 and submitted a written statement of the previous testimony. He added that in the annual elections for 1935, "92.2 percent of the 45,950 workers operating under the employees' representation plans cast their ballots," thereby constituting a "virtually unanimous endorsement of the plans . . . in the face of organized agitation against them from the outside." *Legislative History, NLRA*, vol. II, 1753.

9. *Legislative History, NLRA*, vol. II, 1746, 1749. For Desvernine's constitutional views, see National Lawyers Committee of the American Liberty League, *Report on the Constitutionality of the National Labor Relations Act* (Pittsburgh: Smith Bros. Co., 1935).

10. *Legislative History, NLRA*, I, 502–505.

11. Lewis Lorwin and Arthur Wubnig, *Labor Relations Boards: The Regulation of Collective Bargaining under the National Industrial Recovery Act* (Washington, D.C.: Brookings Institution, 1935), 130–156.

12. National Labor Board, *Decisions of the National Labor Board, August 1933–March 1934* [Part I] (Washington, D.C.: Government Printing Office, 1934), 6.

13. NLB, *Decisions*, 83–84.

14. Lorwin and Wubnig, *Labor Relations Boards*, 143, 149.

15. NLB, *Decisions*, 69–71.

16. Stenographic Report of Hearing, January 17, 1934, 24–25, Cleveland Knitting Mills, National Labor Board, Entry 21, Transcript No. 159. Record Group 25, National Archives, Suitland, Maryland.

17. Wolman said: "If we follow the thing out logically, which I do not think is the way that it ought to be followed out, because that is the way we deal with abstractions, and I am trying to get away from that—if we follow it logically, if new representatives were elected, it might be said that there was the necessity for an election, which you now deny." But the lawyer was not willing to settle for Wolman's obfuscation of the very important conceptual dilemma of whether a contract could be set aside on the basis that one of the contracting parties—the employees—acted under some form of delusion in selecting an agent to act on their behalf. The exchange continued:

Mr. Stanley: All right. A number of our employees are perfectly satisfied. I think I might say all of them are satisfied. If you have new representatives that necessarily means a new contract.

Dr. Wolman: Not necessarily; not if they are satisfied. To follow it out logically, the whole thing becomes contradictory. I am asking the employer to get the state of mind of his employees. There is an issue as to their method of set up, their plan of employee representation, their plan of electing their representatives. Now, either you are familiar with the attitude of mind of your employees, or you are not. Either this thing that happened a while ago in the middle of November really expressed their wishes or it did not. If it did not express their wishes, there is all the more reason for an election. If there isn't, there isn't any problem of a controversy.

Stenographic Report, 33–34.

18. NLB, *Decisions*, 70.

19. National Labor Relations Board, *Decisions of the National Labor Relations Board, July 9, 1934–December 1934* [vol. I] (Washington, D.C.: Government Printing Office, 1935), 195.

20. NLRB, *Decisions*, 199.

21. NLRB, *Decisions*, 173.

22. NLRB, *Decisions*, 175–176.

23. NLRB, *Decisions*, 35.

24. NLRB, *Decisions*, 36–37.

25. *Pennsylvania Greyhound Lines, Inc.*, 1 NLRB 1 (1935), 11, 13.

26. *NLRB v. Pennsylvania Greyhound Lines, Inc.*, 303 U.S. 261 (1938).

27. The Third Circuit Court of Appeals held that the Association was entitled to compete in a secret election with the outside union. *Pennsylvania Greyhound Lines, Inc. v. NLRB*, 91 F.2d 178 (1938).

28. 303 U.S., 270–271.

29. 8 NLRB 866 (1938).

30. 8 NLRB, 872–873.

31. *Newport News Shipbuilding & Drydock Co. v. NLRB*, 101 F.2d 841 (4th Cir. 1939), 845–846.

32. 101 F.2d, 847.

33. *NLRB v. Newport News Shipbuilding & Drydock Co.*, 308 U.S. 242 (1939), 250–251.

34. Joseph Rosenfarb, *The National Labor Policy and How it Works* (New York: Harper & Brothers, 1940), 130–131. For a discussion of the remedy of disestablishment, see 533–541.

35. For a perceptive discussion of collective bargaining and industrial democracy and the changes in that relationship after Taft-Hartley, see Nelson Lichtenstein, "Great Expectations: The Promise of Collective Bargaining and its Demise, 1935–1965," paper presented at Wilson Center Program on American Society and Politics, Washington, D.C., March 1988.

36. Michael Goldfield, *Decline of Organized Labor in the United States* (Chicago: University of Chicago Press, 1987), 10, Table 1.

37. Harry A. Millis and Emily Clark Brown, *From the Wagner Act to Taft-Hartley: A Study of National Labor Policy and Labor Relations* (Chicago: University of Chicago Press, 1950), 272.

38. Howell John Harris, *The Right to Manage: Industrial Relations Policies of American Business in the 1940s* (Madison: University of Wisconsin, 1982), 23–40.

39. Harris, *Right to Manage*, 24–25. For a somewhat different perspective on the labor policies of the Special Conference Committee firms, see Thomas Ferguson, "Industrial Conflict and the Coming of the New Deal: The Triumph of Multinational Liberalism in America," in Gary Gerstle and Steve Fraser, eds., *The Rise and Fall of the New Deal Order, 1930–1980* (Princeton, N.J.: Princeton University Press, 1989), 3–31. Ferguson describes the conflicts of interests between capital-intensive firms, which were more accommodating toward unions, and the labor-intensive employers, who were overtly antagonistic toward worker organizations.

40. Harris, *Right to Manage*, 27–28.

41. Harris, *Right to Manage*, 32. The labor policies followed at GE during the 1930s and their impact on independent organizing activities are described in Ronald W. Schatz, *The Electrical Workers: A History of Labor at General Electric and Westinghouse, 1923–1960* (Urbana: University of Illinois, 1983), 53–79. Company unions, Schatz notes, were an important part of the "subtle but devastatingly effective nature of the corporation's antiunion policies" (70).

42. Harris, *Right to Manage*, 97–98.

43. Millis and Brown, *From the Wagner Act*, 346–353.

44. Melvyn Dubofsky, "Labor's Odd Couple: Philip Murray and John L. Lewis," in Paul Clark et al., eds., *Forging a Union of Steel: Philip Murray, SWOC, & the United Steelworkers* (Ithaca, N.Y.: ILR Press, 1987), 41–42.

45. See Gilbert Gall, "CIO Leaders and the Democratic Alliance: The Case of the Smith Committee and the NLRB," *Labor Studies Journal*, 14 (1989), 1–27; and also Steven Fraser, "Sidney Hillman: Labor's Machiavelli," and Ronald W. Schatz, "Philip Murray and the Subordination of the Industrial Unions to the United States Government," in Melvyn Dubofsky and Warren Van Tine, eds., *Labor Leaders in America* (Urbana: University of Illinois Press, 1987).

46. An example is the strike at North American Aviation in Inglewood, California, which was broken by federal intervention in 1941. Although the strike was supported overwhelmingly by North American workers, the political climate was such that the president could use military force "backed in turn by CIO officials

who unhesitatingly disowned the strike as the price required to retain their links with the administration and fend off drastic antilabor legislation." Nelson Lichtenstein, *Labor's War at Home: The CIO in World War II* (Cambridge: Cambridge University Press, 1982), 63.

47. U.S. Department of Labor, *The Termination Report of the National War Labor Board: Industrial Disputes and Wage Stabilization in Wartime, January 12, 1942–December 31, 1945*, Vol. I (Washington, D.C.: Government Printing Office, 1947), 5–11; see also generally, Joshua Freeman, "Delivering the Goods: Industrial Unionism During World War II," *Labor History*, 19 (1978), 570–593.

48. *Termination Report*, 186. The Board's application of the principle is analyzed in Abraham L. Gitlow, *Wage Determination Under National Boards* (New York: Prentice-Hall, 1953), 148–167.

49. *Termination Report*, 94. In December 1941, Roosevelt secured a voluntary "No–Strike, No–Lockout" pledge from labor and industry. The pledge consisted of three major points: "(1) There shall be no strikes or lockouts; (2) All disputes shall be settled by peaceful means; (3) The President shall set up a war labor Board to determine finally all disputes not settled by agreement of the parties." George W. Taylor, "Labor's No Strike Pledge–A Statistical View," in Colston E. Warne, et al., eds., *Yearbook of American Labor*, vol. 1 (New York: Philosophical Library, 1945), 137.

50. Constance Williams, "Developments in Union Agreements," in *Yearbook of American Labor*, 109, 116–117.

51. Nelson Lichtenstein, "Conflict over Workers' Control: The Automobile Industry in World War II," in Michael Frisch and Daniel Walkowitz, eds., *Working-Class America: Essays on Labor, Community, and American Society* (Urbana: University of Illinois Press, 1983), 284–311, 301.

52. Neil Chamberlain, *The Union Challenge to Management Control* (New York: Harper & Brothers, 1948), 3.

53. Harry Truman, "President Truman's Opening Address," *The President's National Labor-Management Conference, November 5–30, 1945: Summary and Committee Reports*, U.S. Department of Labor, Division of Labor Standards, Bulletin No. 77 (Washington, D.C.: Government Printing Office, 1946), 37–38.

54. "Statement of Management Members of Committee II," *President's Labor-Management Conference*, 56–59.

55. "Statement of Labor Members of Committee II," *President's Labor-Management Conference*, 61–62.

56. Clark Kerr, "Employer Policies in Industrial Relations, 1945 to 1947," in Colston E. Warne et al., eds., *Labor in Postwar America* (Brooklyn: Remsen Press, 1949), 46–47.

57. Nelson Lichtenstein, "From Corporatism to Collective Bargaining: Organized Labor and the Eclipse of Social Democracy in the Postwar Era," in Gerstle and Fraser, *Rise and Fall of the New Deal Order*, 126.

58. Clinton S. Golden and Harold J. Ruttenberg, *The Dynamics of Industrial Democracy* (New York: Harper & Brothers, 1942), 330. The particulars of Murray's plan are set forth in Appendix I, 343–347, consisting of an excerpt from Murray's report to the CIO Convention in Detroit in November 1941.

59. Golden and Ruttenberg, *Dynamics*, 318.

60. *Termination Report*, 457.

61. John T. Dunlop, "The Decontrol of Wages and Prices," in Warne et al., *Labor in Postwar America*, 16–17.

62. "Summary Report of the Conference to the President," *President's Labor-Management Conference*, 12–13.

63. Kerr, "Employer Policies in Industrial Relations," 45.

64. Barton J. Bernstein, "Walter Reuther and the General Motors Strike of 1945–1946," *Michigan History*, 49 (1965), 261, 262. See also Martin Halpern, *UAW Politics in the Cold War Era* (Albany: SUNY Press, 1988); and Nelson Lichtenstein, "Walter Reuther and the Rise of Labor-Liberalism," in Dubofsky and Van Tine, *Labor Leaders in America*, 280–302. Regarding the GM strike, Lichtenstein points out that while Reuther's program "was formally directed against the giant automaker, it was in practice a union demand against the state as well, for its ultimate success rested upon the Office of Price Administration and other government agencies maintaining price and production controls well into the postwar era" (290).

65. Bernstein, "Walter Reuther," 277.

66. Millis and Brown, *From the Wagner Act*, 272.

67. Charles Morris, ed., *The Developing Labor Law: The Board, the Courts, and the National Labor Relations Act*, 2d ed. (Washington, D.C.: Bureau of National Affairs, 1983), vol. 1, 36.

68. U.S. Senate, Committee on Labor and Public Welfare, *Legislative History of the Labor Management Relations Act, 1947* [hereafter *Legislative History, LMRA*] (Washington, D.C.: Government Printing Office, 1974), 915.

69. Pub. L. No. 80–101, 49 Stat. 449 (1947), codified at 29 U.S.C. § 151 et seq.; see generally Benjamin Taylor and Fred Witney, *Labor Relations Law*, 5th ed. (Englewood Cliffs, N.J.: Prentice-Hall, 1987), 199–245.

70. Morris, *Developing Labor Law*, 46–48.

71. For example, *International Harvester Co.*, 29 NLRB 375 (1939).

72. Millis and Brown, *From the Wagner Act*, 109–110.

73. 29 U.S.C. §§ 159(c), 160(c).

74. See Millis and Brown, *From the Wagner Act*, 427. The Board in 1948 chose to disestablish a labor organization only where there was proof of employer domination rather than mere assistance, and the remedy was applied to both affiliated and nonaffiliated unions. *Carpenter Steel Co.*, 76 NLRB 670 (1948).

75. *Legislative History, LMRA*, 56.

76. *Legislative History, LMRA*, 324.

77. *Legislative History, LMRA*, 376.

78. *Legislative History, LMRA*, 826.

79. *Legislative History, LMRA*, 549.

80. 211 F.2d 317 (7th Cir. 1954).

81. 211 F.2d, 320–321. Judge Rives in dissent pointed out that Congress had enacted a specific proviso to section 8(a)(2) authorizing an employer to confer with employees during working time without loss of pay. In view of the proviso he inquired, "how can it be doubted that permitting the Independent's officers to take not one but four trips on company time without loss of pay, two of those trips in respondents' motor vehicles, and one of them with all expenses paid by respondents, amounted to contributing 'financial or other support to it'?" (324).

82. 221 F.2d 165 (7th Cir. 1955).

83. 221 F.2d 167–168. The quotation is from *NLRB v. Sharples Chemicals, Inc.*,

209 F.2d 645, 652 (6th Cir. 1954). The *Sharples* decision, however, upheld a Board's order of disestablishment of a dominated organization. In context, the language reads as follows:

The disestablishment of a company dominated employee organization may be necessary to completely dissipate the former relationship. The test of whether an employee organization is employer controlled is not an objective one but rather subjective from the standpoint of the employees. The complete disestablishment of the organizations was within the discretionary power of the Board.

As support for its statement, the *Sharples* court cites the Supreme Court's decision in *Newport News*. Thus, the most plausible reading of the Sixth Circuit's opinion is that the Board need not make an "objective" showing through some type of evidence that an employer exercised power over an employee organization, but rather that the Board, on a given set of facts, might infer that employees were subject to being influenced by the employer's actions. The *Chicago Rawhide* case simply inverts the meaning of the quotation.

84. 503 F.2d 625 (9th Cir. 1974).

85. 503 F.2d, 630–631.

86. 724 F.2d 535 (6th Cir. 1984).

87. 724 F.2d, 545, 547.

88. 360 U.S. 203 (1959).

89. Cabot Carbon Co., 117 NLRB 1633 (1957).

90. Cabot Carbon Co. v. NLRB, 256 F.2d 281 (5th Cir. 1958), 289.

91. 360 U.S., 211–212, 214, 217.

92. For an argument that the Court of Appeals' reading of the legislative history is the correct one and that the Supreme Court was wrong, see Martin Feldman and Sylvan Steinberg, "Employee-Management Committees and the Labor Management Relations Act of 1947," *Tulane Law Review*, 35 (1961), 365–386.

93. 691 F.2d 288 (6th Cir. 1982).

94. 249 NLRB 396 (1980).

95. 691 F.2d, 295.

96. Julius Getman and Bernard Pogrebin, *Labor Relations: The Basic Processes, Law and Practice* (Westbury, N.Y.: Foundation Press, 1988), 314. The decision is also criticized in Raymond Hogler, "Employee Involvement Programs and NLRB v. Scott & Fetzer Co.: The Developing Interpretation of Section 8(a)(2)," *Labor Law Journal*, 35, 21–27 (1984). The Sixth Circuit attempted to distinguish *Scott & Fetzer* as a "narrow holding" where there was individual rather than representational communication and no antiunion animus was present. *Lawson Co. v. NLRB*, 753 F.2d 471 (6th Cir. 1985). More recently, the court has reverted to the *Scott & Fetzer* mode of analysis based on employer motivation. *Airstream, Inc. v. NLRB*, 877 F.2d 1291 (6th Cir. 1989). The Sixth Circuit's lack of consistency and failure to provide a convincing rationale for its decisions are simply one more illustration of the problematic nature of section 8(a)(2).

97. Note, "Collective Bargaining as an Industrial System," *Harvard Law Review*, 96 (1983), 1662, 1673.

98. Note, "Collective Bargaining," 1680.

99. Legal commentary has applauded the "freedom of choice" thesis since its judicial inception. See Note, "Section 8(a)(2): Employer Assistance to Plant Unions

and Committees," *Stanford Law Review*, 9 (1957), 351, 365, which cites Chief Judge Magruder's concurring opinion in *Coppus Engineering Corp. v. NLRB*, 240 F.2d 564, 573 (1st Cir. 1957) as an example of the better construction of section 8(a)(2) based on employee free choice.

100. Note, "Participatory Management Under Sections 2(5) and 8(a)(2) of the National Labor Relations Act," *Michigan Law Review*, 83 (1985), 1736, 1750.

101. Note, "Participatory Management," 1767–1768. The interpretation is criticized in Shaun Clarke, "Rethinking the Adversarial Model in Labor Relations: An Argument for Repeal of Section 8(a)(2)," *Yale Law Journal*, 96 (1987), where Clarke asserts that the plain language of section 2(5) does not require that the organization be representational in nature, but only that "employees participate" (2034). The authors of a Department of Labor study, conversely, believe that Congress in 1935 was concerned with plans based on representation and that Board cases allow an interpretation that focuses on that element of section 2(5) as determinative of legality. Department of Labor, Bureau of Labor Management Relations & Cooperative Programs, *U.S. Labor Law and the Future of Labor-Management Cooperation, First Interim Report* 42–59 (BLMR No. 113, February 1987).

CHAPTER 4

Participation in the Modern Workplace

THE INSTITUTIONAL BACKGROUND

The history of employee participation makes clear several points. To begin with, the idea of conferring autonomy, responsibility, and authority on workers through methods of workplace democracy has an impressive lineage in American industrial thought, dating at least from the Straiton and Storm plan in the 1870s, and that context helps to inform our understanding of participation. Second, participatory devices serve a variety of managerial ends. According to their proponents, such techniques reduce conflict, improve morale and productivity, and align the incentives of workers with those of the enterprise. For Storm, Porter, and the Filenes, representation systems facilitated the attainment of mutual goals of workers and managers, and both parties perceived benefits from the arrangement. But as they evolved, employee representation plans at CF&I, Midvale Steel, Bethlehem Steel, and many other major corporations became tools with which to undermine workers' attempts at self-mobilization. The plans defused overt challenges to management authority and substituted internal procedures for mediating conflict and discontent. Modern plans, likewise, may display elusive dimensions of participation, presenting, on the one hand, uncontroversial goals of economic efficiency and worker satisfaction, and, on the other, pernicious strategies for controlling and manipulating employees.

Between the late 1940s and the mid-1960s, worker participation programs were a matter of little academic or practical significance in America. The resurgence of interest in participative systems can be located in the worker unrest and social turmoil of the late 1960s and early 1970s. The demand for autonomy and self-determination in the workplace, and its connection with broad political movements, was so pervasive that the authors of a 1970 study of developments in industrial relations complained about the abuse of the term "participation," calling it "one of the most overworked words of the decade." They observed that "along with 'meaningful' and 'involvement' it appears in a variety of forms and contexts. For example, it is a prime demand in the student revolts which have girdled the earth, while for hippies the term describes a central tenant [sic] in a life-style."[1]

But worker militancy was more than a superficial fad lamented by unsympathetic academics; it also constituted a major force in the economic transformation that accompanied the political change taking place during the period. The most significant feature of that transformation was the declining industrial productivity and profitability of American corporations, which resulted in one of the periodic crises of capitalism. According to one analysis, "the American GNP had grown, on average, by 3.7 percent annually between 1941 and 1973; growth slumped to 2.1 percent between 1973 and 1983. Inflation was higher, unemployment grew, real wages stagnated, and major industries and industrial regions declined."[2] Profit rates, measured as a ratio of return to capital, had attained record postwar highs in 1965. But they fell sharply from that point, sinking in 1974 to levels approximately one-half as great as the 1965 peak.[3] Worker resistance to managerial control was correlated with falling profits. The costs of job loss to workers declined through most of the 1960s, and, correspondingly, workers' willingness to accept the existing conditions of employment decreased substantially. Thus, the "resistance index" of labor, composed of measures of strike activity, ratios of quits to layoffs, and nonmonetary bargaining demands, indicated dramatic levels of militance and activism that peaked in 1968 and did not moderate until the recession of the early 1980s[4]

Certain examples of those trends, such as the experience of General Motors at its plant in Lordstown, Ohio, are notorious in the field of labor relations. When its profit margin declined from 10 percent to 7 percent in the late 1960s, GM imposed stringent efficiency standards on its workers. Among the consequences were a three-week wildcat strike at Lordstown in 1972 and other episodes of sabotage and disruption.[5] The unraveling of the social structure of accumulation—that set of institutional arrangements determining the conditions of capitalist political economy—led employers to explore new methods of dealing with shop-floor relations, productivity, and profits. Participative programs offered a convenient response.

With an increase in workers' ability to resist managerial control, traditional forms of workplace discipline such as discharge were less effectual. Employers, as a consequence, sought other means of eliciting desired behavior from workers. In his perceptive treatment of American labor relations, Richard Edwards described a system of "bureaucratic control" that emerged in large modern corporations to supplant the outmoded disciplinary tactics previously used by managers. Bureaucratic control, he said, is above all organizational and institutionalized. Rules and procedures do not depend on personal discretion but are depersonalized and embedded in the structures of the organization. A complex arrangement of rewards encourages desired levels of performance, punctuality, attendance, and a cooperative attitude. Further, Edwards notes, "the most sophisticated level of control grows out of incentives for workers to identify themselves with the enterprise, to be loyal, committed and thus self-directed or self-controlled. Such behavior involves what may be called the 'internalization of the enterprise's goals and values.'"[6] Worker commitment through internalized motivation is obviously more valuable than coerced obedience. As a leading authority on management practices observed of the early 1980s, superior workforce performance could no longer be achieved through the authoritarian methods of scientific management because "changing expectations among workers have prompted a growing disillusionment with the apparatus of control."[7] Productivity was linked to motivation and, in turn, to participation.

Work in America, the landmark report prepared in 1973 by a special federal task force to the Secretary of Health, Education, and Welfare, set the terms of the debate about the motivation of American workers.[8] The authors documented the "blue-collar blues" and "white-collar woes" prevalent in the American economy and attributed the lack of worker motivation to stultifying, unchallenging jobs. Their solution was radical reform and innovation in the design of jobs, specifically including the creation of autonomous work groups and the diffusion of decisionmaking power throughout the enterprise. "It follows," the report concluded, "that if autonomy, participation, challenge, security, pay, mobility, comfort, and the opportunity for interaction with co-workers are increased, the satisfaction of workers with their jobs should increase."[9] And, in confirmation of the *Work in America* hypothesis, General Motors' successful experiment in work design at the Tarrytown, New York, plant led to a reduction of grievances, productivity improvements, and a general diminution of conflict in the operation.[10]

Impelled by the breakdown of the structure of capitalist accumulation, employers seized on organizational design as a means of dealing simultaneously with productivity and labor relations. While some employers relied on worker participation techniques already familiar in American industry, another important influence was the Japanese model of quality control and its dominant organizational model of participation, the Quality Circle (QC). The spread of Japanese-inspired employee involvement (EI) programs into the United States occurred gradually through the 1970s. As early as 1967, an article by Joseph Juran disseminated information about the QC phenomenon occurring in Japan.[11] Japanese Quality Circle leaders toured selected U.S. industries in 1968, and in 1973 a team of six Lockheed managers traveled to Japan to learn more about the technique. This resulted in the formation of the first Quality Circles at Lockheed in 1974. Some three years later, only five additional companies were users of Quality Circles, but in 1977 the situation changed. After the formation of the International Association of Quality Circles (IAQC) by Don Dewar, one of the original Lockheed managers to travel to Japan, the popularity of QCs spread dramatically. In 1980 the companies using Quality Circle-type EI structures numbered 230 and the estimated figure increased twenty-one-fold only a few years later.[12]

By the 1980s EI programs had attained a substantial reputation in two important areas: increased productivity and democratization of the work environment. The claims of higher quality and quantity production attributed to EI programs were widely publicized. One expert, Robert Cole, stated to a Honeywell Quality Circle Conference that the primary purpose of QC was to increase productivity, and any other benefits were peripheral. According to Cole,

Quality Circles do contribute to improved QWL [Quality of Worklife] but their primary purpose is to improve quality and productivity. The further the focus moves from there, the further you get from the technological base, the quality control tools that make them work. Hardnosed line people—managerial and labor—respond better to the technical core. They know how to make it fly. The QWL is a side effect, not a reason for being.[13]

Similarly, Dewar and Bearsdley, authors and consultants on QCs, stated in the foreword of their book that "Quality Circles can be the most effective tool with which to effect genuine productivity and work quality improvement in any industry, business, institution, or government agency in any culture or country."[14] In a 1989 survey of Fortune 1000 firms conducted by researchers at the Center for Effective Organizations, 70 percent of the respondent managers said that an important reason for implementing an EI program was to improve productivity, and 72 percent said that an important reason was to improve quality.[15]

The financial stimulus for EI programs was reflected in early reports of economic savings generated by the programs. Lockheed attributed a saving of over $3 million from 1974 to 1977 to improvement ideas coming from QC members.[16] The federal government claimed savings of $215,000 at a cost of $40,000 by using the technique at the Norfolk Shipyard.[17] Clyde H. Molde, an operations vice-president at Honeywell, said that his division realized savings in excess of $1 million owing to the installation of Quality Circles. Westinghouse Electrical Corporation has over 2,000 Quality Circles in operation and conducts a Quality College, which trains those from other corporations on how to organize QCs. QCs as productivity tools are the topic of countless seminars held by major consulting firms as well as practical articles in a variety of publications.[18] And in their highly popular account of American economic decline and the solution offered by participation, John Simmons and William Mares echoed the themes of *Work in America* analyzing a number of specific cases in which job redesign and participation improved productivity and lowered labor conflict in major firms.[19]

But despite acclaim for the improved productivity achieved through employee participation and QCs, the evidence to support the proposition is not altogether convincing, particularly in nonunion workplaces. For example, after a careful review of the literature, David Levine and Laura Tyson offered only limited and qualified conclusions about the effects of participation. In summary, they said: "Our overall assessment of the empirical literature from economics, industrial relations, organizational behavior, and other social sciences is that participation *usually* leads to small, short-run improvements in performance and *sometimes* leads to significant, long-lasting improvements in performance." They found that participation usually has a small positive effect on productivity and "almost never a negative effect," but the magnitude of the effect varies according to the dispersal and degree of decisionmaking power in the participatory process.[20] Focusing on the relationship between unions, participation, and performance, Maryanne Kelley and Bennett Harrison recently analyzed productivity in the American metalworking industry and found "no evidence whatsoever" that a participation program by itself resulted in greater economic efficiency. To the contrary, they determined that nonunion plants with a labor-management committee were somewhat less efficient than plants without such committees and substantially less efficient than unionized plants.[21] The productivity improvements associated with participation, then, may be questionable in the absence of meaningful worker representation.

Another asserted benefit of participation is that it creates a more "humane" working environment by increasing the degree of mutual cooperation in shop-floor decisionmaking. When EI works according to the "ideal participative model" presented in most program descriptions, satisfaction is presumed to increase because of an increase in decisionmaking responsibilities for the workers involved. Workers' ideas are heard, evaluated, and, if found worthy, implemented. With their knowledge of the production process, workers help management overcome the problems that impede greater efficiency, and workers gain self-worth and esteem.[22] Rather than opposing management, the individual strives with management toward common goals. The conflict between worker and manager is eliminated, and, instead, there is participation, cooperation, and democracy.

Empirical research dealing with worker participation and the democratization of the workplace is fairly limited.[23] In Japan, where consensus decisionmaking and joint consultation are central to the industrial relations system, the issue of democratization is clearly secondary to economic outcomes.[24] Even Robert Cole asserts that quality control EI programs in Japan very often take on a coercive aspect with top-down control continuing to dominate the small group environment. Quality Circles are developed not for "people building" but for increased productivity. Consequently, the rhetoric of democratization is subdued and employee involvement is viewed as a direct control mechanism intended to improve the efficiency of the worker as a producer.[25]

In this country, however, workers often respond positively to the ideals of democratic participation associated with EI programs, which in turn may further managerial aims. One worker described his reaction to a QC scheme: "Several positive circle results include the opportunity to voice my gripes concerning work problems, the chance to be heard on solving problems, more awareness of other problems within my group, and the application of Quality Circle techniques in finding solutions to problems in my private life."[26] Through such experiences, workers may develop attitudes more congenial to management. At the A.O. Smith Corporation in Milwaukee, an employee said that after the company decided to implement an EI program in its automotive parts plant, managers "turned over control of the shops to us."[27] A Union Carbide employee succinctly expressed one of the managerial goals of the EI structure: "We have learned a new appreciation of management by our being able to participate." The ease with which such attitudes can be fostered is the foundation of the "people building philosophy" of EI programs. Says the Monsanto Quality Coordinator at the Decatur, Alabama, facility: "I love to see people develop, and I've seen people who have gone from being shy and who would jump if you said 'boo!' to being assertive people." Indeed, some managers claim that this is the primary reason why teams are implemented. "We hope for quality and cost improvements along the way, too, but the main thing is people building. . . . We already have a good esprit de corps developing. . . . It's a team spirit."[28]

Inculcated with the proper attitudes, workers learn to respect the responsibility of management and to moderate their resistance to the commands of management. Because the potential for labor power is all that employers purchase, and not its actual expenditure, labor output requires that management exert power over workers in order to eliminate behaviors that do not contribute to production. In the capitalist enterprise, accordingly, "freedom" is necessarily defined within the constraints of productive needs. Allowing workers to participate in limited decisionmaking is a method of linking performance with managerial requirements of the job, and an EI program is the ideal structure to control decisionmaking while keeping separate the power to implement decisions. "People building" thus becomes synonymous with developing a cooperative team spirit in workers consistent with managerial priorities. If the appropriate team spirit is developed, management can safely delegate decisionmaking, otherwise its exclusive prerogative, without fear of disruptive conflict.

The assumption that workers want a more democratic workplace, and that EI is a way of achieving it, is based on the relatively unexceptional proposition that alienation is reduced by increased control over the immediate environment.[29] Collective bargaining, a traditional mechanism for the extension of workers' control, is arguably as suitable as nonunion systems of participation, since it provides a broad array of democratic processes.[30] Perversely, there is no widespread attempt by managers to introduce unionism into the workplace. Employee involvement programs, promoted heavily by management consultants and usually initiated by managers, allow management to maintain control not only over the affected work force but over a larger portion of the total operation by creating the impression that a democratic work place can exist without unionization. The function of a union as an organization is to demand a voice in the enterprise, and, as Kelley and Harrison show in their important study, participation without a secure and meaningful voice is less than optimal. They conclude that productivity improvements generated by joint labor-management committees in the absence of a strong union "may enhance the position power of managers at the expense of workers." But managerial exploitation frustrates the basic purposes of involvement: "The resulting deterioration of trust and demoralization of the work force could be responsible for our finding that, in [branch plants] with [labor-management committees, LMCs] but without a union, productivity levels are actually *lower* than in setting in which both LMC and union are present."[31]

The emphasis devoted to firm efficiency and democratic concepts makes it appear that current participatory schemes have a greater affinity with the benign plans of Storm, Porter, and the Filenes than with the antiunion machinations of Rockefeller, Schwab, and the Iron and Steel Institute. In fact, however, contemporary programs may be a very sophisticated and richly articulated network of control that can be readily adapted to any particular purpose desired by management, including antiunionism. Combining small-group dynamics with participative control schemes increases the power of employers while sustaining the disorganization of workers and removing the threat of collective opposition, which continues to be a hazard to production in the modern firm.[32] We next explore some theoretical dimensions of participation that have special pertinence to present conditions of employment in this country.

DISCIPLINE, POWER, AND ORGANIZATIONAL DESIGN

The coalescence of civil rights laws, judicial erosion of the employment-at-will rule, and changing relations of production have, as mentioned, hampered direct disciplinary control over employees. One management expert comments, for example: "In spite of their greater liberty [than unionized companies] some of the nonunion companies appear to err in the direction of not firing people. Some seem to lean so far over backwards to retain employees that it may hurt the organization."[33] With the declining efficacy of discipline to managers, other means of dealing with workers increase in importance.

Stewart Clegg's treatment of organizational power sets forth two different models that help to refine our understanding of the contemporary work environment. The first model is based on a Hobbesian conception of power as mechanistic, causal, and embodied in a sovereign; it is, Clegg says, power as "a supreme agency to which other wills would bend." That type of power corresponds to the unadorned exertion of managerial authority, such as a mass firing of employees or the summoning of armed state forces. In contrast, Clegg postulates a Machiavellian view of power as "imprecise, contingent, strategic and organizational."[34] Central to the Machiavellian understanding, and to a postmodern theory of power, is organization. Power is transmitted though "agency," Clegg argues, and "organization is essential to the achievement of agency. . . . It is the stabilizing and fixing factor in circuits of power." Because power is fluid and contested and "does not belong to anyone nor to anyplace," it is appropriate to focus on "strategies" of power. Power, from this perspective, can be defined as the effectiveness of strategies for acquiring "for oneself a greater scope for action than for others implicated by one's strategies."[35] Translated to the workplace, power furthers the material interests of employers by ensuring their continuing domination and control over workers, and ideology plays an important part in strategies of power in the organization.

Since the work of Weber and Bendix, ideology has been essential to the sociological analysis of organizations. Organizational legitimacy is attained through managerial ideologies, which Bendix defined in his classic study as "all ideas which are espoused by or for those who seek to explain and justify that authority."[36] The importance of legitimacy in maintaining the political power and public prestige of corporate bureaucracy was alluded to in the earlier discussion of employer welfare policies during the 1920s; to underscore that contention in the present context: "Corporate social policies originated as an expression of a new ideology of business power. They represented an attempt to legitimize that power in the eyes of government and other groups."[37] Such concerns are no less critical to the modern organization, because public opposition to corporate activities has significant effects on productivity.[38]

Within the organization, ideological structures are an important constituent of dominance over workers; even such apparently altruistic projects as alcohol recovery programs may be imbued with an ideology of social control.[39] The term "ideology," one study argues, by definition connotes the production of knowledge impelled by the material interests of a dominant group. Because that point is typically overlooked in management theory, "the analysis of ideology has come to be construed as focused on shared norms and beliefs, rather than on the bases of political contention." In fact, the important organizational issue is "*why* individuals hold and promote the beliefs, attitudes, and values that they do," especially when interests are not compatible.[40] One answer is that the shared meaning and culture of an organization are produced through organizational discourse that is biased in favor of owners and managers. Dennis Mumby, for example, argues that such discourse "functions to articulate contexts of meaning through which members are able to perceive and make sense out of their organization," and it is ideological "when certain meaning formations are legitimated to the exclusion of others for no other reason than that it serves the vested interests of a particular group to frame organizational reality in this way."[41] Power structures are thus permeated with ideology.

The sociological approach to organizational control sketched above is related to developments in legal theory, and the insights from each discipline enrich one another and in turn deepen the analysis of participation. "Critical" legal theory asserts that rules of law are often "indeterminate" and permit judicial interpretations that are not dictated by an internal logic or coherence, but are based on the maintenance of existing relations of wealth and power within our society. Legal principles appear to be neutral and objective, thereby commanding general adherence to the rule of law, and, at the same time, law helps to constitute a system of beliefs that effectively reinforces the existing social structures and has the "effect of making the social world as it is come to seem natural and inevitable." Domination is most complete "when both the dominant and dominated classes believe that the existing order, with perhaps some marginal changes, is satisfactory, or at least represents the most that anyone could expect, because things pretty much have to be the way they are."[42] In short, the order of things is not vulnerable to challenge.

The application of the sociological and legal theory to participative schemes is straightforward. Employers have economic incentives to devise ideologies that further their control over workers. Effective ideologies legitimate the actions of management, and, on a profound level, shape the worker's understanding and interpretation of workplace reality. Like the ambiguous, manipulable, and indeterminate rules of law that govern our social relations, articulations of power in the form of employee involvement, worker participation, and other innovative designs are arenas of contest. Management surrenders some measure of its prerogative and allows workers to contend within established limits for a share of power; management's actual motive for doing so is an anticipated increase in financial wealth at some point in time, but its expressed intention may be largely ideological. The theme can be further elaborated using a well-known example of critical legal scholarship.

In an essay dealing with corporate organization and the legal system, Gerald Frug examined the structure of American law governing corporate bureaucracy. Frug concluded that the "stories" offered by the body of legal doctrine to justify and protect the immense powers of corporations "are no more than variations on a single story about the acceptability of bureaucratic organization and that this story, far from building a convincing case for bureaucracy, is a mechanism of deception."[43] The "deception," in Frug's view, is our belief that bureaucracy satisfactorily accommodates human needs for freedom and autonomy by providing legal safeguards to regulate bureaucratic control over individuals. Consequently, the same explanatory appeal underlies corporate law as well as organizational theories of participation—in both cases, an apparent solicitude for the person.

Frug identifies the first element of bureaucratic ideology as the problem of objectivity. Organizations, Frug says, must seem to be subject to a meaningful degree of external control. "Objectivity is thought to protect people within the bureaucracy from domination and to ensure that the interests of constituents are not threatened by the consolidated power exercised by the bureaucracy itself." One method of attaining objectivity is by emphasizing "values of organizational life that everyone is considered to hold in common. It is the fact that these values are shared that makes them 'objective.'" The second, and antithetical, element essential to the ideology is the adjustment of conflict arising out of personal and individual desires, or "subjectivity." The organization must demonstrate that it "does not limit the opportunity for personal self-expression," and that while there are common organizational values, "individuals can escape from the enforced commonness of objectivity and be themselves." Although the two aspects of the bureaucratic ideology are ultimately irreconcilable, they form the basis for efforts at legitimation: "All the stories of bureaucratic legitimation . . . share a common structure: they attempt to define, distinguish, and render mutually compatible the subjective and objective aspects of life." The line between subjectivity and objectivity thus becomes the focal point of all legitimating efforts, and "it is this line that allows bureaucratic theorists simultaneously to separate and combine the values of subjectivity and objectivity—to present bureaucracy as both an enhancement and a protection of liberty—and that therefore permits them to present bureaucracy as legitimate."[44] Employee involvement is an excellent device for mediating claims of individual workers that are in opposition to organizational imperatives.

Following Frug's thesis, participation programs are effective because they have an apparent humanizing tendency in a bureaucratized work environment. They instill a personal relationship between co-workers and the processes of production. Rules and regulations become less formal and are not associated directly with management but rather are seen as a natural outcome of the social relations of production. Where managerial power is disguised, workers accept more responsibility for conforming to rules and policies. Consequently, a "debureaucratization" of control serves as the cornerstone of involvement programs. In the debureaucratized workplace, peer pressure is institutionalized as the predominant source of control. Under the guise of participation, workers are told that they have increased authority over hiring, disciplining, and firing of fellow workers. Management power becomes more "democratic," more innovative, and more responsive to workers. At the same time, the system of property rights in our capitalist economy, which confers final authority on managers regarding entrepreneurial decisions, remains intact.

Practically, analysts have suggested several ways in which control mechanisms can be embedded in the social relations of the workplace through organizational design rather than externally imposed as rules. First, workers can be made to understand the work environment from the perspective of management. Second, management can limit worker participation to the unimportant aspects of plant operations, in which case no genuine power is surrendered. Third, managers can employ a variety of "intimidation rituals" to make workers in a participative setting submit to the managerial interpretations of the problems of work.[45]

Further, participation programs fragment the collective voice of workers through the use of small group dynamics, with several important consequences. Employees, first of all, have a sense of belonging to and identifying with a specific work group. For that reason, they have little sense of community with all other workers in the plant. The segmentation into small groups engenders an "us-them" view of work relations and obscures the common interests of workers as opposed to the interests of managers. The small group allows management to more closely monitor employee behavior and attain conformity to the organizational norms.[46] Similarly, participatory structures encourage workers to confront managers on an individual basis, thus impeding collective activity on the part of workers. Conflict is to be resolved by personal interaction and not through institutional methods such as a negotiated labor agreement. The supervisor appears to be "one of the workers," and the goals of workers and supervisors are perceived as common and mutually attainable, rather than class-based and adversarial.

Stratifications of power and influence are reinforced through disparities of knowledge and status. The ostensibly superior knowledge of managers as compared with that of workers results in levels of inequality. As William Winpisinger comments, "workers often have a 'leave it to the experts' attitude when it comes to many issues of management. This puts them at a disadvantage when talking with managers 'equally' about a problem."[47] Likewise, certain values within the group, such as hostility toward unions, may be rewarded by superiors. Workers who are "loyal" to the company achieve greater respect and are perceived as part of an "elite" group within the work force.

Last, the techniques described above may be coupled with an explicit or implicit antiunion philosophy. In a nonunion firm where workers have no formal representative, the employer's stated objective may be to maintain a "personal" relationship without the "intervention of a third party" who would disturb the cooperative atmosphere, and those sentiments are often communicated directly to workers. One company's employee handbook contains fairly explicit advice for employees seeking to organize. "[Our company's] position is that unionism . . . would not help [our workers] in terms of pay and benefits or job challenges and satisfaction, and that unionism definitely would cost [our workers]—perhaps a great deal."[48] Even in a unionized setting, participatory schemes can have the result of weakening the representative and fragmenting the solidarity of workers.[49]

A case study conducted by Grenier describes precisely how an employee involvement plan developed by management was an important part of a comprehensive control structure of an organization, including the managerial counteroffensive against a unionizing drive by the Amalgamated Clothing and Textile Workers Union. A comprehensive discussion of the antiunion campaign is set forth in Grenier's earlier book.[50] Here, additional material is used to explain how the employee involvement program, which was typically referred to as a "Team," shaped the attitudes and behaviors of workers by controlling particular elements of the work culture such as employee selection and socialization, allocation of rewards and punishments, and leadership patterns, all of which were eventually directed toward the end of maintaining a nonunion operation.

TEAMWORK IN ACTION

Ethicon, Inc., the world's largest producer of sutures, is one of the oldest subsidiaries of the Johnson and Johnson (J&J) family of international companies. With its five locations in the United States and one in Canada, Ethicon supplies the North American medical profession with a large share of all sutures and ligatory clips on the market. Throughout the 1980s, J&J had a strong position in the surgical instrument and supplies market as well as in hospital supplies, a position made possible by the strong tradition and commitment to the professional and pharmaceutical corporate sectors within J&J. Some Ethicon plants are unionized, including the bargaining unit at Somerville, New Jersey, represented by the Amalgamated Clothing and Textile Workers, Local 630, where the parties enjoy a stable collective bargaining relationship.[51]

Prior to locating an Ethicon plant in Albuquerque, J&J surveyed the area in the late 1970s and decided to accept the incentives offered by San Angelo, Texas. In 1979, however, thanks to Albuquerque's commitment to support an Industrial Development Bond issue for $10 million, and a government subsidy of $1.5 million in the form of an Urban Development Action Grant, the city was selected as the site of the next Ethicon plant. Within a short time, plant construction was completed and the facility began operations.

During 1982–83, Ethicon was one of the best places to work in Albuquerque. The employee benefits were unsurpassed in the area. Even the local university did not match the excellent health insurance coverage and maternity care benefits, which were fringes that particularly appealed to the mostly female labor force. The clean-room working conditions lent a dignity to the monotonous manufacturing process that was difficult to quantify. The fact that most of the workers wanting to work at Ethicon had a tradition of low-paying jobs, sometimes in sweatshop-like conditions, made the work seem all that much better in spite of its low wages. Approximately 288 workers were employed at Ethicon, most of whom worked on the assembly line, in maintenance, or shipping and receiving. More than 80 percent of the work force was female and included 114 Hispanics and 55 non-Hispanics. The majority of the women were also working mothers.

Despite existing union relationships, one important reason why J&J chose the location in the Southwestern part of the United States was its potential for remaining a union-free environment. The issue was a matter of economics for the employer. As one manager at the new Albuquerque plant stated, "Ethicon simply has to cut back on employee wages and benefits. The company is paying out the nose in wages and benefits. Most of our plants are union. Here [in the west] we have a better chance of keeping them out not just for now but forever."[52] The nonunion operation in turn translated into lower labor costs, perhaps the single most important facet of American employers' opposition to unions.[53] As the QC developer admitted, the parent corporation decided in 1979 before "brick one" was laid for the plant, that it would remain nonunion at all cost and that the QC would be developed as an alternative to unionization.

The manager in charge of QC development was not an engineer or production expert. Rather, the task of QC development was assigned to a social psychologist from one of the major behavioral science departments in the country. In one of his candid moments, he confided that he was hired for three reasons: he was a Chicano, he hated unions, and he was trained in manipulating people. He understood that the main reason why the QC concept was being used at the plant was to keep out the union, with the attendant economic benefits to the company. In his words: "We have made out five and ten year projections and they are based on the assumption that we will not be a union plant. Each year we keep out the union we make $3 million dollars. . . . When we reach our top [employment level] we will be making $5 million dollars every year we keep out the union."

From the beginning, the techniques of employee selection followed management's desire to identify individuals who fit into the corporate union-free culture of the "new design" plant. According to the social psychologist, the company selected in part based on an applicant's manual dexterity. But he continued:

The second criteria [sic] is person-environment fit. Here we have to cull out those people that might have a negative impact on the environment of the plant. One of those impacts is unionization. . . . They have to fit the QC environment and keep out the union environment. . . . We have to catch them at the door.

Thus, the effects of the QC on the work force began even before an applicant was officially hired. Each potential employee was first interviewed by a member of the personnel department and, if she survived the initial interview, was referred to the plant manager or a department supervisor for another interview. The final stage in this process was an interview by two QC members or future "peers" from the Circle to which the applicant would be assigned. Those two workers had the authority to hire or to veto the hiring of the applicant. Consequently, the new employee realized during the hiring process that she was dependent upon her fellow QC members for her job; and after an employee was hired, the QC program continued to function as the primary structure socializing the employee into the normative patterns of the plant work culture.

When the Amalgamated Clothing and Textile Workers Union (ACTWU) began its union organizing campaign in June 1982, management mobilized the QCs as the focal point of the attack against the union and its supporters, attempting to eradicate an influence they considered detrimental to production and to the harmonious social environment of the plant. Team meetings served as the major dissemination point for information concerning management's views of the union as well as the most efficient medium for the identification, and subsequent isolation, of employees who deviated from these views. To make full use of the control potential of the QC, management developed a three-pronged strategy against the union, using the QC as the basic mechanism of control. Each one of the strategic decisions had a profound impact on the work relations between workers themselves and between supervisors and workers. A quote from the QC developer summarizes the elements of the antiunion strategies used at the QC level:

We are using the "traditional" management approach [against unionization] where management gives the workers information not necessarily solicited by them but nevertheless important in informing them about the anti-union stance of the company.

Another approach is the "pro-active" approach [used by some teams]. The facilitator sort of orchestrates and initiates the discussion of the union at QC meetings and in that way gets across certain ideas about the union to employees.

The third approach is the "individual conflict" approach where individuals already known to be pro-union are isolated at the QC level and individual level. We try to keep them isolated from other QC members and at the same time confront them individually concerning the union issue.

Three distinct socializing mechanisms of the QC structure thus could be arrayed against members of the group who expressed pro-union sentiments.

In QCs where there was sizable union support, management usually had two supervisors present during meetings. Besides the QC's leading facilitator, the social psychologist or another member of the personnel department was present. This often enabled the development of a scenario in which facilitator and personnel administrator, seemingly in a spontaneous manner, brought out an interesting topic concerning the union. Not all facilitators were skilled enough to utilize the "pro-active" approach, according to the social psychologist, but one QC was utilizing it very efficiently.

An observation of the particular QC made clear the design and purpose of the pro-active approach. At one meeting, following a discussion of the weekly production numbers, the facilitator noticed that one of the employees up for evaluation was not present. He remarked that she was probably home "watching TV." Immediately after this, he said, "By the way, did any of you watch '60 Minutes' last night?" Several people raised their hands, including the female personnel administrator present. The facilitator asked her what she thought of the piece on the "union and Coors." She replied that it had been interesting because it showed how unions "don't leave people" alone, even if voted out. The facilitator then asked her to talk about it, "for the benefit of those who didn't see it." The personnel administrator related the major points of the report, emphasizing the intransigence of the union in the face of employee opposition and the company's good will. After she finished, two employees made remarks supporting the company's position against the union. The facilitator commented that the show was a good example of how "unions don't care about people, they just care about dues."

In November 1982 the company informed the corporate headquarters that it was instigating a "psychological strategy" against the pro-union people. The key to this strategy was the identification of pro-union people and this was best done at the QC level. Facilitators were instructed to maintain a "rating scale" for each QC member. On this scale, a $+2$ designation represented a strong antiunion stand while a -2 identified those employees with strong pro-union attitudes. Consistent with the valence of the ratings, official management rhetoric labeled union supporters as "negative" influences and "losers" while antiunion employees were referred to as "positive" forces and "winners."

For the psychological campaign to be effective at the individual level, the "button" or weakness of each pro-union worker had to be identified, and the "personal touch" in authority soon became the customary method of controlling the work force. When deviation from management's expectations occurred, there was direct confrontation. Facilitators approached pro-union workers to express their "surprise" and "disappointment" at the workers' attitudes and to ask if there was anything the facilitator could do to make working conditions more pleasant. If the worker responded, as many often did, by asserting her belief in unionism while also continuing to work "for" the company, the facilitator typically responded with "then there is nothing more to say." The line drawn, the personal touch was withdrawn as if it had been a benefit of compliance with company norms. The noncompliant were treated, if they were lucky, with indifference, and more likely with open hostility from fellow workers as well as management.

Production and quality issues became less and less important to the agenda of QCs as the psychological strategy developed. Again, quoting the QC developer: "As the guy in charge of QC development, I have to keep the QC in tune with company goals. The goal now is to keep out the union. . . . If production suffers, we have three other plants that can take up the slack." Most of the time was spent elaborating the managerial perspective on unionization. Indeed, the QC format allowed management the opportunity to give "captive audience speeches" every week. The personnel director admitted that the QCs had become "conflict groups" rather than production groups, and facilitators were given a confidential document on the type of behavior expected of them during the union campaign. Instructions included detailed answers to anticipated questions by QC members, followed by this explicit order: "When talking to employees, make sure you stress that *you are giving your personal views and opinions and are not expressing the views and opinions of management.*"

If a facilitator was unable to control the "negative" influences in his or her QC, the existence of the QC was undermined and the abilities of the supervisor questioned. One particularly verbal pro-union QC had its meetings suspended indefinitely because of the facilitator's inability to "control" his QC. In that case, the union supporters had exerted their influence to become the informal QC leaders. Although they did not discuss the union during QC meetings, they set the tempo of the meeting and, in effect, usurped the facilitator's agenda. One worker in the QC reported the facilitator's frustration when she demanded clarification of a certain work rule and would not be put off by his attempts to move on with the agenda. He objected that her insistence made it impossible for them to "work as a team." She, on the other hand, asserted her right to know why a certain aspect of the work process was organized as it was. Soon after the incident, meetings for the team were canceled. The social psychologist reported that the QC was "moving away" from the facilitator, who required a bit more training in the "art of workplace manipulation."

That particular event provided management with a benchmark for measuring the ability of other facilitators to control their QC interactions during the campaign. After termination of the recalcitrant QC's activity, other facilitators were pressured to put an end to pro-union discussions in their areas. Sometimes this resulted in undisguised threats against pro-union people at QC meetings. The following statement made by a facilitator to employees during a QC meeting illustrates an effective managerial response to the "counterproductive" activities of union supporters.

And another type of counterproductive activity which is the most blatant . . . and . . . I can see some people losing their job over this real soon, that is, creating an atmosphere [that] in anyway harbors failure or excessive frustration for people out there on the floor. And that is someone coming over to you and saying . . . "you are being treated unfairly." Now if any of you have ever worked at another plant . . . [you know] you've got it good here. . . . Anyone that is going around telling you over and over that "it's not right, they're treating you unfairly," that person is on their way out as far as [another facilitator] and I are concerned. . . . And unfortunately I'd hate to see it happen to someone I really like, [that] I think is doing a good job overall. That kind of attitude does more to hurt productivity than anything else. And that attitude has gotten to be the norm of [our production unit] and we can't allow that. . . . I think part of the problem is a lot of people in manufacturing have given too much as far as some of the freedom we've gotten. . . . [Now we are back] to this point . . . where this is the alternative, "Get your butt in gear and do your work or get out." . . . If you don't want to do that, there are plenty of places out there that will take you . . . but there won't be too many.

Such coercion utilized by QC leaders was typical during the campaign, and it was ultimately successful. As a result of its intense antiunion campaign, the company won the Board election by a substantial margin.

The failure of the union's attempted organizing drive in the face of such opposition was hardly surprising. Through legal maneuvering, the company delayed the election for as long as the NLRB would permit in order to strengthen its multifaceted campaign. Eventually, the election was held, and two out of every three workers voted against the union. The final vote was 141 against representation and 71 in favor of it. The night-shift workers described the party atmosphere at the plant following the company's victory. So exuberant were the managers that they treated the antiunion leaders to the night off, and invited them to pizza and champagne at a local restaurant. This prompted one union organizer to remark: "Well, now we have the slogan for the next campaign. 'Do you want pizza and champagne or do you want your rights?'"

The union filed charges protesting the conduct of the company and its representatives during the campaign. The organizers believed that the behavior of the company had been sufficiently unlawful to warrant overturning the election; altogether, the union filed over sixty unfair labor practice charges during the course of the campaign. The NLRB responded by issuing a record number of complaints (for the ACTWU Western Region) against the company. All counted, Ethicon faced over fifty unfair labor practices complaints alleging violations of the sections 8(a)(1) and (3) of the Act, a number comparable to the complaints issued against the J.P. Stevens company in the 1970s. Ethicon–Albuquerque, with its open and manifest antiunion sentiments, thus managed a very respectable showing of outlawry.

After lengthy delays, the case was settled, but the settlement was neither amicable between the union and the company nor equitable to Ethicon workers. In February 1984 the company offered for a second time back pay without reinstatement to the four workers who had been fired for their pro-union activities. Three of the four wanted to accept the back pay, while the fourth wanted her job back. The NLRB called the fourth worker and informed her that they had the power to settle the three cases, separating her charge and trying it alone. This tactic infuriated the union, which saw one charge alone as a weak and pointless solution to the issue. The worker, too, after consulting with her lawyer, decided that her case by itself was not something she was willing to see through. She agreed to settle. The union refused to accept the settlement, insisting that the only just solution should include reinstatement. However, because the aggrieved parties had voluntarily agreed to the terms, the NLRB had the legal authority to put the settlement into effect without the union's approval. In February 1984, nearly a year after the election and nearly two years after the beginning of the campaign, the government ordered Ethicon to pay nearly $50,000 to six workers. The union refused to sign the agreement, insisting on reinstatement. Said the head union organizer of the settlement: "It's significant. But $50,000 is a small price for the company to pay for what they did to their employees." And there ended the long struggle where the clear winner was the company and the clear losers were the union and its supporters.

PARTICIPATION AND UNION ORGANIZING IN THE 1990s

The evidence that employee involvement programs in nonunion environments can be an effective weapon against unions is, in light of the Ethicon case, compelling, but certainly not unusual. As we have shown in earlier chapters, participation schemes have a traditional place in management history as a device for controlling labor, and that they should have a continuing presence in the antiunion arsenal of employers and corporate consultants is not surprising. According to surveys conducted by the AFL-CIO Organizing Department in 1984 and 1988, EI-style programs are among the most effective antiunion strategies utilized by companies. Of the 226 organizing campaigns surveyed in 1982–83, unions won 43 percent of the elections. Against companies with some sort of EI/QWL programs, however, unions could muster only a 16 percent win rate. "Fortunately," according to the authors of the report, "only 8 percent of the companies had these programs."[54] At the time of the 1988 survey, 6 percent of the companies out of the 187 campaigns surveyed had EI/QWL programs and unions again won only 17 percent of those elections.[55] As other sources suggest, there are undoubtedly instances in which unions are discouraged from even approaching companies with participation programs.

Richard Bensinger, the Director of the AFL–CIO Organizing Institute, worked as the Western Regional Representative of the Amalgamated Clothing and Textile Workers Union and was the lead organizer for ACTWU in the Ethicon campaign. After the Ethicon loss, Bensinger went on to establish a reputation as one of the most effective organizers in the history of the AFL–CIO by winning sixteen consecutive campaigns. In the words of Dick Wilson, former director of the AFL–CIO's Organizing and Field Services Department, Bensinger is "an organizing genius." Bensinger believes that management-initiated employee involvement programs are an extremely effective and complex organizational method of controlling, and sometimes subverting, the will of the workers. And, he concedes, participation is appealing to workers over the short term.

It is difficult to generalize but when a union is not involved in these things workers usually end up being manipulated. This might have its attractions, since usually it means that the company will change their routine for a while and it will seem as if something will come out of this change. But in most cases it's all smoke and mirrors. . . . Especially in these days, when companies are looking for flexibility, which really means absolute control, you find that employers will put in some sort of quality circle model to avoid other models which might require that they really listen and respond to the people, like a union. . . . Employers create these things to create an illusion of participation when in reality the purpose is the opposite: to control and manipulate the workers.

Bensinger adds that "the first thing employers did out west was run and set one of these programs up right as a campaign became public. It is an incredibly cynical way of dealing with people."[56]

In the field, many union organizers have encountered employers who implemented EI programs immediately upon suspecting an organizing drive, or have used them to avoid signing a contract after the union has won representation rights. One worker's experience recorded in a 1988 Senate hearing is illustrative. After a successful two-month period of organizing, during which the Steelworkers obtained authorization cards from fifty of the approximately eighty employees at Crane Resistoflex in Jacksonville, Florida, the company began its antiunion campaign. According to the employee's testimony:

We made no secret of our campaign, and well before we filed with our petition with [the] NLRB the company launched a tremendous campaign against us, or against the union, if you will, the organization.

First, the company set up weekly small group meetings on every shift, and we were required to attend. At these meetings, for the first time, supervisors asked us for suggestions on safety and productivity. They also told us that these meetings were to show us that they cared about us and that we therefore did not need a union, and that the company would do anything to keep a union out of the plant.

The witness made the point of his testimony clear to the committee. "I hope my experience will help show you that employers can make a mockery of the law in order to prevent unionization."[57]

Charlie McDonald, executive assistant to the secretary-treasurer of the AFL–CIO, represents a unionist's view on participative techniques and organizing. McDonald says: "I find that quality circles help the employer take advantage of their ability to communicate very forcefully the disadvantage of trade unionism, from the employer's perspective." That advantage is not always apparent from NLRB election statistics, because employers may discourage unions from even filing an election petition. According to McDonald, "I think employers have become quite skilled at keeping incipient campaigns from assuming the fifty-five, sixty, seventy percent level of support. It requires a much greater challenge to the union organizer."[58] Confirming McDonald's perception, the Council on Union-Free Environment of the National Association of Manufacturers (NAM) has acknowledged the value of EI in thwarting organizing drives by publishing a pamphlet detailing how to use EI programs to stave off unionization.[59]

Unions leaders, of course, are cognizant of the limitations of our labor law. Not only does section 8(a)(2) afford scant protection against antiunion organizational techniques, the delay between the filing of a petition and the date of an election allows employers to intensify their resistance to a union drive. That particular feature of the law, in the view of many unionists, destroys any genuine freedom of choice for workers. One proposal for change is to eliminate such delays. "Somehow, we have to compress the process [leading to elections]. If people want a representative, that decision has to be made quickly. A mandatory time period to conduct an election has to be paramount. There has to be a way, that if the majority chooses, that's the end of it."[60]

To compensate for the weaknesses of the labor law, many unions are developing new strategies that sidestep the NLRA and appeal more directly to workers, while simultaneously attempting to neutralize employer resistance. The United Electrical (UE) Workers Union has had considerable success with its "mass organizing strategy." David Cohen, International Representative of the UE, describes the strategy. He says that mass organizing is, in essence, a union election conducted by a respected member of the community, such as a judge or member of the clergy. Cohen continues:

This does one basic thing to start with—it proves to workers some of the myths of our democracy. Everyone's had their free chance to vote in a secret ballot election.

The workers are under no pressure. The company hasn't started its terror campaign yet because it is still waiting for a petition to go to the NLRB. And those elections are winning by, normally, about 80 percent.

Should the employer demand an NLRB election, Cohen adds, workers are reluctant to accede to the employer's wishes. "They voted in their own election. It was run by a priest, state representative, sheriff, mayors or people like that." The UE's approach to organizing demonstrates not only the deficiencies of NLRB procedures, but the willingness of workers to unionize in an atmosphere free of coercion. Cohen notes: "Last year, using the community election tactic, we won eleven campaigns out of eleven. There were two campaigns we figured we wouldn't win, so we pulled out of the NLRB election."[61]

Similarly, the International Ladies Garment (ILG) Workers Union has adopted a strategy designed to circumvent Board election procedures as a means of gaining recognition. The ILG describes its tactic as "total war" aimed at gathering broad community support and bringing pressure to bear on the employer. Their drive begins with workers inside the operation. "Through them, we try to identify the institutions within the community that they respect. Quite often it is a church, or a social organization. We try to form an alliance with those organizations." Using such alliances, the ILG forces employers to reduce or completely forego resistance to the organizing effort. The ILG acknowledges that its approach requires arduous effort, but the union believes that labor law is simply ineffectual for workers. "It works for the employer. So we cannot depend on the NLRA, or any other laws."[62] Such frustration amply attests to the failure of our labor policy. But it also hints at a direction for future reform.

In summary, then, what of participation in today's workplace? It is clearly nourished by many of the same impulses that characterized the plans after World War I and just prior the Wagner Act. Power and profits remain abiding concerns of employers. Rockefeller's philosophy of mutual interests has been absorbed into a textured ideology of corporate munificence, democracy, and individual fulfillment through organizational design. Meanwhile, the unremitting hostility of most American employers toward unions threatens to emasculate independent collective bargaining in the near future. The National Labor Relations Act has become the nemesis, not the guarantor, of workers' rights. Accordingly, it is imperative that our national policy, which expressly condones and encourages collective bargaining, be revitalized.

NOTES

1. George Strauss and Eliezer Rosenstein, "Workers' Participation: A Critical View," *Industrial Relations*, 9 (1970), 197.

2. Richard Edwards and Michael Podgursky, "The Unraveling Accord: American Unions in Crisis," in Richard Edwards, Paolo Garonna, and Franz Tödtling, eds., *Unions in Crisis and Beyond: Perspectives from Six Countries* (Dover, Mass.: Auburn House, 1986), 30–31. For a more recent and detailed treatment of the postwar economic cycle, see Andrew Glyn, Alan Hughes, Alain Lipietz, and Ajit Singh, "The Rise and Fall of the Golden Age," in Stephen Marglin and Juliet Schor, eds., *The Golden Age of Capitalism* (Oxford: Clarendon Press, 1990), 39–125.

3. Samuel Bowles, David M. Gordon, and Thomas E. Weisskopf, "Power and Profits: The Social Structure of Accumulation and the Profitability of the Postwar U.S. Economy," *Review of Radical Political Economics*, 18 (1986), 136, fig. 1.

4. Bowles, *et al.*, "Power and Profits," 141, fig. 2. The authors examine the decline of American capitalism between the late 1960s and the election of Ronald Reagan in a recent book that also assesses the Reagan agenda for business ascendancy through the 1980s and its impact on workers. Samuel Bowles, David M. Gordon, and Thomas E. Weisskopf, *After the Waste Land: A Democratic Economics for the Year 2000* (Armonk, N.Y.: M. E. Sharpe, 1991). See also Michele Napels, "The Unraveling of the Union-Capital Truce and the U.S. Industrial Productivity Crisis," *Review of Radical Political Economics*, 18 (1986), 110–131.

5. For a good account of the Lordstown strike and its underlying causes, see Stanley Aaronowitz, *False Promises: The Shaping of the American Working Class* (New York: McGraw Hill, 1973), 21–50.

6. Richard Edwards, *Contested Terrain: The Transformation of the Workplace in the Twentieth Century* (New York: Basic Books, 1979), 150.

7. Richard Walton, "From Control to Commitment in the Workplace," *Harvard Business Review*, 63 (March–April 1985), 79.

8. Report of a Special Task Force to the Secretary of Health, Education, and Welfare, *Work in America* (Cambridge, Mass.: MIT Press, 1973).

9. Report, *Work in America*, 96.

10. The facility was transformed from having "one of the poorest labor relations and production records in GM" to "one of the company's better run sites." Robert H. Guest, "Quality of Work Life—Learning from Tarrytown," *Harvard Business Review*, 57 (July–August 1979), 76. David Fairris similarly argues that "quality of work-life programs have their origin in particular programs begun in the late 1960s and early 1970s by employers to address the emerging contradictions in shopfloor dispute resolution, and the jammed grievance procedures in particular." "Appearance and Reality in Postwar Shopfloor Relations," *International Contributions to Labour Studies* (forthcoming).

11. Joseph Juran, "The QC Circle Phenomenon," *Industrial Quality Control*, 23 (1967), 329–336.

12. See, generally, Don Dewar, *The Quality Circle Guide to Participation Management* (Englewood Cliffs, N.J.: Prentice–Hall, 1980).

13. "Honeywell Imports Quality Circles as Long-Term Management Strategy," *Training/HRD*, August 1980, 94.

14. Don Dewar and Jefferson Beardsley, *Quality Circles* (Menlo, Calif.: International Association of Quality Circles, 1977), 13.

15. Edward Lawler III, Gerald Ledford, Jr., and Susan Mohrman, *Employee Involvement in America: A Study of Contemporary Practice* (Houston: American Productivity and Quality Center, 1989), 12.

16. Dudley Lynch, "Circling Up Japanese Style," *American Way*, April 1981, 36.

17. Steve Bryant and Joe Kerns, "The Quality Circle Program of the Norfolk Naval Shipyard," *Manufacturing Productivity Frontiers*, September 1981, 34.

18. See, generally, "Productivity Teams," *Small Business* 5 (1980), 21–25; D. Hutchins, "Quality Circles in Context," *Industrial and Commercial Training*, 15 (1983), 80–82; "Mind the Quality, Feel the Effect," *Employee Gazette*, 91 (June 1983), 220.

19. John Simmons and William Mares, *Working Together* (New York: Alfred A. Knopf, 1983).

20. David Levine and Laura Tyson, "Participation, Productivity, and the Firm's Environment," in Alan S. Blinder, ed., *Paying for Productivity: A Look at the Evidence* (Washington, D.C.: Brookings Institution, 1990), 183–243, 204 (emphasis in original). See also Michael Conte and Jan Svejnar, "The Effects of Worker Participation in Management, Profits, and Ownership of Assets on Enterprise Performance," in *New Developments in the Labor Market: Toward a New Institutional Paradigm* (Cambridge, Mass.: MIT Press, 1990), 59–83, who report similar results.

21. Maryanne Kelley and Bennett Harrison, "Unions, Technology, and Labor–Management Cooperation," in Lawrence Mishel and Paula Voos, eds., *Unions and Economic Competitiveness* (Armonk, N.Y.: M. E. Sharpe, forthcoming), 7–8.

22. This is the theoretical rationale for participation described by Levine and Tyson, "Participation, Productivity," 187. Cooperation among members of a group resolves the "prisoner's dilemma" of individual self-maximizers competing in the zero-sum game predicated by agency theorists.

23. One exception is John F. Witte, *Democracy, Authority, and Alienation in Work: Workers' Participation in an American Corporation* (Chicago: University of Chicago Press, 1980). Witte defines "democracy" as a condition where there is a reasonable assumption of political equality and where a set of formal decisionmaking mechanisms exists. Democracy increases "if the influence of those lower in the organizational structure is increasing" (7). Witte's study was limited to a single nonunion firm, and one important conclusion he drew was that "meaningful democracy in an organization is not a minor adjustment of style and priority but requires a radical shift away from traditional norms of corporate organization" (156). Those norms include managerial assumptions about hierarchy, property, and meritocracy. See also Edward Greenberg, *Workplace Democracy: The Political Effects of Participation* (Ithaca, N.Y.: Cornell University Press, 1986) (studying worker-owned plywood cooperatives in the Pacific Northwest).

24. See Masanori Hashimoto, "Employment and Wage Systems in Japan and Their Implications for Productivity," in Blinder, *Paying for Productivity*, 245–294. The author notes that consultative practices are "the cornerstone of the Japanese industrial relations system" and a key to that country's greater productivity (271–272).

25. Robert Cole, *Work, Mobility and Participation: A Comparative Study of American and Japanese Industry* (Berkeley: University of California Press, 1979).

26. W. E. Courtright, "Hughes Circles: An Update." *The Quality Circle Journal*, 4 (1981), 34.

27. John Hoerr, "The Payoff from Teamwork," *Business Week*, July 10, 1989, 58.

28. B. Lloyd, "Does More Input from Employees Mean Higher Mill Efficiency and a Better Product?" *Daily New Record*, August 2, 1982, 5–6.

29. Jon Shepard, *Automation and Alienation: A Study of Office and Factory Workers* (Cambridge, Mass.: MIT Press, 1971).

30. Seymour Lipset, Martin Trow, and James Coleman, *Union Democracy* (New York: Anchor Books, 1962).

31. Kelley and Harrison, "Unions, Technology, and Labor–Management Cooperation," 44 (emphasis in original).

32. For an excellent case study of the team concept in the auto industry that illustrates the managerial fear of collective action, see Mike Parker, "New Industrial Relations Myth and Shop Floor Reality: The 'Team Concept' in the U.S. Auto Industry," paper presented at the Woodrow Wilson International Center, Program on Industrial Democracy and Work Relations, March 28–30, 1988. Parker analyzes the Japanese influence on the "new work design" and its American antecedents. Publicized as an innovative development in auto manufacturing with both management and labor benefitting from the arrangement, the team concept is actually used "to create convenient myths to disguise a relationship that entails giant steps backward for workers and unions" (4). The team design, in fact, enables the employer to implement a system of "management by stress," in which workers are continually forced to intensify their efforts so as to maintain production standards. Because the system is especially vulnerable to collective challenge, management has two alternatives regarding labor unions: "either prevent unionization in the first place, or keep a subdued union which helps prevent any collective action and defuses any sense of solidarity and militancy on the shop floor" (29).

33. Fred Foulkes, *Personnel Policies in Large Nonunion Companies* (Englewood Cliffs, N.J.: Prentice-Hall, 1980), 341. For a discussion of the evolving relationship between the management of work and the employment-at-will rule, see Raymond Hogler, "Employment at Will and Scientific Management: The Ideology of Workplace Control," *Hofstra Labor Law Journal*, 3 (1985), 27–58.

34. Stewart Clegg, *Frameworks of Power* (London: Sage Publications, 1989), 4.

35. Clegg, *Frameworks*, 17, 32.

36. Reinhard Bendix, *Work and Authority in Industry* (New York: John Wiley, 1956), 2.

37. Neil Mitchell, *The Generous Corporation: A Political Analysis of Economic Power* (New Haven, Conn.: Yale University Press, 1989), 7.

38. Analyzing the slowdown in productivity growth using 1948–66 as a base, Bowles, Gordon, and Weisskopf constructed a model based on five variables. One of those variables, which they designated "citizen protest," accounted for 17 percent of the slowdown in productivity growth in 1973–79. *After the Waste Land*, 115.

39. Richard Weiss has demonstrated, for example, that the recent managerial focus on employee assistance programs relies heavily on a "disease ideology of alcoholism" and actually enhances the degree of social control within the organization—"social control" signifying the presence of "mechanisms to ensure conformity with the will of corporate management." Weiss notes that "domination is easier if those subordinated can be rendered willing to accept the relationship as, in some sense, right and proper (in Weber's terminology, *legitimate*)." *Managerial Ideology and the Social Control of Deviance in Organizations* (New York: Praeger, 1986), 37 (emphasis in original).

40. Richard Weiss and Lynn Miller, "The Concept of Ideology in Organizational Analysis: The Sociology of Knowledge or the Social Psychology of Beliefs?" *Academy of Management Review*, 12 (1987), 108, 114.

41. Dennis K. Mumby, *Communications and Power in Organizations: Discourse, Ideology, and Domination* (Norwood, N.J.: Ablex, 1988), 92–93.

42. Robert Gordon, "New Developments in Legal Theory," in David Kairys, ed., *The Politics of Law: A Progressive Critique* (New York: Pantheon, 1982), 286, 288.

43. Gerald Frug, "The Ideology of Bureaucracy in American Law," *Harvard Law Review*, 97 (1984), 1278.

44. Frug, "Ideology," 1286–1287. Indeed, the tension between economic hierarchy and the individual's psychic needs may be reproduced as a "legitimation crisis" at the most basic level of social analysis. See William Connolly, "The Dilemma of Legitimacy," in William Connolly, ed., *Legitimacy and the State* (New York: New York University Press, 1984), 227.

45. Michael Moch and Anne Huff, "Power Enactment Through Language and Ritual," *Journal of Business Research*, 11 (1983), 305.

46. William Ouchi, "The Relationship Between Organizational Structure and Organizational Control," *Administrative Science Quarterly*, 22 (1977), 95–114.

47. William Winpisinger, Personal Interview, May 1984.

48. Foulkes, *Personnel Policies*, 53 (emendations and ellipsis in original).

49. Mike Parker and Jane Slaughter, *Choosing Sides: Unions and the Team Concept* (Boston: South End Press, 1988).

50. Guillermo Grenier, *Inhuman Relations: Quality Circles and Anti-Unionism in American Industry* (Philadelphia: Temple University Press, 1988).

51. With the cooperation of Local 630, Ethicon–Somerville developed an employee involvement program in 1980 that had some degree of success. See U.S. Department of Labor, *The Ethicon/ACTWU Work Involvement Process*, Bureau of Labor–Management Relations and Cooperative Programs, BMLR 111, 1987.

52. All quotations are taken from Grenier's field notes compiled during the time he was an independent researcher at Ethicon. Further details of Grenier's involvement are set out in *Inhuman Relations*.

53. Henry Farber concludes that the decline in unionization since 1977 is explained by two factors. The first is "an increase in employer resistance to unionization, probably due to increased product market competitiveness." The second, which reflects the importance of the managerial ability to influence workers' perceptions, is "a decrease in demand for union representation by nonunion workers due to an increase in the satisfaction of nonunion workers with their jobs and a decline in nonunion workers' beliefs that unions are able to improve wages and working conditions." "The Decline of Unionization in the United States: What Can Be Learned from Recent Experience?" *Journal of Labor Economics*, 8, Part 2 (1990), S76. The Ethicon experience in New Mexico amply substantiates and documents the abstract propositions.

54. Department of Organization & Field Services, *AFL–CIO Organizing Survey* (Washington, D.C.: AFL–CIO, 1984), 6.

55. Department of Organization & Field Services, *AFL–CIO Organizing Survey*, 5.

56. Richard Bensinger, Personal Interview, June 1, 1991.

57. U.S. Senate, Committee on Labor and Human Resources, Hearings before the Subcommittee on Labor, January 29–February 5, 1988, *National Labor Relations Act Practices and Operations* (Washington, D.C.: Government Printing Office, 1988), 21 (testimony of Norman Medows).

58. Charlie McDonald, Personal Interview, June 3, 1989.

59. On this point, see Mike Parker, *Inside the Circle: A Union Guide to QWL* (Boston: Labor Notes/South End Press, 1985), 113–118.

60. McDonald, interview.

61. David Cohen, "The Shift to Mass Organizing," *L[abor] R[esearch] A[ssociation]'s Economic Notes*, 58, nos. 9–10 (November–December 1990), 4–5.

62. Jeff Hermanson, "New Tactics for New Times," *LRA's Economic Notes*, 8–9.

CHAPTER 5

Changing Labor Law

THE CONDITION OF AMERICAN UNIONISM

In March 1990, *Time* magazine conducted a survey of public attitudes regarding unions in the United States. Nearly three-quarters of those interviewed said that American workers still needed labor unions to protect their interests, but almost the same number believed that labor unions had either "too much power" or the "right amount." Directly contradicting the public's perception of union power, the *Time* feature article was devoted to an analysis of unions' inability to win bargaining concessions through strikes. Labor's impotence, the report notes, has become a fact of industrial life: "As more and more employers move quickly to replace striking workers, some union leaders are beginning to view their biggest weapon, the refusal to work, as little more than labor suicide." Employers are increasingly willing to deal with strikes through the hiring of permanent replacements, a strategy dictated by competitive pressures and a "declining union influence," which lessens the "fears of reprisals or sympathy strikes."[1]

The disparity between popular perceptions of organized labor's strength and the reality of its decline is tellingly illustrated by union membership data. According to one estimate, private-sector union membership fell from 16.8 percent of the nonagricultural work force in 1983 to 12.9 percent in 1988.[2] The authors' projections suggest that future union growth under existing conditions may have deteriorated "beyond all chances of even a moderate recovery." Following a severe curtailment of organizing activity in 1981–82, most major unions evidenced slight recovery as of 1988. Consequently, "there is sufficient support for the worst-case scenario to conclude that although the certification election process may not have run completely dry for unions, it has come very close to doing so in the years since the recent recession, and there are no signs of a significant recovery."[3] An example that particularizes the academic data is the United Food and Commercial Workers' (UFCW) recent defeat in a representation election at Be-Lo grocers in Norfolk, Virginia. The UFCW invested some $1.5 million in its efforts to organize 5,000 workers at three Be-Lo locations, where employees earn minimum wages and have few fringe benefits. The first election, held in March 1991, was considered "a crucial test of organized labor's ability to organize new members." Following the union's initial loss, one UFCW official asked: "If the labor movement can't convince these people they need our help, who can we organize?"[4]

One solution to labor's dilemma would be to modify the legal rules concerning representation elections. If the period between the filing of the NLRB petition and the election were eliminated, for example, employers would lack the opportunity to intervene in the organizational activities of workers. That simple alteration of the law might greatly stimulate union growth, for, according to one authority, "relatively modest differences in the institutions that govern labor relations exert a substantial influence on the evolution of unionism."[5] Yet changing the current law is extremely problematic. Employers as a class would oppose, and most probably defeat, any such legislation. Further, as the *Time* survey indicates, public attitudes are not generally supportive of expanded power for unions. The schism between popular beliefs about unions and the reality of economic power in American labor relations is attributable in part to the tenacious set of ideas concerning workers, employers, and unions in a free market economy; those ideas generally can be referred to by the term "industrial pluralism."

Industrial pluralism was organized around certain core assumptions that furnished the theoretical components of the industrial relations system. To begin with, pluralism held that the collective bargaining process in the United States reached a stage of maturity during the postwar period in which responsible unions negotiated on a basis of rough equality with management, thereby producing industrial compacts inuring to the benefit of the concerned parties and to society in general.[6] Although conflict was inherent in the system, differences between labor and management could be adjusted satisfactorily through compromise at the negotiating table, and such adjustment required neither governmental oversight nor active state intervention. Rather, labor agreements themselves reflected the appropriate delineation of power and interests; in exchange for the wage bargain, unions conceded managerial prerogatives in operating the enterprise and fulfilling any entrepreneurial functions attaching to ownership. When disputes arose concerning the interpretation or application of the agreement, those differences were resolved by means of contractual grievance and arbitration procedures.[7] Particularly compared with trade unionism in other industrialized nations, American labor pursued collective bargaining goals through decentralized negotiating units rather than broad social and political objectives through classwide movements.[8]

Similarly, according to the accepted view, labor law provided a workable fabric of state regulation to accommodate the dynamic process of union-management relations. Although the Wagner Act was excessively pro-labor in orientation, the 1947 Taft-Hartley amendments to the Act restored balance, fairness, and a recognition of individual rights to the statutory framework. Once Congress had corrected the major flaws of the NLRA, the National Labor Relations Board and the federal judiciary rendered interpretations of the statute that clarified the congressional intent, furthered the Act's stated policies, and developed a body of doctrine that was relatively stable, relatively predictable, and internally coherent. The legal environment thus mirrored the institutional maturity reached by trade unions and employers. Labor law, consistent with this interpretation, was not subject to the vagaries of the political system, but was analogous to the "mainstream" perception of judicial decisionmaking, in which law and politics are differentiated, conceptually bounded realms of activity.[9]

Further reinforcing pluralist themes, academic research gradually adopted a perspective that ignored history in favor of practice. George Brooks, an eminent industrial relations scholar, observed in 1961 that "the relevance of labor history to industrial relations is negligible or nonexistent." He attributed that "distasteful conclusion" to the attitudes of labor relations practitioners who "are not interested in subjecting industrial relations to the searching light of historical research, and would quite naturally regard any suggestion of the kind as subversive." Personally deploring the trend away from historical studies, Brooks explained that a powerful series of events during the postwar era had produced "an astonishing degree of unanimity in our judgment of industrial relations. Almost all the articulate members of the community now accept the same objectives in industrial relations, variously called maturity, industrial stability, responsibility, or statesmanship." Because stability was a primary ingredient of the system, disruptive influences such as rival unionism, communism, and anticapitalistic views were unattractive to industrial relations participants. And, Brooks pointed out, "a commitment to these attitudes may have a high degree of political and social value, but it is deadly to the writing of history."[10]

The decline of historicism had important methodological consequences. By treating collective bargaining as a self-contained dynamic from which "institutional" or nonquantitative features could be excluded, industrial relations researchers could redirect the field along social scientific lines, drawing most heavily upon economics and psychology. As a result, "industrial relations itself shrank down into a kind of minidiscipline, confined as before to the union sector, but striving belatedly to assert its own credentials as a rigorous social science."[11] The theoretical amalgam was eventually proclaimed as the "new" study of industrial relations, and quantitative analysis became its research model of choice.

During the 1970s, declared the authors of one survey, "the method of inquiry in the study of unions and collective bargaining underwent profound change," with the consequence that "analytical research firmly established itself in this field. The earlier work of the institutionalists, seen as being inadequately rigorous, was supplanted in large part by model-building and testing which were judged the preferred way to advance knowledge."[12] In contrast to the institutionalists, the prevailing orientation emphasized empirical methodology drawn from social sciences and a model of behavior based on individual, maximizing decisions rather than on concepts of ideology, power, and historical evolution. The deductive method was "particularly useful for developing explanations that can be verified empirically, and the verification methods can be neatly connected with the laws of statistical inference." Observation, description, and statistical relations are also "neatly connected" with a bounded process impervious to sociopolitical contingencies. Compared with British industrial relations research, which was more policy-oriented and qualitative in nature, American scholars tended to treat the microanalytical level of workplace relations. Disciplines not lending themselves to that approach became marginally attractive. "Economics and psychology, the fields of ascendancy, approach problems from the perspective of the individual; sociology and political science, the fields on the decline, from the perspective of the group."[13]

Even as the social science paradigm was claiming the field of industrial relations, a number of important historical and legal studies were undermining pluralism's basic premises of equality of power, neutrality of the legal regime, and the acquiescence of capital in the procedures of collective bargaining.[14] The new scholarship examined the unregenerate antagonism of American employers, actively pursued through the legal and political systems, to all forms of collective action by workers. Although apparently accepting a stable and peaceful accord in which unions enjoyed a legitimate existence, American capitalists initiated strategies to weaken unions in organized plants, to prevent unionization of nonunion facilities, to eviscerate the power of organized labor in the political sphere, and to weaken the effectiveness of labor law. Those strategies came to fruition in the workplace of the 1980s with a redistribution of wealth and consolidation of political power in favor of employers.

The 1977 defeat of legislation designed to assist unions—the Labor Reform Act—revealed with striking clarity the antagonism of business interests toward labor's political aspirations. Although those proposed legislative changes were framed as minor "procedural" revisions of the NLRA, they provoked a massive and unanticipated response from the business community. The corporate attack relied on arguments about individual employee rights, economic efficiency, and legal equity, all of which were successfully arrayed against labor's most sustained attempt at collective bargaining legislation since the New Deal. After that political defeat, the possibilities of statutory reform to benefit organized labor are tenuous at best.

Accordingly, this chapter explores two related themes. The first theme is that the balance of power in the workplace has steadily shifted toward capital and away from American workers and their union representatives. That shift, accelerating through the 1980s, has taken place along a number of important fronts, including the processes of collective bargaining, the content of our social and political discourse, and the legal environment of labor relations. Second, given the strength of employers, any proposed legislative change in the foreseeable future must concede both the irrefragable managerial antipathy toward unionism and capital's ability to thwart any political initiatives not in its perceived interests. Successful legislation therefore must be narrow in scope, limited in objective, acceptable to the business community, and attractive to the public. The components of a feasible program of reform are, in brief, as follows.

To begin with, we sketch the roots of management's campaign to erode the union presence in American industrial life. The point of the historical analysis is to establish that the existing framework of labor relations is not, in fact, a fair adjustment of the legitimate interests of labor and capital, nor is the law neutral as to the relations of employee and employer. A growing body of evidence suggests that labor law fails to protect workers' rights and actually stifles workers' capacity for self-organization and their mutual protection through concerted activity. No longer is pluralism an appropriate model for understanding the fundamental problems of contemporary industrial relations; to the contrary, the paradigm should be dislodged in order to make way for creative solutions. Toward that end, we offer a specific legislative proposal that has two distinct advantages. In the first place, the proposal is a realistic once that might be adopted even in a regressive labor relations environment. Second, if enacted, our proposal would help to reverse the precipitous decline in union membership by creating new conditions for organizing in which workers could exercise an unimpeded choice regarding representation.

THE EVOLVING INDUSTRIAL RELATIONS ENVIRONMENT

Beginning in the 1950s and continuing through the early 1970s, American unions enjoyed a period of relative quiescence in which collective bargaining was the settled method of labor-management dealings.[15] The accord was limited to workers in the core sector of the economy and to particular industries, and, in any event, it was steadily chipped away by employers pursuing courses of action aimed at containing unions within their established constituencies and defeating them on the industrial perimeters. Employer strategies included shifting employment to nonunion facilities, the implementation of "human resource management" techniques designed to supplant the functions of unions, and a firmer stand on the economic issues of collective bargaining. Among others who have described such developments, Thomas Kochan, Harry Katz, and Robert McKersie produced an influential book in 1986 titled *The Transformation of American Industrial Relations*.[16] While their narrative of union decline is astute, the theoretical framework of their study makes clear the limitations of mainstream industrial relations research. Committed to a narrow perspective that fails to take seriously the relevance of the legal and political systems, their case for reform is ambivalent and lacking in conviction. For that reason, the work serves both as a guide to managerial behavior and as a good example of industrial relations theory hobbled by a predisposition toward pluralist ideas.

According to Kochan, Katz, and McKersie, the decline of trade unionism and the emergence of a nonunion industrial relations system was driven by the particular values of American managers. Stated briefly, their thesis is that "the deep-seated opposition to unions embedded in the ideology of American management and the culture of many American firms serves as the relevant value in explaining the rise of the nonunion human resource management system in American industry."[17] That insight, of course, is hardly a novel one in terms of labor history and, in an important sense, the "transformation" was more accurately a continuation.[18] What Kochan et al. do substantiate, from their managerialist point of view, is that the ostensible labor-management "accord" and the presumed power relations underlying collective bargaining were always exceedingly flimsy.

In the first place, a number of major employers remained nonunion even during the 1940s and 1950s, including Delta Airlines, IBM, and Motorola. The strategy of those firms was to copy, or even surpass, the wage and personnel policies of competitive unionized firms, thereby assuring the long-term entrenchment of managerial power even at the cost of immediate financial sacrifice.[19] The economic policies were linked with an explicit corporate antiunion philosophy. Taking a specific example—and one that substantially supports our case study of the Ethicon facility in the previous chapter—Kochan et al. trace the evolution of the "union-avoidance" strategy in a particular enterprise. This large manufacturing firm successfully defeated unionizing drives during the 1940s and 1950s. In the 1960s, the company diversified and created a new division located in the West, which eventually employed 35,000 employees. The division relied on an established technique for maintaining its nonunion status: "The cornerstone of the company's human resource management policy is an employee participation program." A company publication propounded the appropriate managerial ideology of common interests and nonadversarial relations.

The [IE] program is a system of management—a change in culture if you will—that invites and requires the participation and involvement of each of us in managing our affairs in the company. . . . The program is based on the assumption that every employee wants to work in an atmosphere where practices, procedures and rules make sense and are reasonable. . . . The employee participation program encourages every employee to regularly attend meetings during which all matters relating to their work environment and their jobs are discussed.

To ensure that the point of the company's strategy is clear, the authors state that "a company manager described the employee participation program as 'a real defensive strategy against the prospect of union organization.' No significant union organizing efforts have occurred in this division since its startup."[20]

In addition to worker participation programs, antiunion personnel tactics often duplicated the grievance processes of collective bargaining agreements, thus providing a means of conflict management and employee due process. Particularly, Kochan et al. argue, the new workplace system demanded a more democratic management style and the increased involvement of workers in production matters. The net consequence of the nonunion system was perceived to be greater flexibility, lower labor costs, and improved motivation for substantial portions of the work force.

In unionized firms, the discernible tendency in the postwar era was to intensify programs of deunionization. Antiunion goals typically were implemented through policies of resource allocation between union and nonunion facilities, relocation of new plants to more favorable regions, and the development of "human resource" personnel strategies. Wherever possible, collective bargaining at major unionized companies was conceded to unions that were independent and cooperative toward management. New plants were opened in geographical areas hostile to unions, such as the South. In addition, capital investment decisions were frequently determined by the existence or not of union representation, resulting in increasing disinvestment in unionized facilities.[21] Internally, the labor relations function gave way to "human resource management," whose practitioners had significantly different training and orientation than did the industrial relations staff.

Thus, entering the 1980s, American corporations were equipped with a well-developed repertoire of antiunion strategies available to them and with a system of values dedicated to the objectives of lowering labor costs, increasing productivity, and, in the words of another expert, maintaining "nonunion status for as many employees as possible."[22] Unions were attacked through investment strategies, personnel policies, and shop-floor organizational arrangements. Those efforts, as declining union membership reveals, were quite successful. Yet Kochan, Katz, and McKersie's framework for analysis hardly does justice to the magnitude of the events.

To provide a theory of industrial change, Kochan et al. offer a three-tiered framework of institutional analysis. Employers, unions, and the state carry out industrial relations activities on the respective levels of strategic, collective bargaining, or workplace behavior, respectively. The top level is characterized by strategic decisionmaking, while the second is a functional tier where unions and employers formalize agreements, and the third is the area where policies are applied to shop-floor personnel and their relations. This framework is important, the authors claim, because it permits an analysis of the interrelationships that make up the theoretical and applied dimensions of industrial relations and because all three levels must be integrated into a single field of inquiry for an adequate understanding of industrial relations. Although the authors' categories have a superficial conceptual bite, the infirmities of their scheme are evident early on in the book.

Regarding the historical framework of American industrial relations, for example, the authors begin with the thesis that prior to the 1930s, public policy was shaped by the classical free market conception that viewed labor primarily as a commodity whose exchange was controlled by market forces. The government's role was limited to "promoting and protecting the workings of a free market, the freedom of individuals to enter into contracts, and the property rights of employers to allocate their resources, including their human resources, as they saw fit." But the New Deal collective bargaining system, in contrast, was a pluralist one recognizing a limited conflict of interest between labor and capital and prescribing regulation designed to strike an accommodation of power among those competing interests. The strategic level of the New Deal system was the compact between employers and unions that "in return for acceptance of a union role in setting wages, hours, and working conditions, management would retain the initiative with respect to strategic and entrepreneurial decisions and shop-floor actions." That arrangement, the authors note, particularly suited the American labor movement's philosophy: "Business unionists rejected the view that effective representation of worker interests required that they eventually wrest away from employers control over the enterprise." Union leaders also preferred to avoid involvement in managerial decisions because they feared that a close identification with management objectives would impede the effective representation of their membership.[23] By casting the labor movement's objectives in terms of "business unionism," Kochan et al. in effect dismiss the continuing presence of class adversarialism as a relevant issue in union decline—despite impressive evidence attesting to its importance.[24]

Kochan, Katz, and McKersie's upper or strategic level of analysis focuses on the human resource policies and the investment strategies of firms, emphasizing their impact on the continued decline in union penetration in American industry. The crucial flaw in their analysis, as suggested, is that they accept the power imbalances of the actors on the strategic level without considering the legal and political framework that sustains it. To illustrate, for Kochan et al. the investment decisions of business are unproblematic because the context of "management rights" in which employers have discretion to allocate resources without interference from labor is taken as an environmental condition of our economy. What was actually a judicial rendering of labor law rather than a statutory mandate is, in turn, reinforced by the authors' historical view that unions accepted a narrow role of collective bargaining in exchange for economic benefits. Capital investment, the felicitous tool with which to tame militant unionism, is merely a feature of the economic system lying beyond the legitimate province of union concern.

A more generous appraisal of declining unionism would consider the role of the judiciary in shaping and altering the terrain of industrial conflict. As will be shown, the U.S. Supreme Court took decisive action to restore the eroded power of capital during the period between Wagner and Taft-Hartley, molding the rules of industrial relations in a number of crucial decisions that deprived unions of important economic weapons and structured the NLRA in ways advantageous to employers. That process has persisted through the 1980s, with several important labor law decisions. In mid-decade, Reagan's highly politicized National Labor Relations Board embarked on its pro-employer course, abandoning earlier cases with only the thinnest veneer of logic and avowedly remaking the system of collective bargaining law. Yet in a book purporting to deal with the "transformation" of American labor relations, Kochan et al. do not cite a single court or Board decision, nor do they refer to the work of any of the various legal scholars who have detailed the crucial impact of judicial doctrine on collective bargaining processes. Consequently, the "strategic" level of their model is so incomplete as to be of scant value in understanding union decline.[25]

The lowest, or workplace, level of the Kochan-Katz-McKersie theory deals with the attitudes and values of American workers in relation to the organization. To determine what those attitudes and values are, Kochan et al. marshall survey data from such sources as the Opinion Research Corporation. They then argue that workers desire a voice in how their work is done and in matters affecting their economic well-being. Workers are not abstractly interested in managerial decisions, they conclude, but approach strategic participation from a practical vantage; before workers are attracted to operational issues, they must be convinced that their activities can be linked with their own job expectations. Moreover, the choice of an individual worker to support union representation is characterized as a combination of the worker's dissatisfaction with the job, his or her belief that unionization will improve job conditions, and the absence of negative stereotypes regarding unions.[26] Taking the relevant factors into account, Kochan et al. think it unlikely that most American workers would select union representation, even though workers have indicated declining satisfaction with employer policies. The result is that the New Deal system of bargaining is inadequate to restore a strong union presence in American industry, although, unfortunately, the newer "human resource management" model, with its "participatory opportunities," is not sufficiently widespread to satisfy the general needs of American workers.

In their treatment of worker preferences, Kochan et al. persistently view workers as atomized, maximizing individuals having no social relations with other workers as a class. The dynamic of collective action is absent from their model, which concerns itself only with workers' expressions taken in isolation from other workers. From that perspective, the prospects of increased union success in organizing are slight. But an important element in collective worker action, and one wholly ignored by Kochan et al., is the formation of "cultures of solidarity" engendered by a unique set of conflictual circumstances in the workplace and the accompanying formation of a class consciousness among workers. Such cultures are "neither ideas of solidarity in the abstract nor bureaucratic trade union activity, but cultural formations that arise in conflict, creating and sustaining solidarity in opposition to the dominant structure."[27] The activities of rank and file steelworkers in the Carnegie-Illinois plants during the latter part of 1936 exemplify the development of worker solidarity.

And contrary to the Kochan-Katz-McKersie thesis, much contemporary labor history is animated neither by the study of collective bargaining institutions nor of individual figures in the panoply of organized labor, but by a concern for workers and their social relations.[28] Particularly significant is workers' awareness of class distinctions and the conditions that produce them. As David Montgomery noted of the early twentieth century, "it remains not only possible but imperative to analyze the American experience of the late nineteenth and early twentieth centuries in terms of conflicting social classes." Values associated with property, individualism, and contract rights were less important than attachments arising out of the common bond of labor. The "daily experiences and visible social distinctions taught many workers that although others might wield social influence as individuals, workers' only hope of securing what they wanted in life was. through concerted action."[29] Such forms of working-class consciousness persist in today's industrial environment.[30]

As a result, the more plausible explanation for declining unionism has to do not merely with the attitudes of workers, but with the changing relations of class forces that enabled capitalism to mount a four-decade offensive against labor, a point Kochan et al. obstinately decline to address as an analytical element embedded in the legal, social, and political dimensions of employment. The weaknesses of the neoclassical, behaviorist approach espoused by Kochan et al., and by many other mainstream industrial relations scholars, have been forcefully articulated by Michael Goldfield.[31]

Neoclassicism, he argues, cannot place a worker's behavior in a historical and social context, but merely presumes that his or her actions are explained as a product of economic rationalism. Goldfield suggests that economistic theorizing fails to account for many important factors:

Thus, among other things, this perspective ignores, or at least does not provide a framework for highlighting, the degree of national, racial, ethnic, and ultimately class influence (some might say peer-group pressure or coercion) on the formation and expression of workers' preferences. Second, it fails to account for the role of other class actors with tremendous influence on the expression of "preferences" of the workers for a union. Among these actors, I would include the unions and their organizers, the companies and the state, all of whom make significant efforts at various times toward affecting the outcomes of union certification elections.[32]

From the class conflict approach, the bottom tier of the Kochan-Katz-McKersie model—the worker on the shopfloor—has as little explanatory power as the strategic level peopled by executives, union leaders, and state officials.

In the middle range of the three-tiered model, Kochan et al. examine important changes occurring in the workplace through jointly negotiated organizational innovations. Those changes, they conclude, have the two basic objectives of increasing participation so as to reduce adversarialism and enhance employee motivation and of modifying the work environment to promote flexibility and lower costs. Examining several case situations, they conclude that the results of Quality of Worklife programs are at best mixed. Such programs require high levels of trust for measurable effectiveness, and a number of illustrative cases reveal failures of management to sustain trust relationships. For collective bargaining to succeed with joint cooperation efforts, unions must be involved on the "strategic" levels of managerial decisionmaking. Absent durable "linkages" between rank and file workers, the collective bargaining process, and participation in management's strategic decisions, the competitive gap between union and non-union systems cannot be closed. Ironically, "this integrated set of innovations is not diffusing to a broad range of partially organized bargaining relationships and is not likely to be found in completely unorganized firms."[33] They conclude that managerial power is effectively shared only in participative programs involving strong union representatives.

The inherent contradictions at work on each level of the three-tier model culminate in the authors' prescriptions for future policy decisions. Recognizing that employer resistance to unionization demands more effective legal protection for workers and unions, they suggest that the NLRA be reformed to strengthen election procedures and to clarify the meaning of section 8(a)(2). But their interpretation of conflict as a structural feature of organizational behavior located within the enterprise, rather than a class-driven antagonism reproduced socially, politically, and economically, leads them into a dead end. Kochan et al. concede that they "do not find it easy or fruitful to predict future political trends." Rather, they want to address those policy choices facing decision-makers irrespective of the political context.[34] But their belief that industrial relations policy is forged separate and apart from the political environment is flatly contradicted by the postwar labor relations experience. Power—its acquisition and application within the firm—is the end, and not the beginning, of policy.

In the final section of *Transformation of American Industrial Relations*, the authors present four "scenarios" for the future. The first scenario assumes a continuation of present trends, whereby competitive economic pressures generate further employer attacks on unions, and union density declines to under 15 percent. With the union threat effectively removed, employers will have a weakened commitment to human resource management and participatory projects. The second scenario assumes limited legislative reform of union organizing procedures. Such reform would enable unions to increase organizing in low-wage service industries but would not affect large firms or existing units, and membership would continue to decline. Third, labor law reform might be combined with a "broader diffusion of innovations in existing bargaining relationships," leading to improved economic performance and labor-management relationships. The final alternative combines the first three scenarios but also includes innovative techniques for unionization and bargaining across all sectors of the economy. Because it requires "fundamental shifts" in values, attitudes, and practices, the final scenario is "perhaps least likely, yet the most interesting, to contemplate."[35]

The generalities suggested by Kochan et al. as a means of dealing with the failing capacities of the American industrial system are neither persuasive nor consistent with their own findings. Deliberately ignoring the political arena because it cannot be readily assimilated into their world of industrial relations, the authors focus instead on the competitive difficulties facing American capitalists. That dynamic impels public policy choices, and the New Deal system fails on grounds of economic efficiency. "For competitive reasons employers need increased trust, commitment, and cooperation at the workplace rather than further institutionalization of adversarial relationships." At the same time, the authors admit that employer resistance has undermined the basic processes leading to union certification and that statutory revision must provide for realistic protection of employee choice regarding representation.[36] Finally, then, Kochan et al. spiral into a theoretical gridlock: managerial power erodes union strength, but global competition requires new forms of organization that, in turn, depend on an effective union presence to ensure "linkage" between the shopfloor and the strategic dimension of management.

Short of economic disaster, a scenario involving radical statutory reform that would facilitate union organizing on the magnitude of the Wagner Act is unlikely. As the history of union-management relations since the end of World War II makes clear, the retrenchment of unions and the accumulation of political power by business interests would preclude any major revisions of the NLRA benefitting labor. There is little incentive for capitalism to support a program of industrial change, because capitalism's interests have been abundantly furthered over the past decade by a massive redistribution of wealth under the existing political and economic conditions.

Since the mid-1970s, the relative political power of American workers has steadily deteriorated, with concomitant economic repercussions; as Thomas Bird Edsall demonstrates, "the continued collapse of the broad representation role of political parties in the United States has direct consequences for the distribution of income." Between 1977 and 1988, the average after-tax family income in this country declined by 10.5 percent for families in the lowest decile of income. In the top decile, however, income increased by 27.4 percent. For the income group comprising the top 1 percent, the growth in income over the decade was 74.2 percent. What such figures illustrate "is a major redistribution of economic power in the private marketplace and of political power in the public sector. . . . One of the major characteristics, then, of the post-New Deal period in American politics has been a reversal of the progressive redistribution of income that underlay the policies of the administrations of Franklin Roosevelt and Harry Truman."[37] That reversal of direction in wealth distribution was accomplished to a considerable degree through managerial innovations that "zapped" labor. In the words of Bennett Harrison and Barry Bluestone:

By the middle of the 1980s, the broad outlines as well as many of the details of these [antiunion] experiments could be summarized in the globalization of production, the hollowing of the firm, outright union busting, and revised labor-management relations that included demands for the lowering of wages, the proliferation of part-time work schedules (in opposition to the workers' expressed preference for full-time employment), and the increased subcontracting of work. Together, these developments added up to a realization of the objective—publicly enunciated by a conservative government back at the very beginning of the 1970s—of "zapping" labor.[38]

By comparison, Kochan, Katz, and McKersie's interpretation of the "transformation" explains nothing about the political and legal environment, but treats the industrial relations system as a self-contained sphere of production influenced only by "competition" rather than as a terrain that is actively constituted by political and social forces.

Ultimately, the industrial system depicted by Kochan et al. is a sanitized one untainted by the complexities of class conflict or historical contingency. For that reason, their policy proposals are unconvincing. They offer neither concrete suggestions for change nor persuasive arguments why change should occur. Thus, the reining exemplar of mainstream industrial relations research offers little basis for political action. A signal omission of their work—the legal rules governing the relationship between unions and employers—is examined next.

LABOR LAW AND INDUSTRIAL RELATIONS

The struggle to establish a statutory framework for collective bargaining in the United States culminated in the Wagner Act of 1935. But the fashioning of labor law did, and does, remain largely the province of the judiciary and the National Labor Relations Board. In a pathbreaking, controversial 1978 essay, Karl Klare laid the groundwork for a new interpretation of labor law based on critical legal theory.[39] As sketched by Klare, and later elaborated by other legal scholars, critical analysis explores the inherent bias of labor law jurisprudence and the ways in which federal courts have successfully dampened the potential for militant worker action and reinforced the system of property rights underlying collective bargaining in America.[40] Klare's point of departure is that the Wagner Act, so ambiguous in its language and purpose, offered "a significant opening in the direction of radical change." That it failed to produce any lasting alteration in the basic organization of the workplace, or in the relationship of the state to private economic activity, is the problem to be explained; the role of the Supreme Court supplies a partial answer.[41]

The formative period of judicial revisionism occurred in the four years following the 1937 *Jones & Laughlin* case, when the Court issued a number of crucial decisions interpreting the Wagner Act. Among them were cases permitting employers to permanently or temporarily replace strikers, authorizing the employer to discharge workers engaging in sit-down strikes, and establishing the superiority of a collective bargaining agreement over workers' rights to engage in concerted economic action.[42] But of greater importance than the bare principles generated in the cases, the Court also fashioned an ideology of workplace relations that persists in contemporary legal doctrine. Collective bargaining law, Klare contends, "articulates an ideology that aims to legitimate and justify unnecessary and destructive hierarchy and domination in the workplace." Accompanying the ideology is an elaborate "institutional architecture" that sustains the power arrangements within the enterprise. Under those arrangements, unions are obliged to regulate employee unrest in furtherance of industrial peace and to take part in an "industrial jurisprudence" that reinforces managerial control over the production processes.[43]

In *Jones & Laughlin* itself, the Court insisted that the NLRA "does not compel agreements between employers and employees. It does not compel any agreement whatever."[44] Through the incorporation of older theories of "freedom of contract," the Court retained contractualism as the underlying framework of labor law. The implications of that theory, Klare maintains, are profound. Initially, the ideal of contractualism "was and is that justice consists in enforcing the agreement of the parties so long as they have capacity and have had a proper opportunity to bargain for terms satisfactory to each." Because contractualism is "formal and abstract," the theory precludes inquiry into the nature of the transaction and instead remains "disinterested in the substantive content of the parties' arrangements." Applied to the realm of labor markets, then, contractualism produces results at once "oppressive and morally defective." In the first place, capitalists exploit the value created by workers over and above labor costs. Second, the employment relationship is social as well as legal. "It establishes an entire system of social relations in the workplace whereby the employer is entitled to control the worker's actions and choices during the major portion of his waking hours. Thus labor contractualism functions as the institutional basis of domination in the workplace." From the contractualist perspective flowed other doctrinal assumptions necessary to the preservation of the economic system in the face of the Wagner Act's radical potential. They included an abiding concern for the sanctity of employer property rights; a reluctance to intrude into the functioning of the labor market; and a reliance on the "expertise" of the NLRB as the guarantor of the state's interest in labor relations.[45]

Extending critical theory into to the postwar period, Katherine Stone examined pluralism's consequences for the administration of collective bargaining agreements. Pluralists, Stone argued, viewed the NLRA as a procedural mechanism that did not confer substantive rights on labor, but rather, through the process of bargaining, employees and union representatives participated in the mutual "governance" of the workplace. The pluralist ideology demonstrates remarkable persistence, according to Stone, because "it serves as a vehicle for the manipulation of employee discontent and for the legitimization of existing inequalities of power in the workplace."[46] Particularly, grievance and arbitration clauses assured that labor conflict was removed from the realm of governmental supervision and channeled into a system of adjudication that precluded collective action and tended to buttress certain assumptions regarding managerial prerogative. Because the federal judiciary initially tried to shield arbitration awards from any substantive oversight, arbitrators were free to develop their own rules of industrial jurisprudence based primarily on the terms of the contract without reference to the statutory objective of promoting employee self-organization.

Beginning with the Supreme Court's 1957 decision in the *Lincoln Mills* case, arbitration was recognized as the cornerstone of federal labor policy.[47] But increasingly, the private ordering of industrial conflict resolution suffers from internal inconsistency and conceptual paradox. Fundamental to the paradigm is the notion that employers and union together regulate all terms of the labor transaction through negotiation of a collective bargaining agreement. Substantive bargaining is free from governmental compulsion, and the parties in theory meet on a basis of common interest and roughly equivalent power. The reality, however, is that a union's right to bargain is narrowly circumscribed to "mandatory" subjects. Matters that are not mandatory subjects include a variety of prerogatives falling within "the core of entrepreneurial control." Moreover, rights of management that are not specifically limited by the agreement are deemed "retained" by management. The retained rights theory and its implications effectively discredit the pluralist conception, Stone concludes:

Under the theory of the workplace as a mini-democracy [pluralists] cannot hold a pure belief in retained rights. Such a position would destroy the illusion of democracy because it would quickly become apparent that only a small number of situations that arise in the workplace are governed by explicit contract language. The overwhelming majority of plant-life issues would still be subject to unilateral management control.[48]

Because the collective bargaining system is skewed in favor of management and its prerogatives, genuine democracy in the workplace is unattainable. The appearance of democratic participation through union representation, however, leads pluralists to conclude that workers acquiesce in the hierarchical order: "The entire panoply of workplace regulations and decisions—disciplinary rules, methods and pace of production, hiring policies, and product quality—is implicitly within the union's consent. Thus virtually all management decisions are legitimated by the theory."[49]

The radical critique of labor law has been challenged by legal scholars arguing from a traditionalist perspective, who defend both the integrity of doctrinal legal analysis and the faith of the industrial relations pluralists in existing collective bargaining arrangements. Matthew Finkin, for example, condemned the work of Klare and Stone because their essays detract from the practice of law and the advancement of legal scholarship.[50] Finkin's general argument is that Klare's thesis concerning the "revolutionary" nature of the Wagner Act is not supported by the Act's legislative history. To the contrary, Finkin asserts, both the House and the Senate emphasized the continuity of the NLRA with previous legislation. Drawing on that history and past decisions, the Supreme Court had no viable "radical alternatives" from which to fashion labor law. Far from mandating participatory democracy on the shop floor, the NLRA presupposed a system of exclusive representation, which is hardly equivalent to the "passivity and exhaustion" of the working class.[51] Finkin similarly rejects Stone's thesis that grievance-arbitration procedures are a pluralist tactic to destroy working-class cohesion; instead, he asserts that Stone interprets the postwar legal evolution "as reflecting neither the statute (or arguable statutory constructions) nor the predisposition of individual Justices, but an ideology fashioned after the war by a bunch of lawyers and economists—primarily identified with Harvard University—whose willing instrument was the United States Supreme Court." Thus, Finkin's rebuttal runs, the criticisms of pluralist theory have no warrant in the reality of industrial relations, and the supposition that the collective will embodied in grievance-arbitration undermines group solidarity is a contradiction in terms.[52]

Klare's and Stone's responses to the Finkin article help to sharpen the discussion of pluralism and its relevance to the matter of industrial democracy. For both Klare and Stone, the normative vision of labor law is its enhancement of participatory processes in the workplace, but its reality is the effectiveness of prevailing legal ideology to thwart such processes. While the Court's interpretations of the statute were a complex mixture of doctrine, precedent, and legislative history, those interpretations nevertheless had a symbolic and legitimating effect that transcended the result in any given case.

Legal images of collective bargaining may combine and coalesce into an integrated, convincing set of beliefs about entitlement, obligation, and equity in the workplace. These beliefs may then be internalized and absorbed by labor leaders at all levels, influencing their actions. To the extent that this is true, that is, to the extent that legal discourse informs or encourages widely held beliefs that existing institutions are either necessary or desirable, legal discourse "legitimates" established arrangements and constrains efforts to forge alternative practices and institutions.[53]

Contractualism, particularly, forces workers' collective activities into the narrow framework of a labor agreement negotiated in a legal environment favoring competitive labor markets and administered through an arbitration system based on the reserved rights of management. Thus, collective bargaining as it now exists in important respects mitigates against the ideal of collective solidarity. Obscuring that point, pluralism prevents our envisioning alternative possibilities "for attaining true equality between management and labor, and true democracy in the workplace."[54]

The antilabor tendencies of the federal judiciary continued to be apparent throughout the 1980s. The Supreme Court's 1981 interpretation of an employer's duty to bargain, for example, left unions virtually powerless to challenge such crucial managerial decisions as plant relocations and shutdowns by removing those subjects from the scope of mandatory bargaining.[55] In an important 1985 case, *Pattern Makers' League v. NLRB*, the Court effectively gutted a union's ability to enforce solidarity through internal rules punishing a member's attempted resignation during a strike;[56] lacking any meaningful perception of the need for group solidarity in labor disputes, the *Pattern Makers'* opinion depicts "a universe populated by isolated individuals whose rights constitute a zero sum and whose relationships with each other are purely contractual and instrumental."[57] And, to take another application of the *Mackay* rule and its pro-employer implications, the Court ruled in the 1989 *Trans World Airlines* case that during a strike the company could award job bids to workers on the job, and returning strikers could not displace them even though the former strikers had greater seniority than the successful bidders. Dissenting, Justice Brennan asked: "If indeed one group or the other is to be 'penalized,' what basis does the Court have for determining that it should be those who remained on strike rather than those who returned to work?" His answer is a revealing glimpse of the Court's predilections in deciding labor law cases. Brennan said, "I see none, unless it is perhaps an unarticulated hostility toward strikes."[58] In general, then, as much contemporary scholarship shows, judicial interpretations of the Act are instrumental in creating a legal regime that defers collective resistance to the operational dictates of the enterprise.

Moreover, after Ronald Reagan's appointees gained control of the National Labor Relations Board in 1984, the Board aggressively fashioned its own pro-employer jurisprudence by overturning many of its earlier precedents. One commentator described the "hit lists" of precedents targeted by the Reagan appointees to the Board; their predicted reversals of Board law, he says, were "chillingly accurate."[59] Although the Reagan Board purported merely to correct the excesses of the Carter Board, many of the overruled precedents dated back several decades. The "mandate" under which the Reagan Board acted was largely the political agenda developed by the conservative Heritage Foundation and Robert Hunter, who became a Board member in 1984. That mandate was actively supported by such business groups as the Chamber of Commerce and the National Association of Manufacturers. Accompanying the doctrinal revolution was an ideology that relied on notions of free choice, individualism, and contractual rights. "Just as political attacks on organized labor are disguised by euphemisms such as 'special interests,'" Levy noted, "so the Reagan Board disguises its real motivations by invoking various legitimating themes that have broader appeal than the mere condemnation of unions." Three major themes routinely appeared in the statements of the Reagan team. First, workers "must be restored the unencumbered right to choose freely for or against union representation; neither choice should be imposed against the will of the majority." Second, in the past, the Board had afforded too little weight to the interests of workers as against the interests of unions and management, to the corresponding detriment of workers. Third, the Board should provide more opportunity "for the private resolution of disputes through the encouragement of collective bargaining." Those animating themes, however, were conveniently discarded when they supported a result in favor of union organizational interests.[60] After his thorough review of the Reagan Board's decisions, Levy reached a sharp conclusion: "The moving force for the Reagan Board is to free the employer from constraint by workers and their organizations. The Board employs any rationale which advances employer power, or which weakens unions."[61]

Even by the late 1970s, the shortcomings of collective bargaining law had become obvious to the labor movement, and trade union leaders initiated a political response to the problem. The Labor Reform Act of 1977, which was passed in the House but defeated by filibuster in the Senate, would have expedited election procedures, strengthened Board remedies, and improved the Board's administrative capabilities.[62] Harrison Williams, author of the Senate version of the bill (S. 1883), declared that the purpose of the legislation was to redress inequities in the NLRA, which "has proven ineffective and impotent in the face of adamant employer resistance." Prominent government and union officials offered their support for the Williams bill. Secretary of Labor Ray Marshall endorsed its remedial measures for unlawfully discharged workers by pointing out that "some employers have found it more profitable to disobey the law than to obey it." Although the number of such employers was small, Marshall continued, their example "causes serious trouble for the implementation of the basic purpose of the act. These violations are rapidly communicated to workers attempting to organize, and it has the effect of killing their enthusiasm for the union and for collective bargaining."[63] Lane Kirkland, then secretary-treasurer of the AFL-CIO, was less enthusiastic concerning the legislation because it was a limited measure. On the one hand, he said, the Carter administration's legislative program did not attempt to correct the unfairness of Taft-Hartley as it affected bargaining relations and therefore left the "current balance of power between organized employees and their employers . . . precisely where it is today." But at the same time, Kirkland recognized that reforms in the area of representation elections were a laudable and necessary objective: "The record compiled since 1960 clearly establishes that the right to organize without employer interference stated in the NLRA does not in fact provide the assured protection that its sponsors intended."[64]

The Labor Reform Act was vigorously opposed by employer groups and their congressional allies, who raised the standard pluralist arguments that the reform proposal created a "pro-labor" law destructive of the existing balance between labor and management and was detrimental to individual employee rights. Senators Hatch and Tower, in a show of concern for American workers, introduced their own legislation as a countermeasure to the Labor Reform Act. Their draft of labor legislation is a distillation of antiunion sentiments in this country and incorporates and summarizes the core ideological elements.

Designated as the Employee Bill of Rights Act of 1977, the Hatch-Tower legislation (S. 1885) was premised on a "balanced approach to modern labor-management relations," the most important aspect of which was the "long-standing national labor law policy of assuring employees the absolute freedom of choice as to whether they want to be represented by a labor organization." Senator Hatch conceded that he was "primarily concerned about protecting employee rights and unconcerned about making it easier for unions to organize at the expense of those employees who are guaranteed the rights to refrain from that activity."[65] Consistent with Hatch's vision of unimpeded choice, S. 1885 guaranteed that no union could represent employees unless a secret ballot election had been held. Individual rights were further assured by new sections requiring a secret ballot referendum authorizing strikes and prohibiting union fines against strikebreakers. Confirming Stone's thesis regarding the centrality of arbitration to pluralist theory, S. 1885 also statutorily mandated that all contractual disputes be submitted to arbitration as the "exclusive forum" for resolution and granted aggrieved employees access to the Board only when the determinations of the arbitrator were "inconsistent with" the rights afforded under the Act.[66]

During the congressional hearings, opponents of the Williams bill marshalled other arguments against the reform legislation, and those views are especially pertinent to the broad policy issues of labor law. Among other criticisms of S. 1883, business interests pointed out that the Reform Act would be economically wasteful and inefficient. "Whatever the merits of collective bargaining," declared the National Association of Manufacturers, "they do not involve a notable record either in improving the efficiency in which manpower is deployed or in achieving noninflationary settlements. Restrictive work rules and wasteful work practices mandated by unions frequently retard the productivity of American business." Monopoly wage gains, moreover, "often far exceed any subsequent increases in productivity among the members they represent." The true purpose of the reform bill, NAM concluded, "is to unfairly assist union organizing efforts," at an unwarranted cost to consumers and society.[67]

Despite strong congressional support, the Labor Reform Act eventually died in early 1978. The House adopted its version of labor reform in October 1977 by a vote of 257 to 163. The legislation was then referred to the Senate, where the strategy of the pro-business contingent shifted to a procedural derailment of the bill rather than its modification. Realizing that any Senate amendments would be subject to compromise in the conference committee, the employer group opted for a filibuster. On June 22, 1978, after nineteen days of debate, the Senate failed for the sixth time to invoke cloture, and the legislation was sent back to committee. Shortly thereafter, labor conceded that the reform attempt had failed.

Union leaders were dismayed at their "betrayal" by American management. AFL-CIO officials were convinced that they could avoid a direct political confrontation with the business community because top executives, at least, would abide by the terms of the supposed labor-management accord and "would recognize that unions have a role in our society, as in all modern industrial societies, plus some rights to, and needs for, security." But in that belief, organized labor had simply succumbed to a delusion: "Perhaps for the first time in recent years, AFL–CIO leaders came to believe, without qualification, that the expressed commitment of the AFL–CIO to the American process of collective bargaining within a free enterprise system was not shared by the business community."[68] The pluralist mythology had been exploded.

Given the fate of the Labor Reform Act, the likelihood of any future legislative alteration of our collective bargaining law is slight. Under Ronald Reagan, organized labor suffered a number of setbacks, including the Air Traffic Controllers Strike of 1981 in which Reagan sent an antilabor "message" to the management community, and the disaster of the 1984 election, when Reagan received 46 percent of the union vote.[69] The political outlook for the 1990s suggests that labor will remain a negligible force in national politics, incapable of developing a working-class movement to counter the trends emerging from the Reagan years. "In the long run the prospects are for the maintenance of a strong, conservative Republican party, continuing to set the national agenda on basic distributional issues, no matter which party holds the White House."[70] Confirming such predictions, President Bush's advisors recommended that he veto any law interfering with an employer's right to replace strikers. Secretary of Labor Lynn Martin informed congressional leaders in early 1991 that she would oppose pending legislation dealing with strike replacements because it "could shift the balance of power between labor and management to labor."[71]

To summarize the argument to this point, American industrial relations research generally disdains issues of social and political policy. It manifests a pluralist disposition toward acceptance of collective bargaining practices as they exist and rarely debates the need for, or possibility of, fundamental reforms. Thus, little intellectual momentum for change is generated. A related hurdle to legislative change is the nature of labor law doctrine in this country. Statutory provisions are sufficiently flexible as to permit disparate and conflicting interpretations of the law, as occurs under section 8(a)(2). Court and Board opinions can be clothed in appealing ideologies that disguise true configurations of power, such as the judicial concern for individual employee rights or the sanctity of contractual orderings. Union efforts to change the legal environment were defeated in 1978. Despite a growing awareness among legal experts that our labor law has "failed" in its objectives,[72] few observers are optimistic about reform in the near future. In his assessment of employment law, for example, Paul Weiler suggests a number of specific changes, but he concedes that his ideas "would attract even more intense opposition [than the 1977 bill] from the business community and its political action committees, and would arguably have even worse prospects for successful enactment."[73] Under such conditions, only a limited political strategy is worth serious attention. Next, we present and defend a legislative option that could succeed.

A PROSPECT FOR LEGAL REFORM

A New Section 8(c)(2)

Our proposal for modification of the NLRA consists of two parts. The first step we suggest is the elimination of section 8(a)(2), a legal alteration that would permit employers to introduce any organizational schemes they desired, including dealing with employees through a system of representation. But to ensure that employees are not coerced by antiunion strategies, we argue that the Act should be further modified to require an employer to bargain with any representative who demonstrates through authorization cards, *without the requirement of an election*, that a majority of employees desire representation by the agent for purposes of collective bargaining. The result would be "immediate recognition" and bargaining, a method currently used in Canada.[74]

Both modifications could easily be accomplished by adding a second clause to the present language of section 8(c) of the Act. That clause would consist of the proposal drafted by Representative Hartley in 1947 as section 8(d)(3), and additional statutory language dealing with union recognition. Specifically, Congress should alter the NLRA by repealing section 8(a)(2) and inserting a new section 8(c)(2), to read as follows:

The forming or maintaining by an employer of a committee of employees and discussing with it matters of mutual interest, including grievances, wages, hours of employment, and other working conditions, shall not constitute or be evidence of an unfair labor practice under any other provisions of the act, provided the Board has not certified or the employer has not recognized a representative as their representative under section 9; and provided further, that if a majority of the employees in an appropriate unit designate a collective bargaining representative through authorization cards, the Board shall order the employer to bargain with the representative for a reasonable period of time not to exceed one year.

The modification, which combines the language of the proposed Hartley bill and a provision for recognition without an election, accommodates the interest of employers, workers, unions, and the public. Further, the proposed changes are wholly consistent with early versions of labor law doctrine. The National Labor Board, under Senator Wagner's leadership, effectively dealt with company unions by means of the NIRA's general mandate favoring collective bargaining. Similarly, the NLRB has in the past afforded bargaining rights to unions based on authorization cards; to do so at present would not constitute a radical departure from previous practices. Consequently, our proposal is not disruptive of basic labor law principles in this country. Nor, we contend, does it impinge upon any legitimate interests.

Overcoming Managerial Opposition

The background developed in earlier chapters shows that participation programs historically have furthered a number of uncontroversial management objectives, including improved employee motivation, higher levels of productivity, and the workers' identification with the goals of the enterprise. Likewise, the centrality of participative techniques to modern industrial organization has been documented by a number of sympathetic observers.[75] From the managerial perspective, intensified global economic competition over the past two decades has spurred interest in workplace innovation as a means of improved industrial productivity; and adversarialism in labor relations is correspondingly viewed as wasteful and destructive, placing American industry at great disadvantage in the world economy. In recognition of that point, the federal government has endorsed worker participation as a matter of policy: "The Department of Labor has taken a strong position in support of labor-management cooperation as an important prerequisite to America's return to preeminence in the world marketplace."[76] More urgently, the Commission on Workforce Quality and Labor Market Efficiency warns of the impending crisis facing the American economy and recommends legal reform to encourage participation programs. "Many observers believe that our labor laws and policies are an outmoded remnant of an era when adversarial relationships were the norm."[77]

Even commentators otherwise critical of our political economy have rejected simple adversarialism as a suitable means of attaining greater democracy in the workplace. Karl Klare acknowledges, for example, that the adversarial model of industrial relations has undisputed weaknesses, including "reliance on an idealized portrait of collective bargaining; an inability to see the need and contemporary potential for democratic work reorganization; and the failure to come to grips with the present context of profound economic transformation and of crisis within the labor movement."[78] Barry Bluestone, an influential economist and an ardent supporter of trade union principles, also agrees that adversarial unionism is no longer a viable strategy for labor. "The union, no matter how militant its stance, has little power to tame the global marketplace or for that matter reign in the multinational firm that moves its operations abroad or outsources its production to avoid the union." Bluestone adds that economic pressures on employers are now more compelling than in the earlier postwar decades. "Wage and benefit differentials that are not offset by higher productivity or better product quality become the prime target of managers who see themselves as constantly battling lower unit-cost, higher-quality producers in order to maintain their profit margins, satisfy their stockholders, and fend off unfriendly corporate raiders."[79] In those circumstances, unions are virtually powerless to prevent organizational innovations.

The 1989 study conducted by Lawler, Ledford, and Mohrman demonstrates the increasing prevalence of participation programs among large employers and clarifies managerial beliefs about participative strategies. The incentives to adopt programs are related to the fundamental managerial concerns of productivity, quality, morale, and motivation. "Simply stated, in this time period [the 1980s] organizations have felt serious competitive pressures and, therefore, have been willing to consider changing their management style."[80] Most power-sharing practices such as participation groups and work teams were initiated in the sample companies after 1982, and, in the vast majority of instances, stimulus toward participation plans came from management and not from unions or employees.[81] The outlook for continued growth of participation is positive: "Given its upsurge in the past 10 years, it might accurately be labeled the Management Phenomenon of the 1980s."[82]

Assuming that worker participation produces the results expected by managers and that participatory techniques continue to flourish in the 1990s, employers have a strong interest in clear, definitive legal rules governing their use. Where a union exists, the employer is obligated to bargain over any change in working conditions directly affecting employees.[83] But in the nonunion situation, where most workplace innovations are now taking place, implementation of a program may constitute an unfair labor practice. The law is complex and unsettled, with different principles controlling Board adjudication and federal appellate review. Moreover, opinions are in conflict among the circuits and are occasionally inconsistent even within the same circuit.[84] An ambiguous legal environment creates uncertainty in the development of participative strategies, and employers concerned with the legality of a program might be dissuaded from such efforts. Even employers who reasonably believed that their actions were lawful would nonetheless remain vulnerable to a Board proceeding and the attendant expense of vindicating their position through years of litigation, a dilemma that recently faced the Du Pont corporation.[85] In addition, for the reasons made clear earlier, no amount of future Board or court interpretation can entirely remove the obstacle posed by section 8(a)(2). The only satisfactory resolution of the problem is legislative repeal of the unfair labor practice provision. Certainly, any congressional action that included the elimination of section 8(a)(2) would command the support of employers.

Protecting Workers' Rights

An argument that has been emphasized throughout this study is that "freedom of choice" for workers cannot be abstracted from its context of workplace relations. Neither the NLRB nor the federal courts have formulated an acceptable general rule under section 8(a)(2) to deal with workers' preferences and participation programs. The reason, simply, is that "choice" is contingent, dynamic, and determined by workers' particularized experience in a given enterprise. In many instances, the desire of workers has been to maintain a program established by the employer, and certainly their desires should be respected—not simply because modern industrial relationships are no longer adversarial, as some judges mistakenly believe, but because workers themselves are best able to ascertain the nature of the employer's program. At the same time, workers must have an effective means of combatting and uprooting those organizational forms they find to be unacceptable.

The case study of the Ethicon program in Albuquerque illustrates the unlawful ends that can be achieved through participatory techniques and why employees are relatively powerless to mount a viable response to such organizational devices. The difficulty is not that employees are unable to separate benign from malignant practices, nor that they are ineluctably spellbound by managerial ideologies, but that they have no direct and immediate means to repel the employer's machinations. Yet the elimination of section 8(a)(2) would not leave the Board powerless against a revival of "company unions." Section 8(a)(1) of the Act prohibits employers from interfering with, retraining, or coercing employees in the exercise of rights guaranteed under the Act, including the right to self-organization. Consequently, legal recourse would remain available to employees.[86] But in addition to statutory remedy, workers would also be afforded the powerful weapon of seeking out a trade union ally to represent their interests. That alternative, in and of itself, virtually eradicates the imbalances of power in participation schemes—and in current representation procedures.

Existing Board law is notoriously inadequate to protect genuine employee choice in selection a union representative when the employer actively opposes their attempt to do so. As a number of scholars have shown, the critical factor in NLRB elections is the employer's antiunion campaign. In their influential book, Freeman and Medoff reviewed the literature on union elections prior to 1984 and reached the following conclusion: "Despite considerable differences among studies, . . . virtually all tell the same story: Managerial opposition to unionism, and illegal campaign tactics in particular, are a major, if not the major, determinant of NLRB election results."[87] Campaign tactics may include both lawful and unlawful conduct. If conduct is unlawful, NLRB remedies often do not eradicate the effects of the employer's unfair labor practices. But even where conduct is lawful, the delays between the filing of the petition and the election are of sufficient duration to erode the momentum of the campaign. Under current labor law and procedure, then, workers' attempts to gain certification and bargaining rights for a representative are easily nullified by employers. Existing labor law offers no meaningful route whereby workers can replace a participation plan with another entity. The card check method of recognition is a practical avenue.

Prior to 1947, unions could claim a right to be certified based on their presentation of authorization cards signed by a majority of employees in an appropriate unit. The Taft-Hartley amendments modified Board certification procedures and provided for certification only through an election. In the mid-1960s, the Board began to accept authorization cards as a means of imposing a duty to bargain where the employer lacked a "good faith doubt" regarding the union's majority status.[88] The Supreme Court's 1974 decision in *Linden Lumber*, however, clarified the rights of employers confronted with a union demand for bargaining. According to the Court, an employer has the right to insist on an election as a condition of recognition, whether or not the employer has a good faith doubt as to employee support. The only situation in which bargaining takes place absent voluntary recognition or an election is when the employer's unfair labor practices warrant issuance of a bargaining order.[89] Accordingly, legislation is necessary to modify existing doctrine and to reestablish the principle that authorization cards are a valid method of indicating employee sentiment and should be given legal effect. The new legal rule, therefore, should stipulate that any designated representative presenting authorization cards from a majority of employees in an appropriate unit, whether the representative is an AFL-CIO affiliate or an independent employee organization, is entitled to bargain collectively with the employer for a reasonable period of time not to exceed one year. Such a principle would guarantee freedom of choice more fully than the existing doctrine.

Organizing Unions

Statutory changes to expedite the formation of a collective bargaining relationship would logically enhance the organizing capabilities of trade unions. One of the greatest obstacles to unionization at present is the tremendous cost of organizing imposed on unions by the existing legal rules. Organizing occurs in a fragmented, decentralized environment, where wages are not taken out of competition and employers have substantial incentives to oppose unionization, where the labor movement lacks any significant degree of coordination and cooperative strategy on the national level, and where unions struggle to negotiate for wages and benefits in localized settings. Those points are central to the "institutional" account of union decline set forth by Joel Rogers.[90]

Collective bargaining in the United States, Rogers contends, is a "low density decentralized case" (LDDC), as opposed to the "high density centralized case" (HDCC) characteristic of many European systems. In the LDDC, unions lack coordinated political power and the ability to extract economic benefits or a "social wage" through state action. Unions are thus compelled to adopt particularized tactics of bargaining that focus primarily on economic issues and that have no meaningful degree of strategic coherence. The pursuit of disorganized, highly specific goals has "tended to divide unions from each other and from unorganized workers. As a consequence, workers as a class were cumulatively weakened and the LDDC status of the United States repeatedly confirmed. This is the basic 'divide and conquer' argument."[91] Comparative studies of union density in "corporatist" or HDCC countries lend credence to Rogers' argument concerning American workers' lack of solidarity; simply put, "the notion that business should engage in a jihad for union-free environment as in the United States is anathema to employers in such a setting."[92] If the key to union decline is employer hostility to unions, and if employers' most powerful weapon against organizing is a campaign period in which management can engage in virulent, often unlawful antiunionism, it follows that an alternative to that method of recognition would greatly encourage organizing by facilitating new structures of union formation.

Assume, to elaborate the point, that a nonunion employer creates an employee involvement program in order to increase productivity and quality control. It soon becomes apparent to workers that the program aims mostly at an intensification of labor output and surveillance and delegates no genuine decisionmaking power to the shop floor. Using the apparatus set up by the employer, workers explore among themselves the option of unionization, and a majority commit to the concept of union representation. With that commitment, a spokesperson contacts various labor unions and selects one, which then distributes authorization cards to be signed and returned. Because the union will receive representation rights with a negligible financial investment, its decision to obtain NLRB certification is virtually risk-free. If the union fails to negotiate a first contract, its only loss is the time expended by its negotiating team. But because workers at the firm initiated the union relationship, they would most likely support the bargaining process in sufficient numbers to secure a contract.

Safeguarding unions against massive losses in organizing activities, such as the $1.5 million spent by the UFCW in the Be-Lo campaign mentioned earlier in this chapter, would promote a new kind of internal union structure. Local bargaining units could be granted considerable autonomy in the conduct of their affairs, since the union representative would suffer no pressure to recoup the expense of organizing. Indeed, workers might well negotiate their own representational contract with the union in exchange for the delivery of their signed authorization cards. Details of the local's and the international's authority could be spelled out in a document fashioned to the needs and desires of the specific work group. Workers, consequently, would have little to fear from a union bureaucracy, and unions would have greater flexibility in dealing with locals. If a work group made unreasonable demands as a condition of representation, the union could simply decline the offer of representation. Such an arrangement would have a salutary effect on the labor movement as an institution.

Recent commentaries have suggested that new conditions of employment demand new forms of unionism. Charles Heckscher, an advocate of union change, proposes a model of "associational unionism" that is "fluid and decentralized," and more responsive to workplace realities. Heckscher's model depends on expanded rights for individual workers, to be enforced through mandated negotiations between employers and work groups and overseen by a "National Employment Relations Board."[93] The tendencies produced by card certification would promote the type of "associational" unionism advocated by Heckscher. Because workers would choose unions, rather than unions choosing workers, workers would select a representative not on the basis of outmoded jurisdictional concepts, but on the basis of competence. Large internationals, then, might bargain for diverse occupational groups and provide a range of employment-related services to the individual employee, such as handling grievances and arbitration, assisting members with unemployment or workers' compensation claims, and advising in matters of civil rights and health and safety laws. Relations between bargaining units would be loosely coordinated by the international along lines of common workplace issues, and the problem of centralized union power would become less threatening to potential members. At the same time, competition among unions would prompt a rejuvenated labor movement, and eventually unions would penetrate into occupations traditionally unresponsive to them. The example of the United Steelworkers union provides a timely illustration of the points just outlined.

Between 1980 and 1990, the United Steelworkers of America (USWA) lost more than one-half its membership, and the USWA is now reduced to approximately 480,000 American members. Launching a campaign in February 1991 to organize office and technical workers in Trenton, New Jersey, the union hired a woman organizer with no previous experience in the steel industry to make house calls. Her reception was "even colder than the weather." Workers feared that unionization would jeopardize their benefits or force them to engage in a strike. "Moreover," the report went on, "many office workers deal more closely with managers than each other, making them more susceptible to employers' antiunion campaigns. And those campaigns, facilitated by diluted interpretations of labor laws, are becoming quite slick." Unions, to recoup their membership share, are attempting to broaden their appeal and to break down traditional stereotypes, and while the USWA's effort in Trenton was unsuccessful, their approach indicates the most promising future direction for the American labor movement.[94] Recognition through authorization cards would have leveled the playing field in the Trenton campaign by taking away the employer's "slick" campaign and by reducing the employer's incentive to coerce workers. The result might well have been a union victory in the representational matter and a low-risk opportunity for workers to experience a union relationship tailored to their specific needs as an occupational group.

Fairly clearly, if employers were denied their most potent antiunion weapon, union membership would increase, labor's power to negotiate agreements would be augmented, and, in turn, its ability to attain political gains in workers' wages, hours, and working conditions would be enhanced. Over time, labor might justifiably claim once again to speak for American workers. But does public policy support those sanguine prospects for labor? Critics of unions typically stress the negative consequences of labor monopolies in a market economy, and those arguments tend to command a powerful following. As a result, any proposal for reform must confront the deeply rooted notion that unions benefit a few workers in this country but are bad for "the rest of us."[95]

Unions and Public Policy

Senator Wagner explained the economic role of trade unions in terms of their ability to redistribute wealth on a class-wide basis.[96] True to Wagner's faith in the collective bargaining process, unions have demonstrated a significant "monopoly" effect on wages by consistently attaining wage differentials substantially higher for union workers than for comparable nonunionized workers. While the union wage effect has varied from time to time and is not uniform across sectors, there is nevertheless no dispute that such a differential exists and continues to provide higher wages and economic benefits for unionized workers.[97] Despite the benefits it confers on unionized workers, the monopoly wage effect is often criticized by market-oriented economists as inefficient and socially destructive. Moreover, the effect of the wage differential on a firm's profitability is an important determinant of the extent of managerial opposition to unionization.[98]

One of the most energetic critics of collective bargaining in America is labor economist Morgan Reynolds, who castigates the system of special legal immunities and privileges granted to trade unions. Marginal theory, he argues, demonstrates the economic inefficiencies that are imposed by union wage demands. Even though higher wages may result in productivity increases, "it is nothing to applaud because previously inefficient production techniques become economical after the price of labor is boosted." Consequently, productivity gains following unionization offer little benefit to the general welfare: "From a social point of view, this is inefficient because too much scarce capital and too little labor are used to produce a lower rate of output; the lower rate results from a rise in costs and, in the longer run, a rise in output price, which reduces consumer purchases."[99] Reynolds contends that the impact of collective bargaining is an unwarranted burden on our economic system; in his calculation, "the cost of unions in the U.S. private sector is at least $126 billion per year, or 3.15 percent of gross national product (GNP), and a good case can be made for much higher estimates."[100] Thus, rather than a justification for the existence of trade unions, the monopoly effect constitutes an argument for elimination of federal labor law. Reynolds says "the proper remedy is deregulation. . . . This prescription includes getting rid of the Railway Labor Act of 1926, the Norris-LaGuardia Anti-Injunction Act, the National Labor Relations Act of 1935 (Wagner Act) as amended, and their pro-bargaining counterparts in the public sector."[101]

In an intensely competitive environment, policy arguments grounded on economic efficiency have undeniable appeal, and congressional action predicated only on a redistribution of wealth through revitalized unionism is unlikely to attract significant public support. Even in Canada, where union penetration is much greater than in the United States, one book-length study analyzes the monopoly feature of collective bargaining from the perspective of the "new classical macroeconomics" and concludes that union wage gains increase unemployment and produce inequitable wage differentials among groups of workers. Further, the author asserts, public opinion in Canada, like public opinion in the United States, reflects the belief that unions have too much power. "More Canadians are now concerned about the power of unions," he says, "than are worried by big business or big government." Strikes and the comitant monopoly wage gains "impose inefficiency costs on society." His solution would be to restrict unions' use of the strike weapon in favor of a system of wage arbitration.[102]

Legal scholars identified with the influential law and economic analysis movement also contribute to the argument against legislation to aid unions. In a widely cited essay, Richard Epstein asserted that the New Deal labor law "is in large measure a mistake that, if possible, should be scrapped in favor of the adoption of a sensible common law regime relying heavily upon tort and contract law." Private contracting between individuals and employers, Epstein contends, is the superior labor relations arrangement, as it distributes wealth based on ability and agreement, thereby producing an efficient allocation of resources. He adds: "To be sure, the common law theory developed here finds no place for the redistribution of wealth from rich to poor so characteristic of the modern state."[103] One segment of the legal community, then, would not only oppose the strengthening of collective bargaining law but would advocate the repeal of all laws conferring rights on unions.

But despite their popularity, market-based labor theories do not establish a convincing case against protective labor legislation.[104] The economic agenda may trace much of its appeal to political propinquity. As Robert Kuttner points out, academic economists arguing from the neoclassical perspective often have a particular affiliation with political conservatives. "Based on its faith in markets, much of the economics profession shares the premise of political conservatism that egalitarianism must harm economic growth. . . . Redistribution, in theory, undermines incentive, thrift, savings, investment, creativity, the efficient use of labor, and the optimal allocation of capital." The illusion fostered by market economists is that redistributive policies are inconsistent with efficiency. In fact, comparison of the American economy with those of other industrialized nations shows that "positive-sum gains tend to be statistically superior in societies where labor and business operate more as equals and where egalitarian values are better entrenched. In practice, redistributive measures take more of a toll on economic efficiency when they are carried out grudgingly, in the inhospitable climate of business supremacy and social conflict."[105] Recent figures support Kuttner's contention that wages and benefits for American workers compare unfavorably to those in other countries. U.S. productivity growth since 1960 is among the slowest in a ten-country group; hourly compensation increases in the United States were slower than in most other industrialized countries since 1979; and absolute poverty among American children stands at 17.1 percent, the highest of eight countries surveyed.[106]

In any event, the crucial proposition that lower wages translate into greater competitive capacity is not uniformly consistent with the economic evidence. Charles Craypo offers the construction industry as an example that disproves the market theory. In that sector, "the union-nonunion wage differential remained constant between 1973 and 1978 and even narrowed after 1978, which should have increased the competitiveness of union contractors and encouraged union growth, yet union density in construction fell from 39 to 22 percent during 1973–1986." The explanation, he says, lies more with "anti-union structural and institutional forces" than with the theory of union wage differentials.[107]

More generally, Freeman and Medoff argue that providing workers with a "voice," or an effective channel through which to express concerns regarding the work environment, reduces turnover and provides a sufficient degree of stability in the work force to substantially offset the economic consequences of the union wage effect.[108] As noted, there is considerable evidence that unions foster rather than impede productivity in the specific context of worker participation. Effective participation requires a long-term employment relationship, guaranteed workers' rights, compensation equity, and a fair distribution of profits.[109] Strong unions assure that those criteria are satisfied, which helps to explain why unionized firms with participation programs are more productive than nonunionized ones.[110] Unfortunately, preserving relations of power and social control within the enterprise may take precedence over immediate concerns of efficiency for American employers as a class.[111]

Given the debatable connections between economic theory, social objectives, and organized labor, a more commodious policy approach would be to acknowledge that in a capitalist democracy the economic functions of unions are closely related to their political ones, and workers' political rights deserve greater state solicitude. In the first place, our system encourages workers to press their short-term material interests in the political arena.[112] Paradoxically, though, we tolerate a vast and growing distance between purported equality in civic affairs and radical inequalities in the private accumulation and possession of wealth.[113] Democracy in the workplace arguably promotes a more democratic society by reducing material inequality in the enterprise and by enhancing the institutional dimensions of democracy.[114] Carole Pateman, one of the leading theorists of participation, suggested that participatory democracy "is built round the central assertion that individuals and their institutions cannot be considered in isolation from one another." A corollary of the principle is that "the existence of representative institutions at [a] national level is not sufficient for democracy; for maximum participation by all the people at that level socialization, or 'social training,' for democracy must take place in other spheres in order that the necessary individual attitudes and psychological qualities can be developed."[115] Pateman's insight is documented by empirical evidence showing that "the experience of direct democracy in the workplace encourages participation in democratic political life outside of the workplace."[116]

Along those lines, scholars have repeatedly urged the expansion of democratic processes within the workplace. The political scientist Robert Dahl, for example, asserts that "*if* democracy is justified in governing the state, then it must *also* be justified in governing economic enterprises; and to say that it is *not* justified in governing economic enterprises is to imply that it is not justified in governing the state." Dahl advocates "self-governing enterprises" that would constitute "one part of a system of equalities and liberties in which both would . . . be stronger, on balance, than they can be in a system of corporate capitalism."[117] And in a more recent work, Dahl offers a model for an "advanced democratic country," which by definition "would deliberately regulate its social, economic, and political structures so as to achieve political equality." Attaining political equality implies the reduction of inequalities caused by the distribution of resources, including economic resources. Thus, Dahl suggests, "the economic order would be seen as intended to serve not merely consumers but human beings in all the activities to which an economic order may contribute." Specifically, he rejects the standard neoclassical view that focuses on individuals as producers and consumers of goods and defines freedom as "above all the primary freedom of choice in the marketplace." Essential to the democratic vision is an internal system of governance for economic organizations. "Of all the relations of authority, control, and power in which people are routinely involved," he comments, "none are as salient, persistent, and important in the daily lives of most persons as those they are subject to at work." For that reason, democratic processes should extend to the operations of the firm.[118]

The role of labor law in furthering democratic ideals in the workplace has likewise received the attention of respected legal analysts. Professor Clyde Summers points out: "The theme that our system of political democracy should be matched by a system of industrial democracy has been an irrepressible one in our history." The disconcerting reality is that labor law falls far short of accomplishing its democratic aspirations. "Our proclaimed national policy of collective bargaining has not only failed to provide seventy percent of employees any voice in industrial government, it has caused us to neglect their need for protection against oppressive conditions and arbitrary treatment which denies their human dignity." Summers warns that "our emphasis on efficiency of production, our dispute over division of shares, and our concern with industrial conflict have caused us largely to forget the more fundamental values of democracy and human dignity. These are the values which must again become central in developing our national labor policy."[119] Karl Klare also underscores the connection between labor unions, workers, and the political system:

Unions, as institutions of working people, can contribute to civic and political democracy. This is particularly so in a political system like ours, which lacks an established social democratic tradition and major labor or social democratic parties. For these and other reasons, it is unfortunate that there is at present no consensus in the United States on the enduring value and potential of collective bargaining to democratic life.[120]

Precisely because of our lack of a strong social democratic tradition, and the lack of an adequate scheme of social insurance comparable to that of other industrialized nations, American unions offer an intermediate step in bridging the gap between equality in the political sphere and the growing economic inequality between classes.[121]

If legal reforms are justified as a theoretical proposition, then it is obvious that legislative action is an urgent matter. A highly publicized government study concluded that we can "ill afford to continue the escalation of confrontation that has traditionally divided labor and management. . . . If our statutes and practices are an impediment to change, we must be willing to consider reasonable alterations in that basic framework to encourage a process that will ultimately benefit society as a whole."[122] For reasons suggested earlier, change must be undertaken by means of legislation rather than judicial or Board construction of section 8(a)(2). Courts are institutionally incapable of formulating broad policy objectives developed though open public debate and dialogue, and cases such as the *Scott & Fetzer* opinion discussed in Chapter 3 demonstrate that the worst extremes of judicial policymaking typically involve a tortured manipulation of fact and law. Precise and unambiguous statutory language will minimize the judiciary's tendency to "interpret" labor law in terms of its views of policy.

The revisions proposed above, and the policy choices supporting them, would move toward resolving crucial labor law problems now facing our society. The reform would encourage the growth of unions, facilitate the preferences of workers, aid managers in developing innovate organizational changes, and encourage genuine industrial democracy. Most importantly, the suggested modification is politically feasible. The proposal is designed as a compromise capable of attracting a broad spectrum of support, and it therefore has little political cost to any legislator voting in favor of it. While the plan does not create fundamental reform, it offers an initial advance toward rehabilitating unionism. The present condition of organized labor is so moribund that a simple, prompt, and definitive forward step, even if apparently slight, would outweigh a plethora of unworkable schemes that are abstractly attractive but practically unattainable.

NOTES

1. Janice Castro, "Labor Draws an Empty Gun," *Time*, March 26, 1990, 56.

2. Gary N. Chaison and Dileep Dhavale, "A Note on the Severity of the Decline in Union Organizing Activity," *Industrial and Labor Relations Review*, 43 (1990), 366–373.

3. Chaison and Dhavale, "A Note on the Severity," 366, 372.

4. Associated Press, "Resistance in south baffles unions," *Rocky Mountain News*, March 23, 1991, 64.

5. Richard Freeman, "On the Divergence in Unionism Among Developed Countries," National Bureau of Economic Research, Working Paper No. 2817 (1989), 20 (emphasis deleted).

6. George Taylor succinctly explained the pluralist view of power: "The national program is essentially designed to maintain industrial relations on as even a keel as possible through a balance-of-power policy. Neither organized labor nor management is to be permitted to possess sufficient power to effectuate demands unilaterally. Neither is it to be permitted to exercise its power to enforce greater demands through collective bargaining than is deemed to be socially desirable." George W. Taylor, *Government Regulation of Industrial Relations* (Englewood Cliffs, N.J.: Prentice-Hall, 1948), 336–337.

7. See, for example, David Feller, "A General Theory of the Collective Bargaining Agreement," *California Law Review*, 61 (1973), 663–856. Feller analyzes the nature of rules in the modern industrial enterprise, noting that firms must be bureaucratically organized. The most significant feature of the collective bargaining process "is the creation of a system of private law to govern the employer-employee relationship" (721).

8. The general characteristics of the American scheme of collective bargaining as of the late 1960s are described in Derek C. Bok and John T. Dunlop, *Labor and the American Community* (New York: Simon and Schuster, 1970), 207–228. For contemporary discussions of pluralism, see Christopher Tomlins, "The New Deal, Collective Bargaining, and the Triumph of Industrial Pluralism," *Industrial and Labor Relations Review*, 39 (October 1985), 19–34; and Katherine Stone, "The Post-War Paradigm in American Labor Law," *Yale Law Journal*, 90 (1981), 1509–1580. Useful historical appraisals of the postwar era include David Brody, "The Uses of Power I: Industrial Battleground," and "The Uses of Power II: Political Action," in *Workers*

in Industrial America (New York: Oxford University Press, 1980), 173–257; Ronald L. Filippelli, "The Historical Context of Postwar Industrial Relations," in Bruce Nissen, ed., *U.S. Labor Relations, 1945–1989: Accommodation and Conflict* (New York: Garland Press, 1990); Mike Davis, *Prisoners of the American Dream: Politics and Economy in the History of the US Working Class* (London: Verso, 1986); and Kim Moody, *An Injury to All: The Decline of American Unionism* (New York: Verso, 1988).

9. The idealized version of a legal system expunged of politics has been described as follows:

(1) the law on a particular issue is preexisting, clear, predictable, and available to anyone with reasonable legal skill; (2) the facts relevant to disposition of a case are ascertained by objective hearing and evidentiary rules that reasonably ensure that the truth will emerge; (3) the result in a particular case is determined by a rather routine application of the law to the facts; and (4) except for the occasional bad judge, any reasonably competent and fair judge will reach the "correct" decision.

David Kairys, "Introduction," in David Kairys, ed., *The Politics of Law: A Progressive Critique* (New York: Pantheon, 1982), 1–2. For a critique of mainstream labor law, see Karl Klare, "Critical Theory and Labor Relations Law," in Kairys, *Politics of Law*, 65–88.

10. George Brooks, "The Relevance of Labor History to Industrial Relations," in George Somers, ed., *Industrial Relations Research Association* [IRRA], *Proceedings of the Fourteenth Annual Meeting* (Madison: IRRA, 1962), 206, 211.

11. David Brody, "Labor History, Industrial Relations, and the Crisis of American Labor," *Industrial and Labor Relations Review*, 43 (1989), 9.

12. Myron J. Roomkin and Hervey A. Juris, "A Critical Appraisal of Research on Unions and Collective Bargaining," in Thomas Kochan et al., eds., *Industrial Relations Research in the 1970s: Review and Appraisal* (Madison: IRRA, 1982), 311. Illustrating the point, the editors of the *Industrial and Labor Relations Review*, which is the leading journal in the field, notified potential contributors to their 1989–90 volume that "institutional" research would be considered for publication. The editors were concerned that "many scholars believed the journal welcomes only papers on labor economics or collective bargaining, and then only if they are laden with quantitative analysis." That perception, they continued, was inaccurate. "Some readers may have concluded that because the proportion of [such] *Review* articles has escalated so rapidly in recent years, we have taken sides in the debate over methodology and have abandoned the institutionalist. That is decidedly not the case." Rather, they said, patterns of research are determined by the nature of training in the field, and most younger scholars view research problems from the social science perspective associated with the "new school" of research. Consequently, the editors observed, "We do not publish as much institutional research as we would like because apparently not much is being done anymore." Editorial Board, "Notice to Potential Contributors," *Industrial and Labor Relations Review*, 43 (1989), 3–4.

13. Peter Cappelli, "Theory Construction in IR and Some Implications for Research," *Industrial Relations*, 24 (1985), 96, 99.

14. For a survey of pertinent research and an able exposition of the antipluralist view, see Christopher Tomlins, " 'Of the Old Time Entombed': The Resurrection of the American Working Class and the Emerging Critique of American Industrial Relations," *Industrial Relations Law Journal*, 10 (1988), 426–444.

15. Richard Edwards and Michael Podgursky, "The Unraveling Accord: American Unions in Crisis," in Richard Edwards, Paolo Garonna, and Franz Tödtling, eds., *Unions in Crisis and Beyond: Perspectives from Six Countries* (Dover, Mass.: Auburn House, 1986), 14–60; Bruce Nissen, "A Post-World War II 'Social Accord?'" in Nissen, *U.S. Labor Relations 1945–1989*, 173–207.

16. Thomas Kochan, Harry Katz, and Robert McKersie, *The Transformation of American Industrial Relations* (New York: Basic Books, 1986) [hereafter cited as *Transformation*].

17. *Transformation*, 56.

18. See, for example, Filippelli, "Historical Context"; Richard Block, "American Industrial Relations in the 1980s: Transformation or Evolution," in James Chelius and James Dworkin, eds., *Reflections on the Transformation of Industrial Relations* (Metuchen, N.J.: IMLR Press/Rutgers University, 1990), 19–48; Sanford Jacoby, "American Exceptionalism Revisited: The Importance of Management," in Sanford Jacoby, ed., *Masters to Managers: Historical and Comparative Perspectives on American Employers* (New York: Columbia University Press, 1991), 173–200.

19. As Fred K. Foulkes showed in his study of nonunion firms, the nonunion personnel system may in fact temporarily cost more than a unionized one, but issues of power are at stake. Foulkes noted: "Whether or not a nonunion plant is more economical, many of the managers interviewed maintained that time spent positively on human relations programs, rather than negatively on grievances, has a distinct effect on employee and management morale." Not only is morale a factor, he continued, but the maintenance of power and control becomes an important character trait of the successful boss. "Many managers took obvious pride in their personnel philosophies and accomplishments, and felt that their efforts had a direct and visible effect on the life on the company. With such belief in the perceived advantages of a nonunion environment, it is not surprising that some looked upon a union as a personal affront." *Personnel Policies in Large Nonunion Companies* (Englewood Cliffs, N.J.: Prentice-Hall, 1980), 60–61.

20. *Transformation*, 57.

21. *Transformation*, 66–76. A comprehensive treatment of the corporate "dismantling" of our industrial sector during the early 1980s is Barry Bluestone and Bennett Harrison's *The Deindustrialization of America: Plant Closings, Community Abandonment, and the Dismantling of Basic Industry* (New York: Basic Books, 1982).

22. D. Quinn Mills, "Management Performance," in Jack Stieber et al., eds. *U.S. Industrial Relations 1950–1980: A Critical Assessment* (Madison: IRRA, 1981), 99–128, 101.

23. *Transformation*, 23–27.

24. See Michael Goldfield, *The Decline of Organized Labor in the United States* (Chicago: University of Chicago Press, 1987), 180–217. Goldfield argues that the "real culprit" in the erosion of union membership is the changing relation of class forces. Those forces include workers' attitudes, state policies, and capitalist resistance to unions. For a more detailed criticism of *The Transformation of American Industrial Relations* on this point, see Raymond Hogler, "Critical Labor Law, Working-Class History, and the New Industrial Relations," *Industrial Relations Law Journal*, 10 (1988), 116–143. Kochan et al. offered a rejoinder to that criticism in their "Response to Hogler's Review of *The Transformation of American Industrial Relations*," *Industrial Relations Law Journal*, 10 (1988), 144–147.

25. Richard Block, for example, comments: "There is very little union or governmental presence at the strategic level of the corporation. The union has been removed from this level by the law, and the principle of governmental nonintervention means that the government will not be a great check on employer strategic decision-making except to the extent that it violates the anti-trust law." "American Industrial Relations," 33.

26. *Transformation*, 216. For other studies of the voting behavior of workers, see Julius Getman, Stephen Goldberg, and Jeanne Hermann, *Union Representation Elections: Law and Reality* (New York: Russell Sage, 1976); William Dickens and Jonathan Leonard, "Accounting for the Decline in Union Membership, 1950–1980," *Industrial and Labor Relations Review*, 36 (1985), 323–334; Henry Farber, "The Decline of Unionization in the United States: What Can Be Learned from Recent Experience?" *Journal of Labor Economics*, 8 (Part 2, 1990), S75–S105.

27. Rick Fantasia, *Cultures of Solidarity: Consciousness, Action, and Contemporary American Workers* (Berkeley: University of California Press, 1988), 19.

28. For further discussion of this point, see generally Tomlins, "Old Time Entombed," and Hogler, "Critical Labor Law."

29. David Montgomery, *Fall of the House of Labor: The Workplace, the State, and American Labor Activism, 1865–1925* (Cambridge: Cambridge University Press, 1987), 1–2.

30. See David Halle, *America's Working Man: Work, Home, and Politics Among Blue-Collar Property Owners* (Chicago: University of Chicago Press, 1984).

31. Two recent studies of trends in union membership provide a contrast between the mainstream industrial relations orientation and Goldfield's class conflict approach. See Gary Chaison and Joseph Rose, "Macrodeterminants of Union Growth and Decline" and Hoyt Wheeler and John McClendon, "The Individual Decision to Unionize," in George Strauss, Daniel Gallagher, and Jack Fiorito, eds., *State of the Unions* (Madison: IRRA, 1991), 3–45, 47–83. While there is general agreement among all of the authors that employer resistance to organization is paramount in explaining union decline, the industrial relations scholars analyze that resistance in economic and psychological, but not political, terms.

32. Goldfield, *Decline of Organized Labor*, 160.

33. *Transformation*, 177.

34. *Transformation*, 230.

35. *Transformation*, 253.

36. *Transformation*, 234–235.

37. Thomas Bird Edsall, "The Changing Shape of Power: A Realignment in Public Policy," in Steve Fraser and Gary Gerstle, eds., *Rise and Fall of the New Deal Order, 1930–1980* (Princeton, N.J.: Princeton University Press, 1989), 270, 274–275.

38. Bennett Harrison and Barry Bluestone, *The Great U-Turn: Corporate Restructuring and the Polarizing of America* (New York: Basic Books, 1988), 51. For a detailed portrait of the worsening condition of the American wage earner, see Lawrence Mishel and David Frankel, *The State of Working America, 1990–1991 Edition* (Armonk, N.Y.: M. E. Sharpe, 1991), 69–127.

39. Karl Klare, "The Judicial Deradicalization of the Wagner Act and the Origins of Modern Legal Consciousness," 62 *Minnesota Law Review* (1978), 265–339.

40. A book-length treatment of labor law from a critical perspective is James

Atleson, *Values and Assumptions in American Labor Law* (Amherst, Mass.: University of Massachusetts Press, 1983).

41. Klare, "Judicial Deradicalization," 290, n. 79. Klare has extended the argument in other works. See, for example, "Labor Law as Ideology: Toward a New Historiography of Collective Bargaining Law," *Industrial Relations Law Journal*, 4 (1981), 450–482; "Critical Theory and Labor Relations Law," in Kairys, *Politics of Law*, 65–88; "Traditional Labor Law Scholarship and the Crisis of Collective Bargaining Law: A Reply to Professor Finkin," *Maryland Law Review*, 44 (1985), 731–840.

42. The decisions that set forth those principles are, respectively, *NLRB v. Mackay Radio & Telegraph Co.*, 304 U.S. 333 (1939); *NLRB v. Fansteel Metallurgical Corp.*, 306 U.S. 1 (1939); and *NLRB v. Sand Manufacturing Co.*, 306 U.S. 332 (1939).

43. Klare, "Labor Law as Ideology," 452.

44. *NLRB v. Jones & Laughlin Steel Corp.*, 301 U.S. 1, 45.

45. Klare, "Judicial Deradicalization," 295–297.

46. Stone, "Post-War Paradigm," 1516.

47. *Textile Workers Union v. Lincoln Mills*, 353 U.S. 448 (1957).

48. Stone, "Post-War Paradigm," 1557.

49. Stone, "Post-War Paradigm," 1574.

50. Matthew Finkin, "Revisionism in Labor Law," *Maryland Law Review*, 43 (1984), 23–92.

51. Finkin, "Revisionism," 57.

52. Finkin, "Revisionism," 55, 83–84. Contrary to Finkin's argument, recent work by labor historians tends to repudiate his position and to support Stone's analysis. In a study of the development of grievance arbitration procedures at General Motors, Nelson Lichtenstein shows how arbitration was effectively used to reduce worker militancy on the shop floor. Under the "umpire" system developed by GM and the UAW, the neutral adjudicator was limited to interpreting the contract language rather than imposing his ideas of "good" labor relations. For that reason, "GM saw the umpire almost exclusively in terms of his ability to facilitate the company's disciplinary regime." The union, conversely, viewed arbitration as a process that would "bring to the factory and mill the protections available to citizens in civil society." The arbitration machinery, consequently, was the arena in which labor-management conflict was mediated. "Great Expectations: The Promise of Collective Bargaining and its Demise, 1935–1965," paper presented at the Wilson Center Program on American Society and Politics, March 28, 1988, 22–29.

53. Karl Klare, "Traditional Labor Law Scholarship and the Crisis of Collective Bargaining Law: A Reply to Professor Finkin," *Maryland Law Review*, 44 (1985), 751–752.

54. Katherine Stone, "Re-Envisioning Labor Law: A Response to Professor Finkin," *Maryland Law Review*, 45 (1986), 978–1013, 1013. For a more recent analysis of labor law and the role of unions in our political economy, see Katherine Stone, "Labor and the Corporate Structure: Changing Conceptions and Emerging Possibilities," *University of Chicago Law Review*, 55 (1988), 73–173.

55. *First National Maintenance Corp. v. NLRB*, 452 U.S. 666 (1981). The underlying premises of the Court's decision are revealed in certain key assertions. For instance, without reference to any authority, the Court explains that "Congress had no expectation that the elected union representative would become an equal partner

in the running of the business enterprise in which the union's members are employed." The rationale for precluding union discussion of certain matters is, apparently, the nature of capitalism itself. The Court said: "Management must be free from the constraints of the bargaining process to the extent essential for the running of a profitable business." One labor law treatise observes that the Court's scope of bargaining doctrine marks a "retreat" from a "broad support for collective bargaining to a new position whereby collective bargaining is seen as a form of interference with managerial efficiency." Julius Getman and Bernard Pogrebin, *Labor Relations: the Basic Processes, Law and Practice* (New York: Foundation Press, 1988), 116–117.

56. 437 U.S. 95 (1985).

57. David Abraham, "Individual Autonomy and Collective Empowerment in Labor Law: Union Membership Resignations and Strikebreaking in the New Economy," *New York University Law Review*, 63 (1988), 1271–1272.

58. *Trans World Airlines, Inc. v. Independent Federation of Flight Attendants*, 109 S. Ct. 1225 (1989), 1237. The Court in *NLRB v. Curtin Matheson Scientific, Inc.*, 110 S. Ct. 1542 (1990), upheld a Board determination that strike replacements would not be presumed to reject continued union representation. While an apparently pro-labor outcome, the decision is by no means indicative of a change of attitude by the Court. First, the narrow holding of the case is an application of the settled principle that Board rulings are entitled to deference if they have a reasonable statutory basis. Second, that unremarkable result commanded only a bare majority, with Rehnquist issuing a half-hearted concurrence. Scalia, joined by O'Connor and Kennedy, asserted that the interests of replacement workers were inherently antagonistic to the interests of the bargaining representative. Blackmun dissented on the ground that the controlling Board precedent was itself inconsistent and irrational. Consequently, a subsequent case with only slightly different facts might persuade Rehnquist to join with the four dissenters, even assuming Justices Souter and Thomas were to agree with the Board. In that event, an employer could challenge a union to strike, hire replacements, and then simply withdraw recognition from the union.

59. Paul A. Levy, "The Unidimensional Perspective of the Reagan Labor Board," *Rutgers Law Journal*, 16 (1985), 269–390, 271.

60. Levy, "Unidimensional Perspective," 277–279.

61. Levy, "Unidimensional Perspective," 390.

62. S. 1883 and H.R. 8410, reprinted in U.S. Senate, *Labor Reform Act of 1977, Hearings before the Subcommittee on Labor, Committee on Human Resources*, 95th Cong., 1st Sess. (Washington, D.C.: Government Printing Office, 1977), Parts 1 and 2, 3–16; 26–46.

63. *Labor Reform Act*, 48.

64. *Labor Reform Act*, Part 2, 1582–1583.

65. *Labor Reform Act*, 101.

66. *Labor Reform Act*, 17–25.

67. *Labor Reform Act*, 665–666, 669.

68. D. Quinn Mills, "Flawed Victory in Labor Law Reform," *Harvard Business Review*, 57 (May–June 1979), 99.

69. Moody, *An Injury to All*, 160.

70. Edsall, "Changing Shape of Power," 286. Edsall's summary of current political conditions is especially pointed:

Cumulatively, developments over the past twenty years—the deterioration of the labor movement; economically polarized partisanship; the skewing of turnout patterns by income; stagnation of the median family income; the rising importance of political money; the emergence of a Republican core composed of the well-to-do and the religious; the globalization of the economy; and competition from foreign producers—have combined to disperse constituencies and groups seeking to push the country to the left, and to consolidate those on the right.

Under the circumstances, an effective coalition for labor law reform is implausible, at the very least.

71. Jill Zuckman, "Bill To Protect Striking Workers Faces White House Veto," *Congressional Quarterly*, March 9, 1991, 608.

72. See House Subcommittee on Labor-Management Relations of the Committee on Education and Labor, *The Failure of Labor Law—A Betrayal of American Workers*, H. R. Rep. No. 98, 98th Cong., 2d Sess. (1984).

73. Paul Weiler, *Governing the Workplace: The Future of Labor and Employment Law* (Cambridge, Mass.: Harvard University Press, 1990), 300.

74. This technique was initially proposed by Paul Weiler in his influential article, "Promises to Keep: Securing Workers' Rights to Self-Organization Under the NLRA," *Harvard Law Review*, 96 (1983), 1769–1827.

75. For a positive appraisal of participation programs during the 1970s, see Richard E. Walton, "Work Innovations in the United States," *Harvard Business Review*, 57 (July–August 1979), 88–98. A good recent survey of literature on the costs and benefits of cooperative labor-management ventures is found in William Cooke, *Labor-Management Cooperation: New Partnerships or Going in Circles?* (Kalamazoo, Mich.: W. E. Upjohn Institute, 1990), 2–17. A substantial majority of employers in Cooke's survey reported that worker productivity and product quality were either much or modestly higher (82–83, chart 4.1).

76. U.S. Department of Labor, Bureau of Labor-Management Relations & Cooperative Programs, *U.S. Labor Law and the Future of Labor-Management Cooperation*, 2 (BLMR No. 104, 1988).

77. Commission on Workforce Quality and Labor Market Efficiency, *Investing in People: A Strategy to Address America's Workforce Crisis* (Washington, D.C.: U.S. Department of Labor, 1989), 34.

78. Karl Klare, "The Labor-Management Cooperation Debate: A Workplace Democracy Perspective," *Harvard Civil Rights-Civil Liberties Law Review*, 23 (1988), 69.

79. Barry Bluestone, "Goodbye to the Management Rights Clause," in Labor Research Review, *Participating in Management: Union Organizing on a New Terrain* (Chicago: Midwest Center for Labor Research, 1989), 68–69.

80. Edward E. Lawler III, Gerald Ledford, Jr., and Susan Mohrman, *Employee Involvement in America: A Study of Contemporary Practice* (Houston: American Productivity & Quality Center, 1989), 13.

81. Lawler, *Employee Involvement*, figs. 6–2 and 1–3. A survey of Pennsylvania employers also indicates that employee involvement programs have grown rapidly since the mid-1980s. Tom Juravich and Howard Harris, *Pennsylvania Employee Involvement Data-Base: A Preliminary Report* (State College, Penn.: Department of Labor Studies and Industrial Relations, 1987).

82. Lawler, *Employee Involvement*, 69.

83. See, generally, Donna Sockell, "The Legality of Employee-Participation

Programs in Unionized Firms," *Industrial and Labor Relations Review*, 37 (1984), 541–556.

84. Compare, for example, *Lawson Co. v. NLRB*, 753 F.2d 471 (6th Cir. 1985) with *Airstream, Inc. v. NLRB*, 877 F.2d 1291 (6th Cir. 1989).

85. The Du Pont corporation discontinued an employee involvement program at one of its plants after an Administrative Law Judge (ALJ) found the program to be in violation of section 8(a)(2). Du Pont declined to appeal the ALJ's decision, fearing that an adverse Board ruling would affect programs throughout the firm. See Amy Marcus and Sonia Nazario, "Labor Board and Unions Challenge Du Pont's Workplace Committees," *Wall Street Journal*, March 26, 1991, B10. The Board is processing several section 8(a)(2) cases, and the matter has important implications for participative schemes. On September 5, 1991, the Board heard oral arguments in *Electromation, Inc.* (Case 25-CA–19818), involving the legality of an employee participation committee. The case attracted considerable attention, and the Chair of the Labor and Employment Law Section of the American Bar Association predicts that "this issue is going to be one of the hottest labor relations issues in the 1990s." Donald Capuano, "*Electromation, Inc.*: The NLRB Reviews the Lawfulness of Employee Participation Committees," paper presented to the Labor Law Section, Colorado Bar Association, September 28, 1991.

86. See, for example, Shaun Clarke's analysis of the point in "Rethinking the Adversarial Model in Labor Relations: An Argument for Repeal of Section 8(a)(2)," *Yale Law Journal*, 96 (1987), 2021–2050. Although the proposed new section 8(c)(2) states that the forming of a committee is not an unfair labor practice under other provisions of the Act, such language would not prevent the Board from finding violations of selection 8(a)(1) where the employer's antiunion statements or actions were made manifest through the committee, as in the Ethicon case; rather, the unlawful act would consist of coercion and restraint of employees, not merely creating a committee.

87. Richard Freeman and James Medoff, *What Do Unions Do?* (New York: Basic Books, 1984), 233. See also Goldfield, *The Decline of Organized Labor in the United States*, 195–205. But see Leo Troy, "The Rise and Fall of American Trade Unions: The Labor Movement from FDR to RR," in Seymour Lipset, ed., *Unions in Transition: Entering the Second Century* (San Francisco: Institute for Contemporary Studies, 1986). Troy argues: "While employer opposition plays a role in thwarting the organizing of the unorganized, most of the decline in membership is associated with losses in employment" (100). The debate is renewed in Richard Freeman and Morris Kleiner, "Employer Behavior in the Face of Union Organizing Drives," *Industrial & Labor Relations Review*, 43 (1990), 351–365; and Leo Troy, "Is the U.S. Unique in the Decline of Private Sector Unionism?" *Journal of Labor Research*, 11 (1990), 111–143. Farber's analysis in "Decline of Unionism" takes into consideration the structural factors emphasized by Troy but nevertheless generally substantiates the Freeman-Medoff-Kleiner thesis regarding the impact of managerial activity.

88. Charles Morris, ed., *The Developing Law Law*, vol. I, 2d ed. (Washington, D.C.: Bureau of National Affairs, 1983), 488–503.

89. *Linden Lumber Div. v. NLRB*, 419 U.S. 301 (1974); *NLRB v. Gissel Packing Co.*, 395 U.S. 575 (1969).

90. Joel Rogers, "In the Shadow of the Law: Institutional Aspects of Postwar U.S. Union Decline," paper presented at the conference on Labor Law in America:

Historical and Critical Perspectives, Johns Hopkins University, March 20, 1990; Joel Rogers, "Divide and Conquer: Further 'Reflections on the Distinctive Character of American Labor Laws,' " *Wisconsin Law Review* (1990), 1–147.

91. Rogers, "Divide and Conquer," 8–9.

92. Freeman, "On the Divergence," 16.

93. Charles Heckscher, *The New Unionism: Employee Involvement in the Changing Corporation* (New York: Basic Books, 1988), 226.

94. Dana Milbank, "Far From the Mill," *Wall Street Journal*, May 23, 1991, A1. Katie Gohn, the union organizer described in the article, began her union career as head of Nittany 9 to 5, an organization of clerical workers at The Pennsylvania State University.

95. This argument against the collective activities of workers first appeared in American law in 1806, when Judge Moses Levy instructed the jury in the *Philadelphia Cordwainers Case* that a combination of workers to raise their wages "tends to demoralize the workmen . . . , destroy the trade of the city, and leaves the pockets of the whole community to the discretion of the concerned." Quoted in Raymond Hogler, "Law, Ideology, and Industrial Discipline: The Conspiracy Doctrine and the Rise of the Factory System," *Dickinson Law Review*, 91 (1987), 720.

96. For a discussion of the economic theory underlying the Act as it was understood by the drafters, see Kenneth Casebeer, "Holder of the Pen: An Interview with Leon Keyserling on Drafting the Wagner Act," *University of Miami Law Review*, 42 (1987), 285–363. The "wage-purchasing power" theory, however, has been questioned by some labor economists. See Daniel J. B. Mitchell, "Inflation, Unemployment, and the Wagner Act: A Critical Reappraisal," *Stanford Law Review*, 38, (1986), 1065–1095.

97. See, generally, Freeman and Medoff, *What Do Unions Do?* 43–56; Barry Hirksch and John Addison, *The Economic Analysis of Unions: New Approaches and Evidence* (Boston: Allen & Unwin, 1986), 116–154.

98. Freeman and Kleiner ("Employer Behavior," 364) conclude their study of managerial antiunionism with the statement: "We interpret our results as consistent with the hypothesis that firms behave in a profit-maximizing manner in opposing an organizing drive."

99. Morgan Reynolds, *Making America Poorer: The Cost of Labor Law* (Washington, D.C.: Cato Institute, 1987), 45.

100. Reynolds, *Making America Poorer*, 188.

101. Reynolds, *Making America Poorer*, 192–193.

102. David Winch, *Collective Bargaining and the Public Interest: A Welfare Economics Assessment* (Montreal: McGill-Queen's University Press, 1989), 5, 138–155.

103. Richard Epstein, "A Common Law for Labor Relations: A Critique of the New Deal Labor Legislation," *Yale Law Journal*, 92 (1983), 1357, 1361.

104. For recent critiques, see Weiler, *Governing the Workplace*, 118–143, and Samuel Bowles, David Gordon, and Thomas Weisskopf, *After the Wasteland: A Democratic Economics for the Year 2000* (New York: M. E. Sharpe, 1990).

105. Robert Kuttner, *The Economic Illusion: False Choices Between Prosperity and Social Justice* (Boston: Houghton Mifflin, 1984), 4, 7. Bowles et al. similarly explain the fallacy of the "no free lunch" argument of mainstream economists. The American economy can avoid "zero sum" tradeoffs between efficiency and equality by elim-

inating the massive waste that characterizes our productive system. *After the Wasteland*, 170–173.

106. Mishel and Frankel, *The State of Working America*, 254–269. The authors concede that America maintains its lead in per capita income measured by purchasing power. At the same time, "income is much more concentrated among the rich in the U.S. than in other industrial countries. In addition, the U.S. also has substantially higher levels of poverty, in terms of purchasing power, than most other industrialized countries" (255).

107. Charles Craypo, "The Decline in Union Bargaining Power," in Nissen, *U.S. Labor Relations, 1945–1989*, 32.

108. Freeman and Medoff, *What Do Unions Do?* 94–110. Although some nonunion employers have grievance procedures, Freeman and Medoff contend that they are not as effective as the third-party arbitration systems in unionized workplaces.

109. See, generally, David Levine and Laura D'Andrea Tyson, "Participation, Productivity and the Firm's Environment," in Alan S. Blinder, ed., *Paying for Productivity: A Look at the Evidence* (Washington, D.C.: Brookings Institution, 1990), 183–237.

110. Maryanne Kelley and Bennett Harrison, "Unions, Technology, and Labor-Management Cooperation," in Lawrence Mishel and Paula Voos, eds., *Unions and Economic Competitiveness* (Armonk, N.Y.: M. E. Sharpe, forthcoming).

111. For insightful criticisms of the neoclassical conception of efficiency, see Samuel Bowles, "The Production Process in a Competitive Economy: Walrasian, Neo-Hobbesian, and Marxian Models," *American Economic Review*, 75 (1985), 16–36; Samuel Bowles and Herbert Gintis, *Democracy and Capitalism: Property, Community, and the Contradictions of Modern Social Thought* (New York: Basic Books, 1986); Karl Klare, "Workplace Democracy & Market Reconstruction: An Agenda for Legal Reform," *Catholic University Law Review*, 38 (1988), 1–68. One study of the historical development of American corporations offers a good analysis of why market theory fails to explain corporate evolution satisfactorily. The author's thesis is that "efficiency" is a social construct built up through state action and the corporate response to government. "Instead of markets calling forth efficient forms of social organization," he says, "political and social interactions produced the structuring of sociologically efficient markets." Neil Fligstein, *The Transformation of Corporate Control* (Cambridge, Mass.: Harvard University Press, 1990), 300.

112. Joshua Cohen and Joel Rogers observed that a capitalist democracy constrains the choices of workers in unique ways. Workers acquiesce in the system neither from fear nor from delusion, but rather because "capitalist democracy is in some measure capable of satisfying the interests encouraged by capitalist democracy itself, namely interests in short-term material gain." But because capitalists control investment, "the satisfaction of the interests of capitalists is a necessary condition for the satisfaction of all other interests within the system." *On Democracy* (New York: Penguin Books, 1983), 51–53. See also Adam Przeworski, *Capitalism and Social Democracy* (Cambridge: Cambridge University Press, 1985).

113. Such disparity is increasingly reproduced within the modern corporation. "In 1979 CEOs made twenty-nine times the income of the average manufacturing worker. By 1985 the multiple was forty. By 1988, *Business Week* said the total compensation of the average CEO in its annual survey had risen to ninety-three times the earnings of the average factory worker." Kevin Phillips, *The Politics of*

Rich and Poor: Wealth and the American Electorate in the Reagan Aftermath (New York: Random House, 1990), 1818.

114. See Cohen and Rogers, *On Democracy*, 161–165. Edward Greenberg confirms that equality of condition is "one of the central values of workplace democracy." *Workplace Democracy: The Political Effects of Participation* (Ithaca, N.Y.: Cornell University Press, 1986, 176).

115. Carole Pateman, *Participation and Democratic Theory* (Cambridge: Cambridge University Press, 1970), 42.

116. Greenberg, *Workplace Democracy*, 131.

117. Robert Dahl, *A Preface to Economic Democracy* (Berkeley: University of California Press, 1985), 111, 162 (emphasis in original).

118. Robert Dahl, *Democracy and Its Critics* (New Haven, Conn.: Yale University Press, 1989), 323–333.

119. Clyde Summers, "Industrial Democracy: America's Unfulfilled Promise" *Cleveland State Law Review*, 28 (1979), 29, 43.

120. Klare, "Workplace Democracy," 4.

121. For a union perspective on the existing disparity of wealth in America and the adverse consequences for most wage workers, see John Sweeney and Karen Nussbaum, *Solutions for the New Work Force: Policies for a New Social Contract* (Cabin John, Md.: Seven Locks Press, 1989).

122. Department of Labor, *U.S. Labor Law*, 32.

CHAPTER 6

Conclusion: Lessons from the Steel Industry

The history of representation plans in the steel industry reveals the ambivalence of managerial motives attending participative techniques. Those plans often contained genuine elements of democratic governance, but even a reformer of William Dickson's integrity succumbed to antiunion sentiments when defending the Midvale representation plan. And on a broader scale, hostility toward independent unionism has been, either implicitly or explicitly, an aspect of participatory techniques since the Rockefeller experiment at Colorado Fuel & Iron; that hostility erupted, to take a modern instance, in the strategic planning of such a progressive corporation as Johnson & Johnson. The aim of section 8(a)(2)—to prohibit organizational impediments to union representation if desired by employees—remains an important concern in today's workplace. At the same time, the basic purpose of the law can be achieved through means other than the express proscriptions of section 8(a)(2).

The complex nature of "freedom of choice" for workers is illuminated by the experience of the Steel Workers Organizing Committee with internal participative schemes. Many rank and file steelworkers were sincere in their dedication to the representation plans, and the legislative history of the NLRA is replete with positive experiences of workers not only in the steel companies but also in other sectors of American industry. Those plans offered the promise of individual expression and personal autonomy within the corporate bureaucracy, while permitting workers to maintain their attachment and loyalty to the employer. The attractiveness of industrial democracy is manifest in our labor history; the fact that it is a promise as yet largely unfulfilled increases, rather than diminishes, its allure.

Another significant dimension of the SWOC organizing effort is that the collective mobilization of the steelworkers was a highly contingent, intensely localized activity, which occurred within a unique industrial setting and was aimed toward precise ends. Steelworkers at Carnegie-Illinois were not driven by a broad national project of political transformation; they were predominantly concerned with the immediate matters of their daily working lives. George Patterson, and the other rank and file leaders, delivered a cohesive and organic unit of workers to the "union"; and Murray's memorandum to the SWOC staff makes abundantly clear that the workers' organizing activities ran far ahead of SWOC's contribution to those efforts. Consequently, any attempt to formulate legal policy by abstract debate about the philosophical nature of individual free choice in the workplace is misguided and obscures more meaningful approaches to statutory reform. A better perspective recognizes that the organizational impulse has its own trajectory determined by the interaction of workers and managers under specific conditions. The validity of that observation is attested to not only by the examples presented in this book, but also by other analyses of collective action. One conclusion is that legal reform should concern itself more with facilitating the dynamics of group behavior and less with ritualistic ceremonies, such as NLRB elections, that have marginal significance for American workers.

Supporting that point, historical analysis makes clear that the formalities of labor law played only a minor part in the SWOC organizing campaign. The rights guaranteed to workers in the Wagner Act were resisted by many employers who believed the law to be unconstitutional; their defiance of legal authority nullified the legislative aims of Congress and forced workers to rely on their own economic strength to enforce the guarantees of organization. The NLRA is no more effective today in protecting workers against widespread corporate outlawry. It is imperative, then, that statutory reform couple workers' legal "rights" with a viable mechanism for their enforcement. Workers who are confronted with organizational forms unilaterally adopted and maintained by the employer, even though those structures are opposed by a majority of the work group, require an efficacious means of challenging the employer's action.

The solution advanced here balances employer, worker, union, and societal interests. Our labor policy should deal with the fact that the period of delay between the filing of an election petition and the election enables the employer to erode the momentum of the organizing drive and in many cases to thwart the attempt at unionization. Any discussion of "freedom of choice" is an unenlightening definitional exercise when divorced from a meaningful avenue for its actualization. The example of Elmer Maloy, John Mullen, George Patterson, and other rank and file steelworkers during the crucial months of the SWOC drive demonstrates the transformative power of participation programs and the ways in which entities created by an employer can, despite the employer's intentions, contribute to the establishment of independent unions. Assuming a more democratic, participatory workplace to be a true goal of our labor law in the postindustrial global economy, the ossified circumscriptions of section 8(a)(2) may well have outlived their usefulness, and it should be recognized that the law no longer has sufficient vigor to serve the needs of those who are most affected by it.

Bibliographical Note

PARTICIPATION IN THE PRE-WAGNER ACT ERA

The earliest participation plan of importance in the United States was implemented at the cigar manufacturing firm of Straiton & Storm in 1883; George Storm's Senate testimony on the subject is recorded in U.S. Congress, *Report of the Committee of the Senate Upon Labor and Capitol*, II (Washington, D.C.: 1885), 803–819. Two other influential early plans are described in H.F.S. Porter, "The Higher Law in the Industrial World," *The Engineering Magazine*, 29 (1905), 641–655, dealing with the Nernst Lamp Company; and Mary La Dame, *The Filene Store: A Study of Employes' Relation to Management in a Retail Store* (New York: Russell Sage Foundation, 1930). Popular contemporary accounts of the experiment with "industrial democracy" include John Leitch, *Man to Man: The Story of Industrial Democracy* (New York: B. C. Forbes, 1919); and W. Jett Lauck, *Political and Industrial Democracy, 1776–1926* (New York: Funk & Wagnalls, 1926). Milton Derber's *The American Idea of Industrial Democracy, 1865–1965* (Urbana: University of Illinois, 1970) is a useful survey of the concept.

Among the historical studies of participation plans before federal regulation are the following: Ernest Burton, *Employee Representation* (Baltimore: Williams & Wilkins, 1926); Robert W. Dunn, *Company Unions: Employers' "Industrial Democracy"* (New York: Vanguard Press, 1927); Carroll French, "The Shop Committee in the United States," *Johns Hopkins University Studies in Historical and Political Science*, 41 (1923), 15–32; Don Lescohier, *History of Labor in the United States, 1896–1932*, vol. III, chapter 18 (New York: Macmillan, 1935); National Industrial Conference Board, *Works Councils in the United States* (Boston: National Industrial Conference Board, 1919); National Industrial Conference Board, *Experience with Works Councils in the United States* (New York: Century, 1922); National Industrial Conference Board, *Collective Bargaining Through Employee Representation* (New York: National Industrial Conference Board, 1933); U.S. Department of Labor, Bureau of Labor

Statistics, *Characteristics of Company Unions, 1935*, Bulletin No. 634, June 1937 (Washington, D.C.: Government Printing Office, 1938), 7–28.

The Rockefeller-King plan at Colorado Fuel & Iron is analyzed in several important works. George West's *Report on the Colorado Strike* (Washington, D.C.: Government Printing Office, 1915) examines the testimony compiled by the Commission on Industrial Relations. A detailed description of the plan and its implementation is Ben Selekman and Mary Van Kleek, *Employes' Representation in Coal Mines: A Study of the Industrial Representation Plan of the Colorado Fuel and Iron Company* (New York: Russell Sage, 1924). On the association between King and Rockefeller, see H. M. Gitelman, *Legacy of the Ludlow Massacre: A Chapter in American Industrial Relations* (Philadelphia: University of Pennsylvania Press, 1988). Rockefeller's philosophy of industrial brotherhood is succinctly expressed in John D. Rockefeller, Jr., *The Colorado Industrial Plan* ([New York: n.p.], 1916), which contains a copy of the plan itself and the company's agreement with employees.

A good summary of the work of the National War Labor Board is U.S. Department of Labor, Bureau of Labor Statistics, *National War Labor Board: A History of its Formation and Activities, Together with its Awards and the Documents of Importance in the Record of Its Development*, Bulletin No. 2987 l(Washington, D.C.: Government Printing Office, 1922). The WLB's case files are located in Record Group 2, National Archives, Suitland, Maryland.

The collection at The Pennsylvania State University Labor Archives is the best source of primary material on employee representation in the steel industry. It consists of interviews, memoranda, and other records, which the United Steelworkers Union donated to the Archives. The collection covers employee representation from the Midvale Plan of 1918 through the formation of the Steel Workers Organizing Committee. Academic studies of SWOC's activity are Robert R. Brooks, *As Steel Goes . . . :Unionism in a Basic Industry* (New Haven, Conn.: Yale University Press, 1940); and Paul Clark, Peter Gottlieb, and Donald Kennedy, eds., *Forging a Union of Steel: Philip Murray, SWOC, & the United Steelworkers* (Ithaca, N.Y.: ILR Press, 1987).

LAW AND PARTICIPATION

With the enactment of the National Industrial Recovery Act, worker participation became a legal issue. The decisions of the National Labor Board dealing with participation under section 7(a) of the NIRA are reported in *Decisions of the National Labor Board, August 1933–March 1934* and *Decisions of the National Labor Board, Part II, April 1934–July 1934* (Washington, D.C.: Government Printing Office, 1933–34). The first or "old" National Labor Relations Board, created under Public Resolution No. 44, continued to enforce the NIRA between June 1934 and May 1935; there are two volumes of its cases: *Decisions of the National Labor Relations Board, July 9, 1934–December 1934* [vol. I], and *Decisions of the National Labor Relations Board, Dec. 1, 1934–June 16, 1935*, vol. II (Washington, D.C.: Government Printing Office, 1934–35). Case files for the NLB and the first NLRB are in Record Group 25, National Archives, Suitland, Maryland. Analyses of the two administrative bodies include Alfred Bernheim and Dorothy Van Doren, eds., *Labor and the Government: An Investigation of the Role of the Government in Labor Relations* (New York: Twentieth Century Fund/McGraw-Hill, 1935); Lewis Lorwin and Arthur Wubnig,

Labor Relations Boards: The Regulation of Collective Bargaining under the National Industrial Recovery Act (Washington, D.C.: Brookings Institution, 1935); Irving Bernstein, *The New Deal Collective Bargaining Policy* (Berkeley: University of California Press, 1950); James Gross, *The Making of the National Labor Relations Board: A Study in Economics, Politics and the Law* (Albany: SUNY Press, 1974); Christopher Tomlins, *The State and the Unions: Labor Relations, Law, and the Organized Labor Movement in America, 1880–1960* (Cambridge: Cambridge University Press, 1985).

Various law review articles discuss Board and court doctrine under section 8(a)(2) of the National Labor Relations Act. Some of the more significant studies are the following, in chronological order: Burton Craeger, "Company Unions under the National Labor Relations Act," *Michigan Law Review*, 40 (1942), 831–855; Note, "Section 8(a)(2): Employer Assistance to Plant Unions and Committees," *Stanford Law Review*, 9 (1957), 351–365; Martin Feldman and Sylvan Steinberg, "Employee-Management Committees and the Labor Management Relations Act of 1947," *Tulane Law Review*, 35 (1961), 365–386; Note, "New Standards for Domination and Support Under Section 8(a)(2)," *Yale Law Journal*, 82 (1973), 510–532; Note, "Does Employer Implementation of Employee Production Teams Violate Section 8(a)(2) of the National Labor Relations Act?" *Indiana Law Journal*, 49 (1974), 516–537; Charles Jackson, "An Alternative to Unionization and the Wholly Unorganized Shop: A Legal Basis for Sanctioning Joint Employer-Employee Committees and Increasing Employee Free Choice," *Syracuse Law Review*, 28 (1977), 809–845; Note, "Collective Bargaining as an Industrial System: An Argument Against Judicial Revision of Section 8(a)(2) of the National Labor Relations Act," *Harvard Law Review*, 96 (1983), 1662–1682; Note, "Participatory Management Under Sections 2(5) and 8(a)(2) of the National Labor Relations Act," *Michigan Law Review*, 83 (1985), 1736–1769; Thomas Kohler, "Models of Worker Participation: The Uncertain Significance of Section 8(a)(2)," *Boston College Law Review*, 27 (1986), 499–551; Shaun Clarke, "Rethinking the Adversarial Model in Labor Relations: An Argument for Repeal of Section 8(a)(2)," *Yale Law Journal*, 96 (1987), 2021–2050; Raymond Hogler, "Worker Participation, Employer Anti-Unionism, and Labor Law: The Case of the Steel Industry, 1918–1937," *Hofstra Labor Law Journal*, 7 (1989), 1–69.

MODERN PARTICIPATION PLANS

Following the renewed interest in participation beginning in the late 1970s and early 1980s, a number of studies appeared. One of the first treatments was John Simmons and William Mares, *Working Together* (New York: Alfred A. Knopf, 1983), which provides a good overview of the topic. More recent book-length treatments include William Cooke, *Labor-Management Cooperation: New Partnerships or Going in Circles?* (Kalamazoo, Mich.: W. E. Upjohn Institute, 1990); and Edward Lawler, Gerald Ledford, Jr., and Susan Mohrman, *Employee Involvement in America: A Study of Contemporary Practice* (Houston: American Productivity & Quality Center, 1989). Valuable analyses of the relationship between participation and productivity are David Levine and Laura Tyson, "Participation, Productivity, and the Firm's Environment," in Alan Blinder, ed., *Paying for Productivity: A Look at the Evidence* (Washington, D.C.: Brookings Institution, 1990), 183–237; and Maryellen Kelley and Bennett Harrison, "Unions, Technology, and Labor-Management Cooperation," in Lawrence Mishel and Paula B. Voos, eds., *Unions and Economic Competi-*

tiveness (Armonk, N.Y.: M. E. Sharpe, 1992). John Witte's *Democracy, Authority, and Alienation in Work: Workers' Participation in an American Corporation* (Chicago: University of Chicago Press, 1980) is an illuminating case study of the effects of participation in one firm.

The controversy regarding participation and labor unions is the subject of several books. Among them are Guillermo Grenier, *Inhuman Relations: Quality Circles and Anti-Unionism in American Industry* (Philadelphia: Temple University Press, 1988); Mike Parker, *Inside the Circle: A Union Guide to QWL* (Boston: Labor Notes/South End Press, 1985); Mike Parker and Jane Slaughter, *Choosing Sides: Unions and the Team Concept* (Boston: Labor Notes/South End Press, 1988); and Donald Wells, *Empty Promises: Quality of Working Life Programs and the Labor Movement* (New York: Monthly Review Press, 1987).

Index

AFL-CIO, 143–45. *See also* American Federation of Labor; Congress of Industrial Relations
Airstream, Inc. v. NLRB, 97 n.96
Amalgamated Association of Iron, Steel, and Tin Workers, 43, 50–51
Amalgamated Clothing and Textile Workers Union (ACTWU): organizing drive at Ethicon, 110–15; unfair labor practices by employer, 116–18
American Federation of Labor (AFL): and employee representation, 34; and Taft-Hartley Act, 77
American Iron and Steel Institute, 2–3; and company unions, 40–41
Authorization cards, 150

Baruch, Bernard, 30–31
Be-Lo grocers, 126, 151
Bensinger, Richard, 117
Berkeley Woolen Mills case, 70
Bernstein, Irving, 2, 24
Bethlehem Steel Co.: employee representation plan, 1–2, 10 n.4; influence of, 43; NLRA legislative history, 67–68; War Labor Board order, 39

Bluestone, Barry, 137, 147
Bohne, Fred, 54–55
Bowers, L. M., 19, 21
Brooks, George, 127
Brooks, Robert R., 39
Brown, H. F., 32

Carnegie-Illinois Steel Co., 8; defense committee, 54–55; employee representatives and CIO, 53–54
Chamberlain, Neil, 79
Chicago Rawhide Manufacturing Co. v. NLRB, 86
Clegg, Stewart, 106
Cole, Robert, 102–3
Collins, John, 69
Colorado Fuel and Iron Company (CF&I), 3–4; employee representation, 27–28; Ludlow Massacre, 18–20; and steel industry, 39
Colorado Industrial Plan, 27–28
Commission on Workforce Quality and Labor Market Efficiency, 147
Committee for Industrial Organization, 1, 10 n.1
Commons, John, 46–47
Congress of Industrial Organizations

(CIO), 1, 50–55. *See also* Steel Workers Organizing Committee
Cope, Elmer, 54–55
Crane Resistoflex Co., 117
Craypo, Charles, 155
Critical legal theory: and ideology, 107; and labor law, 138–41, 159 n.9; and organizations, 108

Dahl, Robert, 156–57
Danbury & Bethel Fur Co. case, 71
Daniels, Josephus, 36
Desvernine, Raoul, 68
Dewar, Don, 102
Dickson, William, 8, 35–39
Du Pont Corp. 32–34, 59 n.72, 77, 148, 165 n.85

Economic conditions and participation, 99–100
Edsall, Thomas Bird, 137
Edwards, Richard, 100–101
Electromation, Inc., case, 165 n.85
Employee involvement, 101–5; and union organizing, 116–18
Employee Representation Plans (ERPs): and antiunionism in 1920s, 31–34; and Bethlehem Steel Co., 38–39; and Carnegie-Illinois Co., 51–55; compared with British system, 33–34; membership data, 35; and Midvale Steel Co., 35–38; and NIRA, 41–42; and SWOC organizers, 1–3; and War Labor Board, 36–39; and Weirton Steel Co., 43–46
Epstein, Richard, 154
Ethicon Corp., 9, 110–16

Fairless, Benjamin, 54–55
Fairris, David, 120 n.10
Farber, Henry, 123 n.53
Federal Knitting Mills case, 70–71
Fernbach, Frank, 1–3
Filene Cooperative Association, 3, 15–16
Finkin, Matthew, 140–41

Firestone Tire and Rubber Co. case, 71–72
Foulkes, Fred, 160 n.19
Freeman, Richard and Medoff, James (*What Do Unions Do?*), 149, 155–56
French, Carroll, 30
Frug, Gerald, 107–8

Gary, Elbert, 36–37. *See also* American Iron and Steel Institute
General Motors (GM): employee involvement programs, 6–7; Lordstown plant, 100; Tarrytown plant, 101; UAW strike at (1946), 82
Gohn, Katie, 166 n.94
Goldfield, Michael, 134–35, 160 n.24
Golden, Clinton, 51, 80
Goodyear Tire & Rubber Co., 18
Grace, Eugene, 39, 43

Haas, Francis, 44–45
Hall Baking Co. case, 70
Harrison, Bennett, 103, 105, 137
Hatch, Orrin, 143
Hatch-Tower bill, 143–44
Heckscher, Charles, 151–52
Heritage Foundation, 142
Hertzka & Knowles v. NLRB, 87
Houde Engineering Co. case, 72–73
Hunter, Robert, 142

Ideology: and law, 107–109; managerial, 77; and organizations, 106
Industrial Conference (1919), 30–31
Industrial democracy, 13–17, 36–39
Industrial pluralism, 126–27, 158 n.6
International Association of Machinists (IAM), 36–37
International Association of Quality Circles (IAQC), 102
International Harvester Co., 4
International Ladies Garment Workers Union (ILGU), 119
Iron and Steel Institute. *See* American Iron and Steel Institute

Johnson and Johnson Co., 110–11
Jones, Mary, 19

Katz, Harry. *See* Kochan, Thomas
Kelley, Maryanne, 103, 105
Kelton, William, 36
King, Mackenzie, 3; at Bethlehem
  Steel Co., 39; and Colorado
  Industrial Plan, 20–24
Kirkland, Lane, 143
Klare, Karl, 50, 138–40, 147
Kochan, Thomas; Katz, Harry; and
  McKersie, Robert (*Transformation of
  American Industrial Relations*): pluralist
  perspective of, 132–36; and union
  decline, 130–31
Kuttner, Robert, 154–55

Labor Disputes Act, 48–49
Labor Reform Act, 128, 143–44
Larkin, Joseph, 68, 92 n.8
Lawson Co. v. NLRB, 97 n.96
Lee, Ivy, 20–22, 39
Leiserson, William, 31–32
Leitch, John, 17–18
Levy, Paul A., 142
Lewis, John L.: and CIO, 1–2; creation
  of SWOC, 50–51; and Philip
  Murray, 51, 78
Lincoln Mills case, 139
Linden Lumber Div. v. NLRB,
  150
Linderfelt, Karl, 19–20
Litchfield, Paul, 18
Long, Billy, 43–44
Lordstown strike, 100
Ludlow Massacre, 18–19

Maloy, Elmer, 52–53
Mares, William, 103
Marshall, Ray, 6, 143
McDonald, Charles, 118
McKersie, Robert. *See* Kochan,
  Thomas
Midvale Steel Co., 8; and employee
  representation, 35–38
Montgomery, David, 13, 134
Mulholland, Frank, 37–38
Mumby, Dennis K., 107
Murphy, Starr, 22–23
Murray, Philip: alliance with

Roosevelt, 78–79; Carnegie-Illinois
  drive, 51–55; corporatism, 81–82;
  formation of SWOC, 51

National Association of Manufacturers
  (NAM), 41–42, 142
National Civic Federation, 29
National Industrial Conference Board,
  29–30, 35, 40–41
National Industrial Recovery Act
  (NIRA), 5; enactment, 40; exclusive
  representation under, 41–42; held
  unconstitutional, 49
National Labor Board (NLB): case
  law, 69–71; creation, 42; and
  Weirton Steel Co., 43–46
National Labor-Management
  Conference of 1945, 79–80
National Labor Relations Act (NLRA):
  economic policy, 5; legislative
  history, 65–69; proposed
  modification of, 8–9, 146
National Labor Relations Board
  (NLRB): and company unions, 71–
  76; creation of, 49; Reagan
  appointees, 142–43. *See also* National
  Labor Relations Act; Taft-Hartley
  Act
National War Labor Board (NWLB)
  (World War II), 78
Nields, Judge, 46–48
Nelson, Daniel, 57 n.17
Nernst Lamp Co., 3, 16–17
New York Conference, 32–34, 59
  n.72. *See also* Special Conference
  Committee
*Newport News Shipbuilding & Dry Dock
  Co. v. NLRB*, 74–76, 87
NLRB v. Cabot Carbon Co.,
  88–89
*NLRB v. Curtin Matheson Scientific,
  Inc.*, 163 n.58
NLRB v. Homemaker Shops, Inc.,
  87
NLRB v. Jones & Laughlin Steel Corp.,
  76, 138–39
*NLRB v. Pennsylvania Greyhound Lines
  Corp.*, 74

NLRB v. Valentine Sugars Inc., 86

O'Brien, John, 38
Ozanne, Robert, 4

Packard Piano Company, 17
Parker, Mike, 122 n.32
Pateman, Carole, 156
Pattern Makers' League v. NLRB, 141–42
Patterson, George, 52–53, 170
Pennsylvania Greyhound Lines case, 73
Porter, H. F., 16–17
Public Resolution No. 44, 49

Quality Circles (QC): antiunion device, 111–16; ideology of, 106–9; origins, 101–3; productivity and, 103–4

Reagan, Ronald, 145
Reagan Board, 142–43
Reuther, Walter, 82, 96 n.64
Reynolds, Morgan, 153–54
Rockefeller, John D., Jr., 3–4; and Colorado Industrial Plan, 20–24; theory of industrial democracy, 26–28; and trade unionism, 24, 26; visit to Colorado, 25–27
Rogers, Joel, 150–51
Roosevelt, Franklin D., 40, 49, 95 n.49
Rumm, John, 59 n.72
Ruttenberg, Harold, 52, 81

Schwab, Charles, 39
Slichter, Sumner, 5
Simmons, John, 103
Smith Committee, 77–78
Special Conference Committee, 59 n.72, 77, 94 n.39. *See also* New York Conference
Steel Workers Organizing Committee (SWOC): and Bethlehem Steel Co., 1–2, 10 n.4; and Carnegie-Illinois Steel Co., 51–55; creation of, 50–51

Storm, George, 13–14
Straiton & Storm Co., 13–14
Stone, Katherine, 139–41
Streamway Div., Scott & Fetzer Co. v. NLRB, 89–90, 97 n.96
Summers, Clyde, 156–57

Taft-Hartley Act: antiunion background of, 76–77; and company unions, 83–85; political forces supporting, 77, 82–83; Truman's veto of, 83
Taussig, Frank, 32
Taylor, George, 158 n.6
Taylor, Myron, 8, 55
Theory Z, 7
Tikas, Louis, 19, 57 n.22
Tower, John, 143
Trans World Airlines v. Independent Fed. Flight Attendants, 142
Truman, Harry: labor-management conference, 79–80; reconversion policy, 81–82; and Taft-Hartley, 83
Tydings, Millard, 66–67

United Auto Workers (UAW): GM strike (1946), 82; labor-management cooperation, 7; no-strike pledge, 78–79
United Food and Commercial Workers Union (UFCW), 126, 151
United Mine Workers of America (UMWA), 3, 18–22, 26, 28
United Electrical Workers Union (UE), 118–19
United States Steel Co., 4, 68
United Steelworkers of America (USWA), 152

Wagner, Robert, 5; on company unions, 65–67; and Labor Disputes Act, 48; and NLB, 42; NLRA enacted, 49; and Weirton Steel Co., 43–46
Wagner Act. *See* National Labor Relations Act
Walsh, David, 69

War Labor Board (WLB) (World War I), 4; and Bethlehem Steel Co., 39; formation and authority of, 29–30; and Midvale Steel Co., 36–38
Weaver, Charles, 66
Weiler, Paul, 145
Weir, Ernest, 43–45
Weirton Steel Co., 43–46
Weirton Steel Co. v. United States, 46–48
Weiss, Richard, 122 n.39
Welborn, J. F., 3, 21–24

Welfare capitalism, 5
West, George, 4, 28–29
Williams, Harrison, 143
Williams, John, 92
Wilson, Woodrow, 22, 29–30
Winpisinger, William, 109
Witte, John F., 121 n.23
Wolman, Leo, 70–71
Work in America, 101

Young, Arthur, 4, 52, 67–68

About the Authors

RAYMOND L. HOGLER is Professor of Management in the College of Business at Colorado State University. Previously, he had practiced labor law, representing employers before the National Labor Relations Board and in collective bargaining activities. He has published many articles in labor and legal journals and is the author of a textbook, *The Employment Relationship: Law and Policy* (1989).

GUILLERMO J. GRENIER is Director of the Center for Labor Research and Studies and Associate Professor of Sociology at Florida International University. His articles have appeared in a variety of scholarly journals, and he is the author of *Inhuman Relations: Quality Circles and Anti-Unionism in U.S. Industry* (1988).